JUDGING CRIMINAL LEADERS

NIJHOFF LAW SPECIALS

VOLUME 55

Judging Criminal Leaders

The slow erosion of impunity

Written by

Yves Beigbeder

Foreword by

Theo van Boven

Published by:
Kluwer Law International
P.O.Box 85889, 2508 CN The Hague, The Netherlands
sales@kli.wkap.nl
http://www.kluwerlaw.com

Sold and Distributed in North, Central and South America by:
Kluwer Law International
101 Philip Drive, Norwell, MA 02061, USA
kluwerlaw@wkap.com

Sold and Distributed in all other countries by:
Kluwer Law International
Distribution Centre, P.O. Box 322, 3300 AH Dordrecht, The Netherlands

Library of Congress Cataloging-in-Publication Data is available.

Printed on acid-free paper

ISBN 90-411-1815-2

Kluwer Law International incorporates the imprint of Martinus Nijhoff Publishers.

Printed and bound in Great Britain by Antony Rowe Limited.

To my wife

TABLE OF CONTENTS

FOREWORD

In his early professional life Yves Beigbeder was legal secretary to the French judge at the Military War Criminals Tribunal in Nuremberg in 1946. It is obvious and natural that this historic involvement in rendering criminal justice to an evil regime and its leaders strongly motivated Beigbeder to apply himself, later in his life, to essential features of international criminal justice. In 1999 his book *Judging War Criminals; the Politics of International Justice* saw the light. The present volume supplements the earlier book against the background of further historical perspectives and with due emphasis on significant recent developments. The wrongs of the past can in all good conscience not be ignored since they have a bearing on life and human conditions of present and future generations. This linkage with the past was highlighted in the preamble of the Rome Statute of the International Criminal Court which recalled that during this century (which meant the twentieth century) millions of children, women and men had been victims of unimaginable atrocities that deeply shock the conscience of humanity. In the same vein recent international debate triggered off by Africans and persons of African descent focussed on the continuing harmful effects of slavery and the slave-trade, which were acknowledged as a crime against humanity on the basis of past and present legal and moral criteria.

New developments in the administration and practice of international criminal justice confirm the positive trend reflected in the title of the present book. It is no longer admitted that criminal political and military leaders escape the imperative prescriptions of justice and benefit from mistaken notions of immunity and impunity in cases where they have to account for grave international crimes that constitute genocide, crimes against humanity and war crimes. In this respect Yves Beigbeder clearly describes the law and practice of the two ad hoc tribunals established by the United Nations Security Council with regard to the former Yugoslavia and Rwanda. They progressively concentrate their judicial activities on the investigation, prosecution and trial of the higher echelons of suspects, up to the level of former heads of state, as illustrated by the case of Slobodan Milosevic. The long and protracted procedures before the British courts as a result of the tenacious and determined activities by the Spanish investigating judge Baltasar Garzon in the case of the Chilean dictator Augusto Pinochet significantly contributed to what Beigbeder calls the erosion of impunity of top leaders. Anyone who is committed to the cause of justice cannot but applaud these developments.

The reader of this book will discover that various models are emerging in making criminal leaders and their collaborators accountable for their schemes and actions. The two ad hoc tribunals for the former Yugoslavia and Rwanda created under the enforcement powers of the Security Council were given priority status over national criminal jurisdictions and can be characterised as supranational bodies of justice. On the other hand, the International Criminal Court established by the 1998 Rome Statute, which should become operational in the near future, is based on the premise that it be complementary to national criminal jurisdictions and that it will only act if the national state is unwilling or unable genuinely to carry out an investigation or prosecution. Other models described by Yves Beigbeder are mixed national/international tribunals still in *statu nascendi*. Among these Sierra Leone's Special Court might prove to be the most innovative and thoughtful in terms of its competence, composition and cooperative arrangements. Further, the Pinochet effect has motivated national magistrates and domestic courts in a number of countries, basing themselves on the principle of universal jurisdiction with regard to the most serious international crimes, to engage themselves in criminal procedures against suspects who may be considered as *hostes humani generis*. These criminal procedures constitute an illustration of an emerging structure of transnational justice.

The successive chapters of the present book are portraying the unfolding pattern of supranational, international and transnational criminal justice which can only bear fruit and become effective in interaction and in interrelationship with national criminal jurisdictions. The struggle against impunity is first and foremost a responsibility of national jurisdictions. However, international criminal law, in devising and reaffirming standards of international criminal justice and in creating tools and mechanisms to enforce these standards, is an indispensable asset whenever national jurisdictions are failing in their duties.

Yves Beigbeder's new book also provides an account of the obstacles that bedevil the creation and development of criminal justice systems as a means to combat patterns and practices of impunity. These obstacles, often presented under the guise of national sovereignty, have stalled progress in the creation of certain mixed national/international tribunals and have led some major powers to wage strong political and diplomatic opposition against the International Criminal Court. The struggle against impunity has a long way to go and is bound to remain, in the destiny of humanity and for many generations to come, a never fully resolved issue of elementary justice and a cause for persistent national and international efforts. Hopeful signs are nonetheless energetic and joint activities of coalitions of non-governmental organisations and groups of like-minded nations that have engaged themselves in working for national and international criminal justice in its various forms and modalities. Another hopeful sign is the moral leadership demonstrated by top United Nations officials, notably the Secretary-General and the High Commissioner for Human Rights.

It is evident that international criminal justice does not function in a political vacuum. The political context can never be overlooked. One of the great merits in Beigbeder's writings is his awareness and his exposition of the political factor which he treats, with the clear insights of a seasoned observer and commentator, in a well-balanced and mature fashion. This book is addressed to a wider readership than specialists in international criminal and humanitarian law. Anyone who takes an interest in the broader dimensions of past and present failures and accomplishments in rendering international criminal justice, will appreciate this book as a source of orientation and inspiration and as a sign of hope.

Maastricht, January 2002 Theo van Boven

Professor of International Law, University of Maastricht; former Director of the United Nations Centre for Human Rights.

INTRODUCTION

On 31 December 2000, Bill Clinton, in the last days of his presidency, authorized his representative to sign the Statute of the future International Criminal Court. While this was taken by the Republicans as a political coup, this late approval, on the last day on which the Statute was open for signature, after years of rejection by the US, was a powerful support to the establishment of the Court, even if ratification of the Statute by the US Senate is more than unlikely for many years to come. Sixty ratifications are needed for the Court's establishment: by January 2002, 48 countries have ratified the Statute.

The probable creation of the Court following the approval of its Statute in Rome in July 1998, is in itself an extraordinary event in the history of mankind. For the first time, a permanent international court will have authority to investigate and bring to justice individuals who commit the most serious crimes of concern to the international community, such as war crimes and crimes against humanity. Kofi Annan, the United Nations Secretary-General, saluted the approval of the Statute by 120 countries by declaring that this adoption was another "giant step forward in the march towards universal human rights and the rule of law – an achievement which, only a few years ago, nobody would have thought possible'.

What is extraordinary and even revolutionary about the creation and development of international criminal justice?

International relations are traditionally based on national sovereignty. The prosecution and enforcement of the law are carefully protected national prerogatives. National courts normally have jurisdiction over crimes committed within their state's territory, irrespective of the nationality of those who perpetrated the crime.

However, in many countries, justice is subordinate to power politics. National political and military leaders enjoy legal or de facto immunity from crimes which they may have committed or allowed to be committed against their own people or against foreign military personnel or civilians. In some cases, impunity through amnesty is the price to pay for the peaceful transition to democracy of a country formerly under dictatorial or totalitarian rule. Even in democratic countries, governments have covered up if not ordered or allowed military abuses committed during colonial or decolonization times, or under emergency conditions through legal amnesty. In many countries, collective amnesia of past criminal offences was often silently encouraged by the authorities, with the help of obliging media, or through censorship.

Hence, a widely-spread culture of impunity under which leaders' abuses, exactions and crimes are neither exposed, prosecuted, judged or sanctioned, leaving victims or survivors to grieve or to seek revenge. However, in the words of Hannah Arendt, 'Men are unable to forgive what they cannot punish'.

Chapter 1 reviews a selected list of massacres and genocides[1] committed in the 20th century, mostly committed with impunity, impunity at times confirmed by the granting of amnesty. These comprise some of the hidden or forgotten crimes of colonialism – the massacres caused by the attempted implementation of the Communist utopia in the former USSR and other Communist countries, including the genocide in Cambodia – the many civil wars in Europe, Africa and Latin America: including the genocide of the Armenians and the genocide in Rwanda – international wars, including the nationalist slaughters of World War I, the Holocaust and other massacres and atrocities of World War II.

International Humanitarian Law

While wars, massacres, torture and other atrocities, and concurrent humanitarian concerns are as old as mankind itself, humanitarian law was only codified at the international level in the second half of the 19th century. Its evolution, since the First Geneva Convention of 1864, has been considerable. Born on the battlefield to 'humanize' war and initially concerned with the protection of wounded and sick soldiers and sailors, prisoners of war and medical personnel, international humanitarian law now also applies to civilians. While this law was originally designed to ensure such protection only during international armed conflicts, the 1949 Conventions and the 1977 Protocols adopted rules to protect civilian populations, who are often the main target of conflicts. Another innovation was to provide protection in non-international conflicts, a more frequent occurrence since World War II. The protection of military personnel placed hors de combat and persons not taking part in hostilities of the Geneva Law was developed concurrently

1 The definition of 'genocide' is that of the 1948 Convention on the Prevention and Punishment of the Crime of Genocide, Art. II: 'In the present Convention, genocide means any of the following acts committed with intent to destroy, in whole or in part, a national, ethnical, racial or religious group, as such:

(a) Killing members of the group;
(b) Causing serious bodily or mental harm to members of the group;
(c) Deliberately inflicting on the group conditions of life calculated to bring about its physical destruction in whole or in part;
(d) Imposing measures intended to prevent births within the group;
(e) Forcibly transferring children of the group to another group'.

The author includes 'political groups' in this list, as originally intended and eliminated at Soviet insistence.

Massacres may be defined as the deliberate and indiscriminate killing by a more powerful or better armed group of a large number of people, often accompanied by atrocities.

with the law of the war, or law of armed conflict, of the Hague Conventions of 1899 and 1907 through restraints on the use of force and the use of certain weapons.

Both the Geneva Conventions and the Hague Conventions rely on states to ensure the respect of these instruments. The state is responsible under classical international law for the violations of provisions of ratified Conventions, and it must submit the violator to national criminal justice. Neither Conventions refer to the possible referral of war criminals to an international criminal tribunal.

Between the two World Wars, two instruments supplemented the Hague Conventions: the Protocol for the Prohibition of the Use in War of Asphyxiating, Poisonous and Other Gases and of Bacteriological Methods of Warfare of 1925 (the Geneva Gas Protocol) and the Protocol to the London Naval Agreement of 1936. After World War II, a number of international arms control agreements were adopted: The 1968 Treaty on the Non-Proliferation of Nuclear Weapons, the Convention on the Prohibition of the Development, Production and Stockpiling of Bacteriological (Biological) and Toxin Weapons and on their Destruction in force since 1975, the Convention on the Prohibition of the Development, Production, Stockpiling and Use of Chemical Weapons and on their Destruction, which came in force in 1993, the Ottawa Convention on the Prohibition of the Use, Stockpiling, Production and Transfer of Anti-Personnel Mines and on their Destruction, in force since 1999.

As inter-state treaties or conventions, ratification of these instruments commit states to the respect of their obligations, without engaging the penal responsibility of their leaders or other officials to national or international tribunals.

A Human Rights Regime

The human rights regime was a creation of the UN, motivated by the horror, pain and repulsion felt in most countries when the Holocaust and other crimes committed by the Nazi regime during World War II were publicly revealed. Human rights instruments offer guarantees of individual freedoms to citizens and their protection against their own government's power and abuses at all times, while humanitarian law provides protection to non-combatant military personnel or civilians only in times of war. The protection of human rights requires an interference with a states' sovereignty, a breach of formal legal frontiers. In 1945, the Preamble of the UN Charter reaffirmed 'faith in fundamental human rights, in the dignity and worth of the human person, in the equal rights of men and women'. The Universal Declaration of Human Rights was adopted in 1948, followed in 1966 by the International Covenant on Economic, Social and Cultural Rights, and the International Covenant on Civil and Political Rights. Also in 1948, the UN General Assembly approved the Convention on the Prevention and Punishment of the Crime of Genocide, a direct 'product' of the Nuremberg judgments. This Convention prescribes that persons charged with genocide are to be tried by a competent tribunal of the State in the territory of which the act was committed, or – a striking innovation – 'by such international penal tribunal as may have jurisdiction with respect to those Contracting Parties which shall have accepted its jurisdiction'. As another follow-up to Nuremberg, the Convention on the Non-Applicability of Statutory Limitations to War Crimes and Crimes against Humanity was adopted by the General Assembly on 26 November 1968. The International Convention on the Suppression and Punishment of the Crime of Apartheid, adopted in 1973, emulates the Genocide Convention in declaring that persons charged with apartheid may be tried either by a national tribunal or by an international penal tribunal. Both Conventions recognise the penal responsibility of individuals, thus voiding the traditional fiction that only the abstract state is responsible for its deeds and misdeeds. The Convention against Torture and other Cruel, Inhuman or Degrading Treatment or Punishment, adopted in 1984, entered into force in 1987. It requires, in part, that wherever the alleged torture occurred, and whatever the nationality of the torturer and of the victim, parties must either prosecute the alleged torturers or extradite them to a country that will, thus giving universal jurisdiction to national courts. This provision was availed of by the British court in the Pinochet affair (see Chapter 5).

International Criminal Tribunals

The first international criminal tribunals to be created were the Nuremberg International Military Tribunal, which met between November 1945 and October 1946 and the Tokyo International Military Tribunal, which sat from 1946 to 1948. The Tribunals' Charters included three categories of crimes: one was based on the Geneva and the Hague Conventions, i.e. war crimes, namely violations of the laws and customs of war, including murder, ill-treatment or deportation to slave labour of civilian population in occupied territory, murder or ill-treatment of prisoners of war or persons on the seas, killings of hostages, plunder of public or private property, wanton destruction of cities, villages, or devastation not justified by military necessity. The other two were innovations: crime of aggression, namely crimes against peace, planning or waging a war of aggression, or a war in violation of international treaties, or participation in a common plan or conspiracy for their accomplishment; crimes against humanity, namely murder, extermination, enslavement, deportation, and other inhumane acts committed against any civilian population, before or during the war, or persecutions on political, racial or religious grounds, whether or not in violation of domestic law of the country where perpetrated. However, this last ground was made conditional and thus limited its impact: it could be considered only if committed in execution of or in connection with any crime within the jurisdiction of the Tribunal. The Nuremberg judges condemned 12 senior German political and military leaders to death by hanging, seven to jail, three were found not guilty. The Tokyo judges condemned seven Japanese defendants to death, 16 to life imprisonment and two to time limited jail.

Criticisms were addressed to both Tribunals. Both applied 'victors' justice', insofar as only the vanquished were called to account for violations of international humanitarian law before the victors' judges and prosecutors. Secondly, the defendants were tried and punished for crimes expressly defined in Charters adopted well after the crimes were committed, a violation of the principle of non-retroactivity of criminal law. Thirdly, the Tribunals' procedural rules inadequately protected the rights of the accused. Fourthly, the victors' governments or armed forces had committed some of the same crimes for which the defendants were tried: they were not subjected to international justice.

In spite of their imperfections and partiality, the Tribunals created a major judiciary precedent: for the first time, high level political and military leaders were made accountable for crimes committed in their name or in the name of their regime: individual responsibility replaced state responsibility. The Nuremberg precedent demonstrated that the creation of an international criminal tribunal was feasible and that it could meet its basic objectives. Nuremberg Law added the concept of crimes against humanity to the crimes defined in the Geneva and Hague Laws. Nuremberg was a first step in the slow evolution from toothless international humanitarian law, poorly enforced by national authorities or courts, to a regime of effective sanctions applied by international tribunals under international criminal law. International law finally addressed individuals, rather than being restricted to relations between states.

Forty-five years later, two temporary ad hoc international criminal tribunals were created. The massive crimes committed in ex-Yugoslavia and the Rwanda genocide induced the UN Security Council, under the pressure of public opinion, to set up in 1993 the International Criminal Tribunal for the Former Yugoslavia and, in 1994, the International Criminal Tribunal for Rwanda. These Tribunals are currently in operation and some of their achievements and problems will be reviewed in Chapters 2 and 3. With regard to the Former Yugoslavia Tribunal, charges by non-governmental organisations that NATO violated the laws of war in its conduct of the Kosovo intervention will also be discussed.

Finally, as noted above, the approval of the Statute of the International Criminal Court in Rome in July 1998 is a major, unexpected advance in the future establishment of international criminal justice at the global level. This approval is the culmination of more than a century of legal and judiciary developments which include at the international level the creation and development of humanitarian law, the creation of a human rights regime and the rise of a long-dormant international criminal law through the creation of international criminal tribunals, and at the national level, the spectacular evolution towards more effective national justice in several countries. The main elements of its Statute, the main obstacles to the work of the future Court, the reasons why a few countries, national constituencies and analysts oppose the creation of the Court are examined in Chapter 4.

More Independent National Justice

In recent years, national prosecutors, judges and courts in a number of countries have assumed a more independent role: in return, they have been exposed to professional accusations and defamation, removal from sensitive cases, damage to their career, and even death threats. In spite of setbacks, they have challenged the impunity of present or past leaders, raising the hopes of victims, their relatives or survivors that justice may finally be rendered. National courts have primary responsibility for judging crimes committed in their own countries, and their capacity, effectiveness and willingness to assume this responsibility is essential to the fight against impunity. The only legal remedy to incompetent or unwilling national courts is a recourse to international courts.

For instance, in the Pinochet case, the tenacious action of Spanish judge Baltasar Garzon and that of Chilean judge Juan Guzman is exemplary. Thanks to Garzon's efforts, retired dictator Pinochet was arrested in London in October 1998 and in March 1999, the British Law Lords ruled that he did not have immunity from arrest and prosecution as a former head of state for alleged offences committed in violation of the 1984 Torture Convention. Even though Pinochet was allowed to return to Chile in March 2000 for medical reasons, his senatorial immunity was lifted in his own country and he was to be judged by a Chilean court for his involvement in the kidnapping and murders of 74 Socialist activists and labour leaders in the first months following his taking power in a 1973 US-supported coup. His trial was however stopped but only on medical reasons.

The impact of the Pinochet case and recent related judiciary developments in Latin American and other countries are reviewed in Chapter 5.

National Tribunals with or without International Participation

In two countries, Cambodia and Sierra Leone, national courts with international participation may be set up to judge major atrocities. In Cambodia, the Khmer Rouge communist-led genocide killed approximately 1.7 million Cambodians between 1975 and 1978. The Cambodian court should judge the Khmer Rouge surviving leaders, after the death of its main leader, Pol Pot. A mixed national/international court will be created in Sierra Leone to try Foday Sankoh, imprisoned leader of the Revolutionary United Front, and other senior perpetrators of egregious crimes and violations of international humanitarian law. War crimes and crimes against humanity committed by Indonesian troops in East Timor may also be tried. The extraordinary trial of two Libyans, accused of murder for killing 259 passengers on board Pan Am 103 over Lockerbie, Scotland in 1988, at an airbase in the Netherlands, under an international agreement which allowed it to take place under Scottish law but at a neutral venue will also be examined. Chapter 6 will report on the current position of these prosecutions and courts.

Chapter 7 provides an assessment of previous findings and a conclusion.

Reasons for this Evolution

Laws evolve in response to the perceived or expressed needs of the people, they sometimes precede and promote the perception that these needs exist and should be satisfied. The rise of an international human rights regime and the creation of the Nuremberg and Tokyo Tribunals were a direct consequence of the horrors of World War II. The creation of the Tribunals for ex-Yugoslavia and Rwanda was also directly linked to the atrocities committed in these two countries. The progressive codification of universal human rights and the belief that their violations by political and military leaders should be punished both at the national and international levels was facilitated by a more favourable climate due to several factors.

One key factor is that more countries, mainly in Latin America, in post-communist Eastern Europe, and parts of Asia and Africa have become democracies. According to Freedom House,[2] in mid-20th century, there were 22 democracies accounting for 31% of the world population – by the end of the century, electoral democracies represented 120 of the 192 existing countries and constituted 58.2% of the world's population. Liberal democracies, i.e. countries which Freedom House regards as free and respectful of basic human rights and the rule of the law were 85 in number, representing 38% of the global population. Under the principle of the equality of citizens, democracy demands that a country's leaders be held accountable for their decisions: they lose their traditional, historical 'sacred' status of being above the law, their de jure or de facto immunity, pseudo 'reasons of state' give way to the rule of law and transparency. Democracy implies separation of powers, the judiciary gaining its independence vs. the executive. As part of the expansion of democracy and as already stated, judges in many countries have broken their links with the political powers and asserted their independence in indicting and judging national political and business leaders: in Europe, Italian prosecutors have been leaders in this process, followed by Spanish, French and Latin American judges. Democracy also implies freedom of thought and expression, freedom of the media. In some countries, the media have supported the action of judges through illegal but effective leaks which prevented the quiet burial of embarrassing disclosures. Finally, the growing influence and loud voice of international human rights non-governmental organisations, such as Amnesty International, Human Rights Watch, the International Federation of Human Rights Leagues, Freedom House and others, echoed by the courageous small voices of national human rights NGOs, have played a decisive role in publicizing massacres and other exactions committed the world over, calling upon governments to respect their obligations and enticing citizens and their national or local associations to protest and defend their rights.

The growing interdependence of countries, the expansion of global communications, the widespread use of the internet, have all contributed to an immediate

---

2 See 'Electoral Democracies, List of Electoral Democracies' www.fordemocracy.net/electoral.shtml, 12 January 2001.

knowledge and moral condemnation of millions of crimes and abuses committed in a faraway country, making it difficult or impossible for leaders to hide their faults or crimes. A symptom of this new imposed transparency is the recent series of public statements of repentance by senior statesmen for past errors, sins or crimes committed by their own country, or a call to penitence by the Pope on behalf of the Roman Catholic Church, which remained silent in the face of the Holocaust, supported Latin American dictatorships and the infamous pro-Nazi Croat Ustachi regime.

More specifically, public prosecutions and judgments of the two international criminal tribunals as well as occasional public statements by the tribunals' prosecutors and Presidents have also played a role in showing international criminal justice in action, even if the media have not fairly reflected the importance of the tribunals' pronouncements.

Considerable Obstacles Remain

At the national level, the main obstacle to an independent, fair and effective justice is the survival and resistance of many despotic leaders and governments which reject or ignore any obligation to comply with human rights and humanitarian law. Other obstacles include the legitimate but often abusive recourse to national sovereignty and non-interference in a country's internal governance and culture as a protection against indiscreet international inquiries into abuses; – the resistance of military authorities to any civilian judiciary control, at the national or international levels, of their actions and possible exactions – the imposition of amnesty by military authorities as the price to pay for a progressive and peaceful transition to democracy – the rejection or unnecessary delays of national authorities in integrating international norms (crimes against humanity, genocide, torture among others) in their national legislation – the passive resistance, refusal or incapacity of national administrations to implementing these norms – the unwillingness or incapacity of national courts to prosecute and judge crimes committed by their own political or military leaders.

At the international level, obstacles relate to political, military, diplomatic, judiciary, commercial, or even religious considerations which delay or block requests for extradition. In many cases, the solidarity between present and former heads of state or of government often assures them of protection against prosecution through extradition. Rejection by some countries of the legitimacy of international criminal tribunals is also a factor.

Judging criminal leaders is first a responsibility of national courts. Should national courts prove unwilling or unable to prosecute and judge these leaders, as an alternative to their impunity, the burden falls on international tribunals or mixed national/international courts. Are the present trends towards more accountability of senior political and military leaders a misperception, a temporary illusion, or a sign that the impunity of criminal leaders is progressively being eroded?

NOTES

As for the preceding book on '*Judging War Criminals – The Politics of International Justice*',[3] the present book is not a legal treatise, although references are made to legal texts and interpretations. The book is an attempt by the author, an independent observer and an internationalist, to describe and assess recent developments in the implementation of international criminal law through the development of universal jurisdiction and the creation of international criminal tribunals, without losing sight of the political limits of this venture. The erosion of impunity of criminal leaders will be a slow and difficult process.

Frequent references to French situations in some Chapters is explained by the author's nationality, upbringing and natural interest in French history. They do not imply that French violations of international humanitarian law have necessarily been more important than those of other countries in comparable situations, such as in colonialist ventures, civil wars or other conflictual and tragic circumstances. However, these references do show the difficulties and obstacles met by such 'civilized' nations as France to be equal to their ambition of human rights promoters.

Finally, the author does not hide his ethnocentric and European approach: he believes in the universality of human rights. He also believes in and supports the creation of the International Criminal Court.

Many thanks are due to those who have given me advice and reviewed this text, including Theo van Boven who has kindly written a foreword to this book, and to the UN library staff in Geneva for their courteous and efficient assistance. The editing skills of Mandy Eggleston are, again, gratefully acknowledged.

Thonon-les-Bains, France
January 2002 Y.B.

[3] Beigbeder, Yves, *Judging War Criminals, The Politics of International Justice*, Foreword by Theo van Boven (Macmillan Press Ltd and St. Martin's Press, Inc., now Palgrave, Basingstoke/New York, 1999).

LIST OF ABBREVIATIONS

AI	Amnesty International
AVCRP	Chadian Association of Victims of Political Repression and Crime
DDS	Documentation and Security Directorate (Chad)
DINA	National Intelligence Directorate (Chile)
ECOMOG	Military Observer Group of the Economic Community of West African States
ECOWAS	Economic Community of West African States
EU	European Union
FIDH	International Federation of Human Rights Leagues
FRY	Federal Republic of Yugoslavia
HRW	Human Rights Watch
HVO	Croatian Defence Council
IAEA	International Atomic Energy Agency
ICC	International Criminal Court
ICG	International Crisis Group
ICJ	International Court of Justice
ICRC	International Committee of the Red Cross
ICTR	International Criminal Tribunal for Rwanda
ICTY	International Criminal Tribunal for the Former Yugoslavia
IHT	International Herald Tribune
ILC	International Law Commission
INTERFET	International Force in East Timor
KFOR	Kosovo (NATO) Protection Force
KLA	Kosovo Liberation Army
MRND	Mouvement républicain national pour le développement et la démocratie (Rwanda)
NATO	North Atlantic Treaty Organisation
NGO	Non-governmental organisation
NPWJ	No Peace Without Justice
OAU	Organisation of African Unity
OHCHR	Office of the (UN) High Commissioner on Human Rights
OIOS	(UN) Office of Internal Oversight Services
OSCE	Organisation for Security and Cooperation in Europe
OTP	Office of the Prosecutor
PLO	Palestine Liberation Organisation
PrepComm	Preparatory Commission for the International Criminal Court
RPF	Rwandan Patriotic Front
RTS	Serbian state radio and television
RUF	Revolutionary United Front (Sierra Leone)
TNI	Indonesian armed forces
UN	United Nations
UNAMET	United Nations Mission in East Timor
UNAMIR	United Nations Assistance Mission for Rwanda
UNICEF	United Nations Children's Fund
UNITA	National Union for the Liberation of Angola
UNOMSIL	United Nations Observer Mission in Sierra Leone
UNPROFOR	United Nations Protection Force (Yugoslavia)
UNTAC	United Nations Transitional Authority in Cambodia
UNTAET	United Nations Transitional Administration in East Timor
UP	Popular Unity Party (Chile)

LIST OF TABLES AND PRESENTATIONS

CHAPTER 1

THE TWENTIETH CENTURY – MASSACRES AND GENOCIDES

You have to be an optimist if you deal with human rights

Mary Robinson (March 2001)

The 20th century started with optimism, with the feeling that progress was continuous and irreversible, improving the quality of life, at least among the 'rich' countries. Mankind was benefiting from inventions of previous centuries, improved communications, thanks to the expansion of railways, the invention of the telephone and of radio, the extended use of electricity. The 20th century saw the development of commercial air travel, space rockets, the invention of radar, the transistor, television, the computer, robots, the nuclear reactor, nuclear weapons, the laser, the revolution in information processing and telecommunications. There was impressive progress in the medical field: the identification of vitamins, the BCG and the anti-poliomyelitis vaccines, DDT, cortisone, penicillin, heart and other transplants, the 'pill', a major tool of women's emancipation, the eradication of smallpox but the surge of new illnesses such as AIDS and Ebola.

The belief and hope in progress was however if not totally destroyed, but at least strongly eroded by the slaughters of World War I and even more by the Holocaust. Technological and scientific progress was not accompanied by social and moral progress – some inventions led to more efficient war tools.

Massacres have long been committed in the history of mankind. The invention and use of more lethal instruments of war have increased the scale of destruction and the number of casualties in conflicts. Conflicts themselves have evolved from traditional country-against-country wars, or wars between coalitions of countries, to conflicts within countries, or civil wars, with the problem of identifying the 'rebels' vs. the 'regular army forces'. Concurrent with this evolution, the increasing impact of wars on civilians, often used by the combatants as targets, hostages or tools to pressure the opposing party. Massacres are part of mankind's make-up and heritage, a part of man's dual and ambivalent nature: saints or believers vs. sinners, love and hate towards oneself and towards others, humanitarian and charitable drives vs. cruelty and killing impulses. The roots of conflicts erupting into massacres are diverse: abusive nationalism, intolerant ideology or religion, territorial disputes, ethnic strife, economic and social grievances, political rivalry for power. But violence is often triggered by irresponsible, greedy, immoral or even criminal leaders who use latent popular grievances to start collective tragedies.

The 20th century is presented as the first Chapter in this study, firstly as an illustration of the many types of conflicts which occur at both the international and national levels. Secondly, massacres and atrocities took place during this century, generally with impunity, in spite of the humanitarian 'progress' constituted by the Geneva and Hague Conventions. Thirdly, this century has acquired notoriety in including genocides, a new category of massacres, among the many others committed in that and previous periods. Fourthly, the relevance of the 20th century is that the extent of its atrocities finally led to the strengthening of international humanitarian law and the development of international criminal law through the creation of international criminal tribunals.

The first section reviews selective samples of massacres committed in a number of countries or territories with impunity, including those committed under the humanitarian cloak of colonialism, and those committed under the mantle of a 'progressive' communism. Others include the first genocide, the genocide of the Armenians and a number of massacres committed during international or civil wars.

A second section covers selective samples of amnesties granted through legislative action, also providing impunity. The purpose of the amnesties is to 'erase the past', to prevent or stop criminal prosecutions on the expectation that political peace and stability will follow, and, in some countries, in order to facilitate the process of transition to democracy.

Finally, in a few cases, national justice has initiated prosecutions and international criminal tribunals have been created to prosecute and judge those leaders mainly responsible for severe violations of international humanitarian law in a few countries.

Unchallenged Impunity

Colonialist Crimes

Starting in the 14th century, Europeans sailed to West Africa in search of gold, ivory and other precious commodities. Initial trade contacts between the Portuguese, the Dutch, the French and the British and the Africans were expanded to include commerce in slaves who were shipped to the Americas and the West Indies to work in sugar, cotton and tobacco plantations. The Portuguese and Spanish expeditions in Central and South America were attracted by gold, silver and diamonds. In the 16th century, they explored Asian countries, looking for spices, Indian cotton, Chinese silk. They were replaced in Asia by the Netherlands, England and France in the 17th and 18th century. The apex of colonial expansion took place in the 19th century.

Decolonization started in the same century, former colonies achieving autonomy or independence: most Latin American countries in the first part of the 19th century, the USA in 1776, Canada in 1867. In 1931, British dominions became independent with their admission to the British Commonwealth. After the second World War, most colonies became independent with the support of both the USA, a former colony and the USSR, a new colonial power over its satellite countries, albeit for different political and economic reasons. Under the leadership of the growing African–Asian group in the United Nations, the General Assembly adopted unanimously on 14 December 1960 the Declaration on the Granting of Independence to Colonial Countries and Peoples. Several factors contributed to the historical decolonization movement: the rejection of brutal domination by a foreign power, the growing aspirations for independence of colonial people, the appeals of charismatic leaders, the formation and action of liberation movements with foreign support – the influence of the Wilsonian rights of people to self-determination and other freedoms – the weakening power of the European colonial empires as a result of military defeats or economic losses during World War II, the moral support of the United Nations Charter and recurrent resolutions condemning the colonialists. The 1960 Declaration declared, in part, that

> The subjection of peoples to alien subjugation, domination and exploitation constitutes a denial of fundamental human rights, is contrary to the Charter of the United Nations and is an impediment to the promotion of world peace and co-operation.

Colonies were non-autonomous territories placed under a quadruple domination by the colonial power: a military conquest and domination, through more potent weapons (guns and cannons against bows and arrows) and the forced recruitment of natives for European wars – a political domination, as government powers were retained by the colonial power and colonies were meant as an extension of the colonial country's strength, population and prestige – an economic domination, whereby the colony provided taxes, manpower (forced labour) and basic commodities (agricultural and mineral products) while the colonial power held a monopoly over colonial products and over finished products sold to the colony – a cultural domination, including religious indoctrination and linguistic imposition.

Colonization was initially due more to individual initiatives, mixing self-interest, greed, lust for power over 'inferior races' with idealism, than to deliberate government planning. Individual adventurers were searching for profit or fortune and expected to improve their social status. Ambitious military leaders hoped for glory on behalf of their country. Colonial Administrators were bringing civilization and order, education, roads, railways and airports, hospitals, they set up administrative structures, they imposed labour and collected taxes. Missionaries wanted to convert the pagans to the Christian faith, clothe them and suppress their 'barbaric' customs.

The Scot David Livingstone (1813–1873) was at the same time a physician, prospector, missionary, the explorer of Central Africa and a promoter of textile trade.

The good conscience of some of the colonizers, of colonial administrators, doctors and missionaries, and of those who supported their ventures in home countries is well expressed in Article 22 of the League of Nations' Covenant: colonies are inhabited by 'peoples not yet able to stand by themselves under the strenuous conditions of the modern world': hence, Kipling's white man's (self-assumed) burden of civilizing the 'barbarians'.

In a book published in 1924, a French author affirmed that France already possesses the 'confident affection' of her colonized peoples', an unlikely illusion probably shared by the population of his and other colonial countries.[1] Fanon's description, which adds nature's hostility to human colonization, is closer to the reality:

> Hostile nature, obstinate and fundamentally rebellious, is in fact represented in the colonies by the bush, by mosquitoes, natives and fever, and colonization is a success when all this indocile nature has finally been tamed. Railways across the bush, the draining of swamps and a native population which is non-existent politically and economically are in fact one and the same thing'.[2]

Besides its basic racism, colonialism is forever tainted by its brutality, its forced labour and its slave trade. One of the reasons used by Europeans to launch colonial expeditions was to stop or prevent the slavery of Africans by Arabs. However the Europeans' transatlantic slave trade surpassed in numbers the slavery of Muslim traders. Historians currently estimate that 11.6 million slaves were deported from Africa across the Atlantic ocean by Europeans – the mortality rate during sailing reached 35% in the 17th century. From the 16th to the 19th century, 5.15 million slaves were sold in Islamic countries.[3]

Slave trade was practised by Europeans from the 15th to the 19th century, on 5000 kilometres of coast of West Africa. Trade bases were sited in territories corresponding to the current states of Angola, Benin, Ghana, Nigeria, Senegal, Togo. European ships brought merchandise to Africa, transported slaves to the Americas, then brought back cargoes of sugar or other commodities. Ports such as Nantes, Bordeaux, La Rochelle, Liverpool, Bristol and others benefited from the trade. African rulers, merchants and middlemen also participated in the trade, thus also acquiring wealth at the expense and suffering of their fellow Africans.

Slavery was first abolished in the State of Vermont in 1777. In 1792, the King of Denmark set 1802 as the date of prohibition of the slave trade. In 1794, a French revolutionary decree abolished 'Negro slavery in the colonies', a decree reversed by

---

[1] V. Beauregard, *L'Empire colonial de la France*, quoted by D. L. Schalk, 'Reflections d'outre-mer on French colonialism' (1998) *Journal of European Studies*, March–June 1998, v. 28 n. 1–2 p. 5(19).

[2] F. Fanon, *The Wretched of the Earth* (Penguin Books, London, 1990), p. 201.

[3] Estimates by P. E. Lovejoy, quoted in W. Reinhard, *Petite histoire du colonialisme* (Bélin, Paris, 1997), pp. 95–96. Historian Roger Botte estimates that Arab slave trade of Africans until the 20th century has involved from 12 to 15 million persons, with the active participation of African leaders: see *Le Monde*, 31 August 2001.

Napoleon in 1801. Initiated by the Quakers, an anti-slavery campaign enticed the English Parliament to abolish slave trade in 1807, followed in 1833 by the abolition of slavery throughout the British Empire. In France, slavery was abolished by the Second Republic in 1848. The US abolished slavery by the 13th Amendment to the Constitution in 1865.[4]

The Final Declaration of the World Conference against Racial Discrimination, Xenophobia and Related Intolerance, held in Durban from 31 August to 7 September 2001, acknowledged, in part, that slavery and the slave trade were a crime against humanity. It recognised that Africans and people of African descent and indigeneous peoples were victims of colonialism and continued to be victims of its consequences. As a last day compromise over this controversial issue, it stopped short from establishing an obligation for reparations for those countries responsible for slave trade and colonialism.[5]

A selection of colonialist massacres and other atrocities follows, as exemplary events but with no attempt to give a complete review of this issue. A common characteristic in the early struggles of the 'natives' against the colonizers is that the former were generally vastly overpowered by the weapons of the latter. Some of the following samples were known to the actors of the events, historians and other specialists, but were only publicized recently, through either lack of interest on the part of the colonial home populations, or deliberate obfuscation on the part of their political and military leaders, and the feeling that the colonized peoples were inferior races who could be enslaved, ill-treated or killed without bad conscience. Until the second half of the 20th century, colonized peoples had no means of publicizing their fate and calling on external support.

The Extermination of the Herero (1904–1907)

This episode of a massacre committed by Germany in its colony of South-West Africa (now Namibia) became public knowledge only in 2000, almost 90 years after the events.[6]

On 12 January 1904, two African tribes, the Herero and the Nama rebelled against the German colonizers, in part as a protest against legal or illegal expropriation of their land in favour of German settlers: 6000 warriors attacked farms, killed settlers and mutilated their dead bodies. Once the fighting began, the new military commander General Lothar von Trotha, who arrived in the colony in June 1904, made his position clear: 'I believe that the nation as such should be

---

4 *Le Monde*, 17, 19–20 April 1988 and http//perso.wanadoo.fr/yekrik.yekrak/chronoeng.htm, 6 November 2000.

5 See *www.un.org/WCAR*.

6 Y. Ternon, *L'Etat criminel, les génocides au XXe siècle* (Seuil, Paris, 1995), pp. 311–313; *Newsweek*, 21 August 2000; T. Dedering, 'The Annihilation of the Herero in German South West Africa, 1904, in M. Levene and P. Roberts (eds), *The Massacre in History* (Berghahn Books, New York/Oxford, 1999), pp. 204–217. South West Africa, now Namibia, had been annexed as a protectorate in 1884.

annihilated'. Before his departure from Germany, he had declared a state of emergency for the whole colony giving absolute power to the military authorities.

Another officer wrote in his battle diary: 'We had been explicitly told beforehand that this dealt with the extermination of a whole tribe; nothing living was to be spared'.

Four thousand German soldiers, equipped with artillery, machine-guns and communications equipment defeated the native fighters. When the extermination order was lifted at the end of 1904, prisoners were herded into camps where many died of malnutrition, overwork and disease. Survivors were allocated as slave labourers to German businesses. They wore copper discs around their necks bearing numbers. There were 80 000 Herero when the rebellion started. In 1911, only 15 000 survived.

In debates in the *Reichstag*, leaders of the Social Democratic Party accused Chancellor Bülow not only of exterminating an African people, but also of being responsible for the brutalization of German soldiers who had been encouraged to abandon any 'civilized' military code of ethics. The extermination of the Herero was opposed by a substantial section of the German public.

Massacre in Madagascar (1947–1948)

Hardly known to the French population at the time of the Malagasy revolt and of its ferocious repression, and unknown to the French public 50 years later, this war caused an estimated 89 000 Malagasy deaths, while the revolt caused the death of 550 Europeans and approximately 1900 Malagasy inhabitants.[7]

Madagascar had been a French colony since 1896. After World War II and the early defeat of France, local leaders were claiming independence for their country, or at least, initially, the status of a free state associated with France within the short-lived French Union, a successor to the former French colonial empire. More concerned with the Indochinese conflict, French politicians reneged on prior promises, relying only on force. They gave priority to the settlers' and other economic interests, to the army's concern for French prestige and the preservation of Madagascar within the Western strategic space – an argument also used to justify the continued fight against the independence of Vietnam and Algeria. Researchers believe that the origin of the rebellion can be traced to secret societies rather than to the Malagasy official political party, the Democratic Movement of the Malagasy Renovation (MDRM). On 29 March 1947, the rebellion started, killing 150 French victims. The local authorities wrongly blamed the MDRM. Its leaders were arrested, its members hunted, the party dissolved. Against approximately 20 000 rebels with a few guns, the repression was carried out by the Foreign Legion, who gave no

---

7 *Le Monde*, 16–17 March 1997; F. Raison-Jourde, 'Colloque AFASPA Madagascar 1947 – Le soulèvement de 1947: bref état des lieux', *Clio en Afrique*, No. 4, Spring 1998. See also P. Vidal-Naquet, *La torture dans la République (1954–1962)* (Les Editions de Minuit, Paris, 1998), pp. 18–19. See also J. Tronchon, *L'insurrection malgache de 1947* (Karthala, Paris, 1986).

quarters: summary executions, burned villages, suspects thrown alive from planes, widespread killings, torture to exact confessions from arrested leaders. The rebellion ceased in December 1948: its failure was due essentially to the lack of armament of the rebels and the movement's international isolation.

The ignorance of the French population at the time of the events was due in part to the French military and administrative censorship, and more generally their lack of interest for this colonial 'accident' and its consequences on the 'natives'. Internally, they were still fighting against the economic deprivations following World War II, externally, the Indochinese war attracted more 'interest'. The French political and judiciary authorities hid or denied the exactions. No sanctions at any level were taken or even envisaged against those responsible for the massacre and torture. It also appears that the Malagasy elite and many families have exerted their own censorship over this period.

Darkness in Leopold's Congo (1884–1908)

In 1876, following a Geographical Conference held in Brussels at the initiative of King Leopold II of Belgium, its participants decided to create the International African Association, to be initially chaired by the King. The Association's official aim was the abolition of the black slave trade: dramatically, this noble aim was disfigured by Leopold's creation of a large slave exploitation carried out by European colonists and traders under his direction. Leopold's agents, including the journalist-explorer Henry Morton Stanley, occupied large territories in the Congo area, to the chagrin of other colonial powers. The Berlin Conference on the Congo, held in1884–1885, acknowledged the transformation of the Association into the Free Congo State, whose sovereign was Leopold. It had rich resources in precious woods, rubber, ivory and copper. In 1891–1892, Leopold, in contradiction with the Berlin Agreement, instituted the principle according to which all land not occupied by Africans was State property and could only be exploited by the State or by a contractor licensed by the State: this established a de facto monopoly on ivory and natural rubber. As the State's agents received bonuses on their production while the natives were subject to forced labour, a criminal exploitation system developed. In 1901, the Congo provided one tenth of the world production of rubber. High profits were used to finance public works decided by Leopold in Belgium.

The horrors perpetrated in the Congo became known in Europe and in the USA through the revelations of missionaries, travellers and Free State's employees. Campaigns were initiated by the British Anti-Slavery Society and the Aborigines Protection Society, now Anti-Slavery International, and by the Congo Reform Association created in 1904. The Association soon had branches in France, Germany, Italy, Norway, Switzerland and in the USA. The latter called for an international investigation of the Congo atrocities. A Commission of Inquiry was set up in 1904: a parade of witnesses offered horrifying testimony concerning black men, women and children: killings, cutting of hands and heads, torture, chained gangs with iron collars, starving porters, burned villages, hostage-taking, repeated lashes of the 'chicotte'. According to specialists, as quoted by Hochschild,[8] between 1880 and 1920, the population of the Congo was cut by at least a half, or an estimated 10 million people. Population losses were caused by massacres, starvation, exhaustion, disease, plummeting birth rate.

Following the Commission's report, Belgium took over the colony from the King in 1908. For many years, these atrocities were first hidden through Leopold's effective public relations campaigns, then forgotten. The Congolese people, scattered over a vast territory and lacking technical knowledge and resources, was unable to disseminate the extent of its suffering.

In French equatorial African territories, similar atrocities took place. An inquiry report written by the explorer Savorgnan de Brazza was suppressed by the government with the endorsement of Parliament and no reforms were initiated. In the 1920s, construction of a railway from Pointe-Noire to Brazzaville cost the lives of an estimated 20 000 forced African labourers.

Joseph Conrad's *Heart of Darkness*, published in 1902, recalls the grim realities of colonialism in the Congo: he observes the 'black shadows of disease and starvation'. Having seen 'the devil of violence, and the devil of greed, and the devil of hot desire', he 'foresaw that in the blinding sunshine of that land I would become acquainted with a flabby, weak-eyed devil of a rapacious and pitiless folly'. Indeed, colonial atrocities were motivated first by greed, and then compounded by the inner cruelty of man to man when not controlled by laws and moral obligations.

Colonialist crimes have long been hidden, denied or presented as forgivable incidents within an overall set of victories of civilization over the ignorant and barbarous natives. These crimes have only recently been acknowledged – they have not been prosecuted. Impunity has prevailed.

Communism: A Criminal Utopia

The implementation of the Communist utopia, in spite of its generous ambition to create a new egalitarian humanity liberated from the 'slavery' of capitalism and imperialism, brought about misery and death to millions.

The Soviet Revolution of 1917 created a totalitarian one-party system, without institutional counter-powers, which effectively destroyed individual rights and freedoms. A regime of terror, intended to keep in power the Bolshevik minority and to promote the revolution, eliminated all forms of opposition. Most of the reality – political repression, forced labour, deportation to concentration camps (the gulags), executions without judgement, forced confessions in well-scripted trials, torture, famines and forced conformity with the official dogma – were carefully hidden from

[8] Facts in this section are based on A. Hochschild, *King Leopold's Ghost, a Story of Greed, Terror, and Heroism in Colonial Africa* (Houghton Mifflin Company, Boston/New York, 1998), Chapter 15. See also Reinhard, pp. 252–254.

the outside world through propaganda and disinformation, with the loyal support, in foreign countries, of local Communist parties' leaders and members, convinced fellow-travellers or cynics: those who dared denounce the Soviet lies and crimes were treated as fascists or betrayers to the cause of the people.

Stalin's crimes were finally disclosed by Nikita Khrushchev in his secret speech to the Twentieth Communist Party Congress on 24 and 25 February 1956. Publications by dissidents in the 1970s confirmed the yet unbelieved rumors of Lenin's and Stalin's crimes. Truth based on facts finally emerged with the opening of Soviet archives after the fall of the Berlin Wall and the dislocation of the Soviet Empire (1989–1991). In France, the publication of the 'Livre noir du Communisme' (Communism's Black Book) in 1997, a best-seller in Europe, was greeted by some intellectuals as finally giving evidence of the extent of the repression in the USSR.[9] Others denounced the book as a manoeuver to disqualify, through the crimes committed in its name, a still worthy ideal. Others challenged the apparent parallel in horror between the Holocaust and the Communist crimes.

The current list of Soviet crimes and estimated number of related deaths are shown in Table 1.1.

The leaders of the new Russia have no intention to investigate crimes committed under Lenin and Stalin, to publicize demonstrated facts and their authors and to prosecute those who are still alive: an impossible task in Russia, when the demise of the USSR has essentially left in positions of political, military, judicial, adminis-

Table 1.1. Current list of Soviet crimes and estimated number of related deaths

(1) 1918–1922: shooting of tens of thousands hostages or persons jailed without judgement and massacre of hundreds of thousands of workers and peasant in rebellion against the new regime;
(2) Liquidation and deportation of the Don Cossacks in 1920;
(3) The famine of 1922 causing 5 million deaths;
(4) The murder of thousands of prisoners in concentration camps between 1918 and 1930;
(5) Deportation of 2 million kulaks (peasants) in 1930–1932;
(6) 1932–1933, 6 million deaths due to the Ukrainian famine, a genocide planned and carried out by Stalin;
(7) 1937–1938, close to 690 000 executions during the Great Purge;
(8) Deportation of hundreds of thousands of Poles, Ukrainians, Balts, Mouldaves and Bessarabians in 1939–1941, then in 1944–1945;
(9) Deportation of Volga Germans in 1941;
(10) Deportation of Crimea Tatars in 1943;
(11) Deportation of Chechens in 1944;
(12) Deportation of Ingouch in 1944.(13)

Altogether, deaths caused by the Soviet regime are estimated at 20 million.

Source: S. Courtois, N. Werth *et al*, *Le Livre noir du Communisme* (Laffont, Paris, 1997), pp. 15 and 22.

9 S. Courtois, N. Werth *et al.* (Eds), *Le Livre noir du communisme* (Laffont, Paris, 1997). See also R. J. Rummel, 'How many did Communist regimes murder', a 1993 study in <www2.hawaii.edu%7Erummel/COM.ART.HTM>, 3 March 2001.

trative and economic power the same persons who held important positions in the Soviet Communist Party hierarchy.

The main senior officials responsible for genocide, other massacres and exactions and their helpers have not been asked to at least show repentance: they are enjoying total judicial impunity for their crimes.

In spite of variations due to different political, economic, social and cultural factors, similar causes resulted in similar effects: in other countries subjected to the Communist ideology and to the one-party system, intransigent leaders were similarly convinced that they held the truth and the key to a happy future for all. Their task was to transform the society and invent a new (Communist) man. Political opponents and 'class' enemies had to be eliminated or forcefully re-educated, while the Communist elite in power was periodically purged to avoid deviations.

Political victims of Chinese Communism are estimated at 20 million: 5 million following the assumption of power, 1949–1954; 8 million during the series of repressions which followed, including 2–3 million during the Cultural Revolution, 1966–1971; at least 7 million who did not survive their detention. To these 20 million should be added 30–50 million deaths caused by the famine resulting from the forced collectivization of the peasants during the 'Great Leap Forward', the outcome of 'erroneous' decisions taken by the 'Great Helmsman'.[10]

In Cambodia, the Khmer Rouge's genocide of their own people was responsible for a large number of executions – between 400 000 and 900 000 – and for the inhuman treatment of between 700 000 and 1 200 000 other victims.[11] Current efforts to set up a Cambodian court, with international participation, to judge the surviving Khmer Rouge leaders are reviewed in Chapter 6.

More victims in Communist North Korea: since its creation in 1948, an estimated 2 million deaths for a country of 23 million inhabitants. In Vietnam, 1 million deaths, in Eastern Europe, 1 million, in Afghanistan, 1.5 million.

Communism imported in Africa caused directly or indirectly an estimated 1.7 million victims in Angola, Mozambique and Ethiopia.

The estimated total for all deaths caused by the Communist utopia from 1917 to the end of the 1980s is 100 million.[12] Those responsible for these crimes have yet escaped any prosecution or sanction, with the exception of the on-going Ethiopian trials. Stalin is still considered an unblemished hero in Russia.

---

[10] J. L. Domenach, 'Le modèle chinois' in 'Les crimes du communisme', *L'Histoire*, No. 247, October 2000, pp. 62–63.

[11] P. Brocheux, 'Pol Pot *et al.* destruction du Cambodge', in ibid, pp. 64–67.

[12] Courtois, p. 15. Rummel's estimate is 110 million.

Impunity in Civil and International Wars

All wars cause deaths, injuries, devastations and suffering. By allowing and training soldiers to kill, the lowest instincts of men and women are released: legal and humanitarian limits are difficult to observe. The scope of casualties and destruction is related to the geographical extent of wars, the duration of the wars, the number of countries in conflict, their relative political, economic and military power, their possession and use of lethal weapons of human and material destruction.

Civil wars oppose citizens of the same state by violent means, as rebels against the authorities of their own government either in order to take over power from then, or to share power with them, or in a few cases, to create a new country from part of the original one. In many cases, such internal armed conflict are supported financially and by the supply of weapons armed forces by external groups or countries. While most conflicts which have erupted in the post-Cold War era are internal conflicts, they are not restricted to that period. The causes for these conflicts are many: they may be due to political rivalries for power, claims for recognition of the rights of ethnic minorities, economic claims, religious conflicts, or to several of these causes. Internal conflicts have included massacres and genocides.

The following conflicts have involved crimes which have generally not been acknowledged nor prosecuted. Impunity has prevailed.

The Genocide of the Armenians (1915–1916)

The Armenian population of Turkey, the main ethnic minority in the country opposed to Turkish domination, suffered a slaughter of approximately 200 000 in 1895–1896. The Armenians supported the 1909 revolution of the Union and Progress Party, the Young Turks, who had promised liberal treatment of ethnic minorities. The Young Turks soon abandoned their liberal programme for an ultra-nationalist pan-Turkism and, in the same year, they killed approximately 30 000 Armenians in Adana.

In the early stages of World War I, in 1915, Russian armies advanced on Turkey from the north and the British attempted an invasion from the Mediterranean. Citing the threat of internal rebellion, the Ottoman government ordered large-scale round-ups, deportation and systematic torture and murder of Armenians, beginning in April 1915. Estimates of casualties vary from 600 000 to 2 million deaths out of the pre-war population of about 3 million Armenians. By 1917, fewer than 200 000 Armenians remained in Turkey. Whatever the exact dimensions of the genocide, Armenians suffered a demographic disaster that shifted the centre of the Armenian population from the heartland of historical Armenia to the safer eastern regions held by the Russians

Turkish crimes against Armenian citizens were recognised in March 1919 by a Commission on Responsibilities and Sanctions created by the Preliminary Peace Conference in Paris. Under Article 230 of the Treaty of Sèvres of 10 August 1920,

'The Allied powers reserve to themselves the right to designate the tribunal which shall try the persons so accused [responsible for the massacres], and the Turkish government undertakes to recognise such tribunal'. However, under Turkish pressure, the Treaty of Lausanne of 24 July 1923, which replaced the Treaty of Sèvres, omitted any mention of violations of the laws and customs of war or of an Allied tribunal.

Turkey's official position is that no genocide occurred: the 1915 'events' are best described as a civil war within a global war. Turkey denies that there was any government-planned-and-executed scheme to exterminate the Empire's Armenian population, an anti-Turkish historical calumny. The main Turkish argument is to equalize the position of the essentially unarmed Armenian population with that of the Ottoman government, its army and police, and to consider that any Armenian 'suffering' was caused by its own provocation and rebellion.

Turkey acceded to the Genocide Convention of 1948 on 31 July 1950. On 29 August 1985, the UN Sub-Commission on Prevention of Discrimination and Protection of Minorities noted the historical fact of the genocide of the Armenians, a resolution endorsed by the UN Commission on Human Rights in 1986. On 18 June 1987, the European Parliament also recognised this historical event as an act of genocide but stressed that neither political nor legal or material claims could be derived from this recognition. In November 2000, the European Parliament invited, in part, the Turkish government and the National Asssembly to recognise publicly the genocide to which the Armenian minority had been subjected before the creation of a modern state in Turkey. The genocide has also been recognised by the Russian Duma, the Greek Parliament, the Belgian Senate, the Italian Parliament and the Vatican. In January 2001, the French Parliament recognised 'the Armenian genocide of 1915'. Turkey retaliated by cancelling an array of contracts with French companies. A resolution condemning the genocide was withdrawn by the Speaker of the US House of Representatives in October 2000, citing President Clinton's warning that a vote could harm national security and hurt relations with Turkey, a NATO ally, thus acceding to an often-used Turkish argument.

Turkey still denies the very existence of an Armenian genocide, the first genocide of the 20th century.[13]

Israel vs. Palestine (1948– ...)

Born with the creation of the State of Israel in 1948, the conflict between Israel and the Palestinians endures in spite of recurrent attempts to find a compromise settlement. A fragile peace has been reached with Egypt and Jordan, but Syria, Iraq and other Arab countries still do not recognise the State of Israel. Following several full-fledged wars, the Palestinians are currently carrying out a second *Intifada*

[13] Beigbeder (1999), pp. 80–87, *International Herald Tribune*, thereafter referred to as *IHT*, 21–22 October 2000; *Le Monde*, 19 and 31 January 2001.

countered by military retaliation from the Israelis, increasing hatred on both sides, feeding Islamist fanaticism and terrorism, with the risk of a regional extension of the conflict. In the 14 months ending in December 2001, more than 800 Palestinians and 200 Israelis have been killed. [14]

The Indonesian Massacres (1965–1966)

The former Dutch Indies became independent in 1949 as Indonesia. On 1 October 1965, the army, under the direction of General Suharto and with the support of the CIA, took power. Its leaders initiated and encouraged the savage killing of Communist Party leaders, members and supporters, with the aid of bands of youths and the local population. With 10 million members in 1965, the Communist Party was seen as a threat to the military in view of its infiltration of part of the airforce and the navy, a threat to landowners because of its collectivist plans, to Muslims because of its anti-religious doctrine, and to the USA, concerned about potential Communist expansion in Southeast Asian countries. In a holy war, Muslims slaughtered atheists. The victims included many thousands of Chinese, suspected because China had become communist, but also targets of long-standing ethnic resentment in view of their domination of commerce and trade. Possessions were looted and houses burned. Eventually, the army re-established order.

The number of deaths is estimated at 500 000 for the period December 1965 to mid-1966 and the number of those arrested also at 500 000. Most were detained without judgement and released only in 1978. The massacres had first a political motivation: to eliminate the Communist threat from Indonesian politics, within the context of the East-West confrontation which provided US support to the Indonesian political and military leadership. In addition, ethnic, religious and economic factors also contributed to the hatred and violence.

These massacres undoubtedly constitute crimes against humanity. Some scholars have labelled them as a genocide, although the massacres were not intended as a total extermination of the groups concerned.

The crisis in **East Timor** (1999) and current judiciary developments in Indonesia and East Timor are reviewed in Chapter 6.

The Biafran War (1967–1970)

Nigeria proclaimed its independence within the British Commonwealth in 1960, which it left in 1963 to become the Republic of Nigeria. Nigeria is a federation of states divided by three major ethnic groups: the Ibo, Hausa/Fulani and Yoruba. The eastern region is dominated by the Ibo (Christians), the west by the Yoruba and the north by the Hausa/Fulani (muslims). Mounting ethnic tension between these

---

[14] *Le Monde*, 1 December 2001.

groups caused the Biafrans – the Ibos and other minority ethnic groups – in the eastern region to fight for their independence by secession from Nigeria.

The war began with ethnic rivalry in the armed forces. In January 1966, a coup led by army officers belonging to the Ibo tribe overthrew the civil government and murdered the Hausa prime minister and the premiers of the north and western regions. A military government led by Major General Johnson T.U. Aguiyi-Ironsi, an Ibo, then instituted a military dictatorship and appointed a military governor in each region. Fearing an Ibo plot to centralise and dominate the federal country, Muslim crowds directed pogroms against the Ibo. In September 1966, massacres of Ibo took place from Kano to Lagos, killing 30 000 Ibo and causing a massive Ibo flight of over a million persons, from the north to the east. On 30 May 1967, Lieutenant Colonel C.O. Ojukwu declared the Eastern Region a sovereign and independent republic. On 30 May, he proclaimed the secession of the Region and the formation of the Republic of Biafra. Fighting broke out between the federal and the Biafran forces. Despite attempts by the Organisation of African Unity to end the civil war, hostilities continued until 1970, when the federal forces had starved the Biafran population into submission. Ojukwu fled the country on 11 January and a delegation to Lagos formally surrendered on 15 January 1970, thus ending the existence of an independent Biafra.

Most of Biafra's military supplies were acquired in the international arms market through unofficial assistance by France via former French African colonies. Britain gave diplomatic support and limited military aid to Nigeria, The USSR was a significant source of arms to the Government of Nigeria. Most African countries did not recognise Biafra, so as not to encourage secessionist trends in the continent.

Biafra was only recognised by Gabon, Ivory Coast, South Africa, Tanzania and Zambia. The US placed sanctions on exports of military goods on both Biafrans and Nigerians.

US and European relief organisations, including Caritas Internationalis, Catholic Relief Services, the World Council of Churches, CARE and others, came to the assistance of the Biafrans in response to Biafran propaganda. Biafra alleged that the Federal Military Government was perpetrating genocide on the Biafran people through the slaughter of civilians by federal ground troops, the indiscriminate bombing of civilian targets, the blockage, its rejection of humanitarian aid and the consequent starvation in the Eastern region. Airlifts brought food, medical supplies and arms to the war zones during the nights. The International Committee of the Red Cross tried to coordinate aid for both sides but was expelled from Nigeria in August 1968.

It is estimated that, during the Biafran war, 2 million people in the eastern region died from the warfare, disease and starvation.[15]

---

[15] Beigbeder (1991), pp. 259–260; Ternon, pp. 313–316; <www.american.edu/projects/mandala/TED/ice/BIAFRA.HTM> , 28 February 2001.

Sri Lanka: An Intractable Conflict (1975– ...)

The Liberation Tigers of Tamil Eelan have been waging a brutal struggle for an independent homeland in the country's northern and eastern provinces since the mid-1970s. The Indu Tamil minority (12.5%) claims that the Buddhist Sinhalese majority (74%) discriminates against them in jobs, housing and education. The violent rebellion counts about 10 000 fighters, including suicide bombers. Members of the Tigers group are responsible for deliberate and arbitrary killings of civilians, torture, hostage-taking and abductions, while the government security forces have also committed human rights violations under the state of emergency. Efforts to solve the ethnic conflict appear deadlocked.

The civil war casualties are estimated at 60 000 deaths.[16]

Angola: The Unending Conflict (1975– ...)

The conflict in Angola between the Popular Movement for the Liberation of Angola (MPLA) whose members later formed the Angolan government, and the National Union for the Total Independence of Angola (UNITA), predates the Angola's independence, which was gained on 11 November 1975. When the Portuguese left Angola, the conflict degenerated into a civil war between the MPLA led by José Eduardo dos Santos, supported by Cuban troops, themselves backed by the USSR, and UNITA, led by Jonas Savimbi, with the support of the South African army, backed by the US. The end of the Cold War led to the withdrawal of the Cuban troops, the independence of Namibia and the end to South African support for UNITA. However, the conflict continued, leaving hundreds of thousands dead and tens of thousands disabled. UN-monitored elections were won by dos Santos: its results were rejected by Savimbi who resumed the fighting. A cease-fire took effect in November 1994, following the signing of the Lusaka Protocol by the two parties. The conflict started again in December 1998. On 23 December 1998, in a Presidential Statement, the UN Security Council called for an immediate cessation of hostilities and, again, said that the primary responsibility for the failure to achieve peace in Angola lay with the leadership of UNITA. In April 2000, the Council voted to tighten its sanctions against UNITA, aimed at preventing the illicit flow of arms and the smuggling of petroleum into UNITA-controlled areas and the sale of diamonds by UNITA. Angola's diamond fields have earned Savimbi and UNITA some $500 million annually. These financial resources together with Savimbi's lust for power and disdain for democracy explain his recurrent stalling of peace negotiations and his war actions, to the detriment of his country's potentially rich economy, causing more deaths and suffering in the Angolan population.

By 2000, an estimated half a million civilians had been killed in the conflict, 300 000 others were wounded, including 100 000 maimed by landmines. Out of

[16] *Amnesty International report 2000*, pp. 221–223; *Newsweek*, 29 May 2000.

12 million inhabitants, one third has been chased from their homes. In addition to these displaced persons, there were about 350 000 refugees outside of Angola. Life expectancy in the country is a low 42.[17]

Sudan: Another On-going Civil War (1983–..)

Sudan achieved independence in 1956, by agreement between Britain and Egypt. The country was then periodically shaken by military coups, while a long civil war opposed North and South. The Christian and animist non-arabic speaking southerners had begun a revolt in 1955, fearing that the new nation would be dominated by the Muslim arabic-speaking north. Following a successful coup by Colonel Muhammad Gaafur al-Nimeiri in 1969, the civil war was ended by an agreement between the government and the Sudan Liberation Front signed in February 1972 at Addis Ababa. The Sudan People's Liberation Army (SPLA) led by Colonel John Garang has been fighting since 1983 to replace the existing government, establish greater autonomy for its region and abolish the universal application of Islamic law. Nimeiri was overthrown in 1985. Following elections in 1986, a civilian government was overthrown by another coup in 1989, led by Lieutenant General Omar Ahmed al-Bashir. He reinforced Islamic law, and continued to pursue the war with the South, diverting relief aid from the famine-stricken south to the north. Despite the prevailing conditions of famine, the government in Khartoum refused either to declare that a food emergency existed in Sudan or to formally make a request for assistance from international donors. A peace agreement was signed between the government and SPLA in November 1999. However, the value of the agreement was cast in doubt when President al-Bashir dissolved the parliament and declared a state of emergency.

The long conflict has claimed an estimated 2 million lives, in part through war-related famine. There are more than 4.5 million internally displaced persons within Sudan, while more than 350 000 Sudanese are refugees abroad. More than 2 million people displaced from the south live in camps around Khartoum.[18]

---

[17] *Basic Facts about the United Nations* (UN, New York, 1995), pp. 33–37; J. Tessitore and S. Woolfson, *A Global Agenda, Issues before the 55th General Assembly of the United Nations, An annual publication of the UN Association of the USA* (Rowman and Littlefield Publishers, Inc., Lanham/New York/Boulder/Oxford, 2000), pp. 23–26. A UN report accused the governments of Burkino Faso, Togo, Rwanda and Bulgaria of complicity in UNITA's sanctions-busting activities: all denied their complicity. See also UN *Press Releases* SC/&& + &, 23 December 1998 and SC/6846, 18 April 2000 and *Le Monde*, 30 December 2000.

[18] R. Bruce McColm, Survey Coordinator, *Freedom in the World, Political Rights and Civil Liberties, 1991–1992* (Freedom House, Lanham/London, 1992), pp. 416–417; *Amnesty International Report 2000* (Amnesty International Publications, London, 2000), p. 223; Tessitore/Woolfson, p. 27.

The Liberia Civil War (1989–1997)

In 1821, the American Colonization Society created Liberia as a home for American slaves, and to christianize West Africa. Liberia's independence was proclaimed in 1947, the first independent country in Africa south of the Sahara. In 1980, Samuel Doe, a 28-year-old member of the Krahn tribe, seized power and killed President William Tolbert. During his tenure, most indigenous tribes co-existed peacefully until 1985, when a coup was attempted against Doe. Since 1985, the indigenous tribes have been fighting against each other. In 1989, Charles Taylor, a leader of the National Patriotic Front of Liberia, invaded Liberia from Côte d'Ivoire to end Doe's dictatorship. Doe was killed in September 1990. The Liberian Civil War has raged since December 1989. From 1990 to 1997, 30 000–60 000 armed fighters (10% of whom were under the age of 15) raped, stole and killed. Since 1990, 150 000–200 000 Liberians have died, 1.5 million of the country's original population of 2.5 million have fled their homes, and hundreds of thousands of them have been injured. The economy has collapsed. Charles Taylor is still President of Liberia.[19]

The Iraq–Iran War (1980–1988)

The Iran–Iraq War began in September 1980 when Iraq invaded Iran and asserted its determination to achieve full control over the Shatt-al-Arab and reverse the Algiers Accord of 1975. In July 1988, Iran accepted the terms of UN Security Council Resolution 598, passed in August 1987, thus ending the conflict. In February 1991, the withdrawal of forces was completed. The eight-year devastating warfare, which had inflicted massive casualties on both sides, accounted for up to a million deaths and the injury and dislocation of millions more, as well as economic losses estimated in excess of $100 million. Recurrent charges by both sides of chemical warfare, bombardment of civilian populations and mistreatment of prisoners of war prompted visits to the front by various UN Commissions. In August 1988, UN investigators concluded that Iraq had been using chemical weapons with increasing frequency since 1984, employing mustard gas, two types of nerve gas, and cyanide gas against Iranian troops and civilians, including a hospital. Late 1988, the Iraqi army reportedly employed chemical weapons as part of a massive campaign by some 30 000 Iraqi troops against Kurdish rebels. The campaign resulted in the flight of 100 000 Kurds into Turkey.[20]

---

[19] 'How Leaders Caused Tribal Conflict in Liberia's War', <www.africalibrary.org/course/papers/sheer.html>, 18 March 2001.

[20] J. Tessitore and S. Woolfson (Eds) *Issues Before the 45th General Assembly of the United Nations, An annual publication of the UN Association of the USA* (Lexington Books, D.C. Heath and Company/Lexington, Mass./Toronto, 1991), pp. 4–5.

The Invasion of Kuwait by Iraq (1990–1991)

On 2 August 1990, Iraqi forces invaded Kuwait. On the same day, the UN Security Council condemned the invasion and demanded Iraq's withdrawal. In November, the Council authorized Member States cooperating with Kuwait to use 'all necessary means' to uphold and implement a series of resolutions 'and to restore international peace and security in the area'. Coalition forces began air attacks against Iraq on 16 January 1991. Hostilities were suspended on 27 February, by which time Iraqi forces had left Kuwait. A cease-fire was ordered and various conditions imposed on Iraq.

The US Defense Department estimated in 1991 that up to 100 000 Iraqi soldiers may have died during hostilities, and experts have further estimated that between 5 000 and 15 000 civilians died during the war, and that up to 86 000 more perished in the four months following the cease-fire due to disease, malnutrition, and civil war. An international team of health experts visiting Iraq in November 1991 concluded that 900 000 Iraqi children were malnourished, and 100 000 were on the brink of starvation.[21]

Massacres in the Congo (1997–2001 ?)

Laurent-Désiré Kabila took control of the Democratic Republic of the Congo in 1997 after a bloody war in which his supporters and Rwandan and Ugandan allies killed tens of thousands of civilians. In August 1998, Tutsi Congolese of Rwandan origin started a rebellion in the Kivu. The conflict became a regional war opposing two coalitions: the Congolese government forces supported by Angola, Zimbabwe and Namibia, against rival factions supported by Rwanda and Uganda, Kabila's former allies. All parties in this internationalized civil war have engaged in indiscriminate attacks on civilians, summary executions, rape and destruction of property, resulting in massive displacement of populations. In October 1997, Kabila forced the UN to recall from Congo a human rights team charged to investigate reports that his Tutsi-dominated troops had massacred Rwandan Hutu refugees (including some of the leaders and participants of the Rwanda genocide). In April 1999, the UN Special Rapporteur Roberto Garreton submitted a report to the UN Commission on Human Rights recording the many cases of exactions committed by the Congolese government forces and their allies and by the rebellion. His recommendation that an international criminal tribunal should be created has not yet been considered seriously by the UN Security Council.

---

[21] J. Tessitore and S. Woolfson (Eds), *A Global Agenda. Issues Before the 47th General Assembly of the United Nations, An annual publication of the UN Association of the USA* (University Press of America, Lanham/New York/London, 1992), pp. 38–39.

The War Between Eritrea and Ethiopia (1998–2000)

A relatively 'small' and geographically limited war between two African countries, this international war, an exception among the many civil wars, was traditional in the sense that it was caused by a border dispute which expanded over two years and unnecessarily caused many deaths and suffering. The fighting started on 6 May 1998 when Eritrea, which had won independence from Ethiopia in 1993 after a 30-year guerrilla war, invaded Ethiopian territory in Badime. The conflict set against each other the two leaders, Ethiopia's Prime Minister Meles Zenawi and Eritrea's President Isaias Afwerki, caused in part by a century-long cultural and economic division between the two countries. Two years of World War I-style trench fighting in the border region took tens of thousands of lives, in a region already beset by famine. The war hindered the distribution of relief supplies, while some donor countries and non-governmental organisations became opposed to sending aid to the parties who gave precedence to war expenditures over their population's welfare.

On 12 December 2000, the leaders of Ethiopia and Eritrea signed a peace agreement in Algiers, after months of diplomatic pressure from the USA and support of Algeria, the UN and the Organisation for African Unity. According to US estimates, 50 000–100 000 soldiers were killed, an unknown number of prisoners captured and 650 000 persons displaced on both sides of the border. The war cost those two poor countries an estimated $1 billion to fight over a barren patch of territory.[22]

Russian Crimes in Chechnya (1999– ...)

The first Russian/Chechen war of 1994–1996 ended with the de facto autonomy of Chechnya and a state of anarchy, kidnappings and killings, followed by Chechen attacks into neighbouring Dagestan in August 1999. The terror bombing of buildings in Moscow in September attributed to the Chechens (300 Russian deaths) triggered the second war, initiated by Vladimir Putin, the designated heir to President Yelstin. Putin won wide popularity by vowing to fight until victory for the Russians. He was elected President on 26 March 2000.

The military operations, started in September 1999, met fierce resistance. On 7 February 2000, Acting President Putin claimed that Russian troops had taken control of Grozny. The city had been devastated by shelling and fighting.

According to Human Rights Watch and other national and international NGOs, Russian troops regularly engage in arbitrary arrests, unlawful detentions, torture, summary executions, disappearances, extortion, violation of medical neutrality and the shelling of population centres. Corruption and lack of discipline and

[22] *IHT*, 13 December 2000.

accountability among the troops remain pervasive. Evidence of atrocities and war crimes has been provided by observers, witnesses and refugees.[23]

The Russian response has been to deny all these charges, to reject any independent international investigation, to refuse access to journalists and observers of human rights organisations. The Russian authorities have delayed the return of an observation mission of the Organisation for Security and Cooperation in Europe (OSCE), to which they had agreed at the Organisation's summit meeting in Istambul in November 1999. A videotape of a mass grave of Chechens released by a German television channel in February 2000 was denounced by a Kremlin official as the 'falsification of the year'. Vladimir Kanavalov, the Russian human rights commissioner said in an interview in July 2000 that he had yet to confirm a single instance of abuse or corruption at detention centres. The only senior Russian officer charged with war crimes, Colonel Iouri Boudanov, considered as a hero by the army and Russian public opinion, may be acquitted. He is accused of having raped and strangled a young Chechen, Elza Koungaieva, in March 2000 in the village of Tangui-Chou. In July 2001, the army announced that it was setting up an alternative military broadcasting station, to counter the focus on 'bad news' by other medias.[24]

Reactions by intergovernmental organisations to Russian war crimes and crimes against humanity in Chechnya have been uneven. The Parliamentary Assembly of the Council of Europe first sanctioned Russia in April 2000 by suspending its voting rights. Russia was admitted as a member in 1996. On 25 January 2001, the Assembly restored these rights to the Russian delegation, while expressing its 'grave concern' regarding the lack of follow-up given to charges of violations of human rights.[25]

A four-day visit to Moscow and Chechnya in April 2000 by Mary Robinson, UN High Commissioner for Human Rights ended in a failure to effect any change in the Russian position. President Putin refused to meet with her. The authorities rejected her proposal to set up an international inquiry as an interference in the country's internal affairs. Mary Robinson finally only asked the Russian government to set up an independent national inquiry commission. On 20 April 2001, the UN Commission on Human Rights adopted a resolution (also) expressing its grave concern about human rights violations in Chechnya. The resolution strongly condemned the use of disproportionate force and serious human rights violations by Russia's forces and called on Russia to ensure that both civilian and military prosecutors undertake credible and exhaustive criminal investigations of all violations of international human rights and humanitarian law. It also raised concerns about the pattern of

---

[23] See Human Rights Watch report on 'The "Dirty War" in Chechnya: Forced Disappearances, Torture and Summary Executions', 21 March 2001; *IHT*, 21 March 2001.

[24] *Le Monde*, 30 November 2000, 13 April 2001; *IHT*, 26–27 February 2000, 27 July 2001.

[25] *Le Monde*, 8 April 2000, 27 January 2001.

forced disappearances, torture and summary executions perpetrated by Russian forces in Chechnya.[26]

On 23 March 2001, President Putin was received by the 15 members of the European Union at the Stockholm Summit. He rejected their request for a 'political solution' of the Chechnya conflict. During the meeting, President Jacques Chirac saluted Russia as a 'strategic partner'. President George W. Bush has given repeated public support to Putin, finding him 'trustworthy', thus virtually silencing almost all other criticism of the brutal war by other Western governments. In a news conference at the Kremlin in July 2001, Putin said: 'I have no intention of changing ... my approach' on Chechnya. Against all evidence, he asserted that Russian cleansing operations 'boil down to passport checks and measures to identify people who are on the federal wanted list' and that alleged crimes by his forces are being investigated and prosecuted.[27]

Putin's assertions were refuted on 11 July 2001 by General Vladimir Moltensky, acting commander of Russian forces in the Northern Caucasus. According to the Itar-Tass news agency, he said that his soldiers had committed 'widespread crimes' when, after mine blasts had killed 11 Russian soldiers and wounded others, they inflicted beatings and electric shocks on 1500 civilians and looted homes in the villages of Assinovskaya and Sernovodsk. The General instructed his subordinate commanders to respond to every citizen complaint filed with prosecutors as a result of the 'mopping up' operation on 3 and 4 July.[28]

Aside of this isolated recognition, promptly rejected by Moscow, the Russian leaders show a genuine 'unwillingness' to carry out reliable investigations and prosecution. National judiciary recourses and sanctions are ineffective, at this stage, and the Russian authorities are deaf to the weak exhortations of a few governments and IGOs and to the direct accusations of human rights groups.

The Russian political and military leaders are not, at present, subject to national or international criminal justice. Russian crimes in Chechnya are not likely to be sanctioned unless or until the Russian government changes its position, as a result of changed opinion of its population and significant political and economic pressures on of Russia.

Following the 11 September attacks, Western countries have accepted Putin's expedient claim that his war in Chechnya was another 'war on terrorism'. They have muted their criticisms, leaving the disclosure of the Russian war crimes and crimes against humanity to human rights NGOs.

[26] *Le Monde*, 6 April 2000, 7 April 2001 and *hrw-news@igc.topica.com*, 20 April 2001.

[27] *Le Monde*, 25–26 March 2001; *IHT*, 23 July 2001.

[28] *IHT*, 12 July 2001; *Le Monde*, 13 July 2001.

Chapter 1

Legal Impunity: Amnesty

The Spanish Civil War (1936–1939)

A prelude to World War II in troubled Western Europe, torn between the combined Fascist and Nazi ideologies and the threatened democratic, pacifist and human rights ideals, the Spanish Civil War was a war by proxy and actual forces and armaments between Mussolini's Italy and Hitler's Germany on the one hand and Stalin's USSR on the other. The fragile Spanish democracy – and the French Republic – were threatened by both rightist Fascism and Nazism, and leftist Communism. The Spanish War also set in opposition an anticlerical government, the Republicans, and leftist parties against the conservative Catholic Church which supported Franco's Nationalists. The war was finally a useful ground for testing new German weapons and strategies against Stalin's Communist expansion plans.

Following the murder, in July 1936, of Jose Calvo Sotelo, the leader of a coalition of monarchists and fascists, the army issued a *pronunciamento* and started military operations against the Republican socialist-communist government. A junta of generals formed a government at Burgos, which was recognised by Germany and Italy. These governments had provided transport for General Franco's African army from Morocco to Spain. In October 1936, Franco was named head of State, with the rank of *generalissimo* and the title of *el caudillo* (the leader).

Moscow provided advisers, logistics experts and some field-grade officers. Foreign volunteers, including more than 2000 from the USA, formed the International Brigades. A conscript Republican army was created. The USSR supplied arms and munitions to the Republic. France provided some aircraft and artillery. The regular army supported Franco's Nationalists movement. Italy dispatched more than 50 000 Italian 'volunteers' (in reality, conscripts) to Spain. The German Condor Legion – who committed the terror bombing of Guernica – provided air support for the Nationalists and tested the tactics and the equipment used a few years later by the Luftwaffe. Germany and Italy also supplied large quantities of artillery and armor, as well as the personnel to use this weaponry. A non-intervention agreement concluded in 1936 only cut off French and British aid to the republic. Germany and Italy did not observe the agreement. The USSR was not a signatory: by 1938, Stalin lost interest in the Spanish War. The weaker republican army, also suffering from internal political dissensions, was losing the war. Its commander surrendered to the Nationalists on 31 March 1939, thus ending the Civil War.

The estimated number of casualties of the Spanish Civil War is 600 000 dead from all causes, including combat, bombing and executions. In the Republican sector, tens of thousands died of starvation, and several hundred thousands more fled from Spain. According to the British historian Hugh Thomas, it is likely that 50 000 persons were killed by the Nationalists during the first six months of the war. These executions were meant to 'clean' Spain from freemasonry, marxism and jewry, considered as pernicious. According to the Spanish historian Antonio

Montero Moreno, 6832 members of the clergy, including 4184 priests and 13 bishops, were killed during the conflict by the Republicans. Churches and convents were often taken as targets, plundered and set on fire. In 1992, Pope John-Paul II beatified 122 martyrs, priests, nuns and lay people, who were killed by the Republicans during the Spanish War, and in 2001, another group of 233 martyrs of the same War.[29]

Following Franco's death in November 1975, Juan Carlos became King. A Parliamentary regime was introduced in 1976 and a democratic Constitution adopted in 1978. Amnesty Acts were issued in July 1976 and October 1977. The collective memories of a cruel civil war, the popular consensus that those involved were equally guilty of atrocities, the obsession of the Spanish people for peace, order and stability, did not trigger a movement for a judiciary process.[30]

Paradoxically, Spanish judges were pioneers in pursuing the practice of universal jurisdiction: the arrest warrant for General Pinochet, then in London, was issued by Spanish judge Baltasar Garzon in October 1998.

Algeria: A 'Dirty War' (1954–1962)

On 20 June 2000, the French daily *Le Monde* published the testimony of Louisette Ighilahriz, a partisan of Algerian independence, tortured by French paratroopers 30 kilometres from Algiers, between September and December 1957. She was saved by a transfer to a 'regular' prison by a French military doctor, whose name she had tried to find for decades.

This publication, almost 40 years after the end of the Algerian war, opened a flood of other testimonies, confessions and controversies in the French press about the practice of torture by the French army during the Algerian war of independence.[31]

Of those in command during the war, one general, Marcel Bigeard, now 84, rejected the testimony as only lies and denied any practice of torture. Another general, Jacques Massu, now 92, who 'won' the battle of Algiers, recognised that the practice of torture was generalised and institutionalized during the Algerian war. He

[29] <lcweb2.loc.gov/cgi-bin/query/r?frd/cstdy:@field(DOCID+es0031>, 28 February 2001; *Le Monde*, 13 March 2001.

[30] See Paloma Aguilar, 'Collective Memory of the Spanish Civil War: The Case of the Political Amnesty in the Spanish Transition to Democracy', Working Paper 1996/85, December 1996, www.march.es/NUEVO/IJM/CEACS/PUBLICACIONES/WORKING%20PAPERS/1996_85.pdf

[31] See *Le Monde*, 22 June, 23 November, 4 December 2000; *IHT*, 3 January 2001. Besides individual and group summary executions, atrocities committed by the French included burning inhabited villages by napalm, asphyxiating prisoners smoked in caves, or in wine cellars, throwing prisoners from helicopters, burying suspects in sand under the sun, rapes. Hundreds of thousands of peasants were deported to 'centres of regroupment', use of electricity current or dumping in water tubs etc. FLN atrocities also included massacres of civilian French and Algerian population, death by cutting throats and other parts of the human body, bombs in cafeterias etc. See also P. Blanchard, N. Bancel, S. Lemaire, 'Le miroir colonial brisé', *Le Monde diplomatique*, July–August 2001, pp. 36–38.

expressed regrets for the practice: 'morally, torture is something pretty dismal'. He said that 'one could have acted differently', although in 1971, he had justified the practice because it led to the quick discovery of explosive devices in the European quarter of Algiers, thus avoiding the death of innocent people. In his recent interview, he said it would be a good thing for France to acknowledge what it did and condemn it officially. Another general, Paul Aussaresses, now 82, described the practice of torture and summary executions, in the full knowledge of the political leaders. He said that this was nothing he 'relished', but something he was resigned to when he went to Algiers. He confirmed that 3024 had disappeared among 24 000 assigned to residence. He admitted that he had personally killed 24 suspected guerrillas. The confessions by the senior military leaders allowed many other testimonies of officers, soldiers required to do their military service in the Algerian undeclared war: some recalled their horror at what they had done, had seen done, being haunted by those memories – others felt that account should be taken of the atrocities committed by the rebels – others attributed the main responsibility to the political leaders.

Algiers was conquered by France in 1830 and the total territory was under French domination in 1847. The conquest was brutal and rebellions brutally repressed. The settlement of French and other Europeans in Algeria was encouraged by the French governments: there were more than a million established settlers in the 1950s. Algeria was considered as part of France, not as a colony, although the natives did not enjoy the status and privileges of French citizens, as did the settlers.

The nationalist movement for independence developed as from 1930. On 9 May 1945, between 8000 and 10 000 Algerians were massacred by French forces to crush a rebellion in Sétif and other Algerian towns, attributed to 'agents of Nazi Germany'. Armed rebellion under the leadership of the 'Front de libération nationale' (FLN) started on 1 November 1954. In 1955, another massacre took place in Philippeville: 12 000 victims.

The Evian Agreements of March 1962 ended the conflict and Algeria became independent on 1 July 1962. Most settlers left Algeria for France, in the fear of retribution by the new Algerian authorities and people, at great material and moral cost, although their resettlement into the French economy was easier than originally feared.

The French population, initially in favour of maintaining French domination in Algeria, found relief in the end of the war and was eager to forget the conflict, including reports of torture committed by the French police and army. The French knew about torture but the vast majority chose to ignore the revelations or warnings given by a few writers, officers and officials.

Up to 2 million French military forces fought during the war. French military deaths are estimated at 25 000, one third of them through accidents, plus 65 000 injured and 485 disappearances; the undeclared war caused, in the civilian population, 2788 deaths, 7541 injured and 875 disappearances; Algerian deaths are estimated at 500 000.[32]

The political leaders, Socialist and Christian-Democrats, with the support of the right, instituted a state of urgency in Algeria as from 3 April 1955 which allowed the extra-judiciary assignment of suspects to residence and press censorship. On 12 March 1956, almost all members of the Parliament (including the Communists) authorized the government to take all exceptional measures to restore order, protect the population and safeguard the territory. All police and justice powers were then delegated to General Massu and the 10th paratrooper Division. Military torture sections were created ('Dispositif opérationnel de protection') and almost 2 million Algerians were regrouped in zones, villages or concentration camps, The government set up three commissions to investigate allegations of torture: they were totally ineffective. Reasons of state, respect for the army and misguided patriotism prevailed over search for facts and condemnation of human rights violations.

Amnesty was granted to the French military and the FLN in 1962 and 1966. Furthermore, according to the French criminal code, crimes such as torture, voluntary homicide or war crimes are subject to a statute of limitation, except for crimes against humanity. But these had to be linked to Nazi crimes until the promulgation of the new criminal code of 1994 extended their definition.

In 1991, a book on '*La bataille de Paris – 17 Octobre 1961*' (The Battle of Paris) by the historian Jean-Luc Einaudi finally brought to light the bloody repression carried out by the Paris police under the orders of Maurice Papon, the Prefect of Paris. A peaceful manifestation organised by the FLN but forbidden by the authorities, was brutally repressed: according to Einaudi's estimates, 300 Algerians were killed by the police, drowned in the river Seine, or shot by bullets, or died as a result of skull fractures. During more than 30 years, the official version was that only three Algerians had been found dead.

Why the long silence over the Algerian war ? Deliberate will of the political and military authorities to obfuscate the war years, refusal of the population to admit a painful past, silence of young soldiers over practices which they were trying to forget, censorship or lack of interest by the medias, or simply lack of concern of the French population towards Arabs who had also committed their own crimes. Or generally, common, ordinary racism towards Arabs, a still prevalent feeling among the French.

Why the explosion of revelations 40 years later ? Perhaps because the time was ripe and silence had become intolerable to many actors in the drama. Perhaps through an evolution of mentalities, the new interest of young generations in their country's past, including the recent revelations on the Vichy government's willing participation in the Holocaust.

Independent Algeria is not at peace. Following the interruption of the 1992 elections by the military powers, elections which would have led to an Islamic majority, armed violence continues to disrupt the country: more than 100 000 deaths

---

[32] *Le Monde*, 20–21 May 2001.

through more massacres, torture and rapes. The recent French revelations on torture and killings has not been paralleled by Algerian disclosures of their own crimes during the independence war and later. As one example, from 120 000 to 150 000 *harkis*, Algerian soldiers who fought with the French, were executed, tortured or burned after the 1962 ceasefire. In any case, Algerian exactions cannot absolve the French violations of the laws of war and of humanitarian law committed by the army and condoned by the political authorities. France signed the Geneva Conventions of 1949 in 1951. The texts were published in the *Journal Officiel* in 1952: French officers were aware of these obligations.

By the end of 2000, 4000 persons had signed an appeal by 12 noted personalities asking the President of the Republic, Jacques Chirac, and the Prime Minister, Lionel Jospin, to condemn by a solemn declaration the practice of torture during the Algerian war. The 12 had rejected Amnesty International's proposal to prosecute the military leaders who had recognised their responsibility: their aim was not to sanction individuals, nor to resort to revenge or to demand penitence or financial rewards, but to expose historical facts. It seemed that neither Chirac nor Jospin wished to initiate a public parliamentary investigation into these facts: they wanted to leave it prudently to historians to continue their research and publish facts, rather than opening another Pandora's box with uncertain political repercussions.

Latin America

Following their independence from Spain or Portugal, most South American countries have suffered from a succession of military coups bringing to power dictators supported by armed forces, determined to crush all real or imagined dissension by terror, torture, disappearances and killings. Dictatorships, mismanagement and corruption by officials on the one hand, and violent rebellions, on the other, have hardened political divisions and caused constant insecurity and large human and economic losses. Some countries have also engaged in international wars, also mentioned in this section. In the latter part of the 20th century, democratic regimes have slowly emerged, still fragile, with the difficult task to deal with past abuses and try to reconcile government forces with rebels or former rebels, and to maintain peace with neighbouring countries. Another characteristic was the strong influence and overt or covert intervention of the 'big neighbour', the USA, to weigh forcefully in favour of rightist military regimes and bring about the ejection of democratically elected leftist governments. The US interventions were then motivated, but not justified, by the anti-Communism of the Cold War and its fear of expansion of Castro-type regimes in Latin America.

In most countries, amnesty was decided, under military pressure, in order to 'extinguish criminal responsibility' of the dictatorships' criminal leaders, for the apparent purpose of facilitating the peaceful transition to democracy.

A few selected samples follow.

Perhaps the longest civil war of Latin America, the 36-year civil war in **Guatemala**, a nation of 10.5 million, began in 1960. The war pitted a rightist military-controlled government against a classic leftist insurgency. At least 100 000 people have been killed, mostly by the army and paramilitary forces; 40 000 are listed as 'disappeared', thousands more have been raped, tortured or illegally detained, and more than a million have been forced into exile or displaced from their homes. On 29 December 1996, the Guatemalan Congress approved a 'law of National Reconciliation' that 'extinguishes criminal responsibility' for offences deemed to be political. The law will not be applicable to the crimes of genocide, torture and forced disappearance. The law was considered as a disguised amnesty by human rights groups. In 1999, the independent Historical Commission, established as part of a UN-supervised peace accord that ended the war in 1996, raised the number of casualties to more than 200 000. Its report said that the army committed acts of genocide against the Mayan people. It listed the US training of the officer corps in counterinsurgency techniques as a key factor in human rights violations during the armed confrontation.[33]

The military dictatorship in **Argentina** lasted from 1976 to 1983. Two years after democracy was restored, the members of the junta received stiff sentences for the torture, kidnapping and the murder of approximately 30 000 people. Thousands of people were dumped in rivers and in the sea, buried in mass graves – made to disappear. However, under Raul Alfonsin, in 1986, the Full Stop law limited further trials. In 1987, the Due Obedience Law excused the vast majority of officers on the grounds that they were only following orders. In 1990, President Carlos Menem pardoned former chiefs of the junta who had been sentenced to life imprisonment.[34]

It is estimated that more than 75 000 victims were killed in **El Salvador** during the military dictatorship period, 1979–1992. On 20 March 1993, the National Assembly approved a government-backed amnesty.[35]

Events in **Chile**, the fall of President Allende and the Pinochet regime, the prosecution of General Pinochet in London and, later, in Chile, are reviewed in Chapter 5. The importance of the Pinochet precedent is also underlined in this Chapter.

National Justice

National Justice in Ethiopia

In Ethiopia, under the dictatorship of Lieutenant Colonel Mengistu Haile Mariam, the Communist regime called the Dergue ruled the country from 1974 until 1994 when it was overthrown by the Ethiopian Peoples' Revolutionary Democratic Front.

33 *IHT*, 20 December 1996 and 27–28 February 1999.

34 *Le Monde*, 4 November 1999; *IHT*, 12 September 2000.

35 Beigbeder (1999), pp. 109, 112.

Emperor Haile Selassie and 59 of his ministers and officers were killed by the Marxist regime. Hundreds of thousands of young people were expelled from Addis Ababa and sent to rural zones for a Marxist re-education. During the Red Terror from 1976 to 1978, tens of thousands of Ethiopians had been killed, mostly young victims. In 1984–1985, 1 million Ethiopians starved in the northern province of Tigré during a famine intensified by the government in order to depopulate rebel areas. The number of deaths is estimated at between 40 000 and 100 000.

The new authorities established a Special Prosecutor's Office in August 1992 with a mandate to create a historical record of the alleged abuses of human rights committed by the former regime, and to bring to justice those who may be criminally liable for gross human rights violations and/or corruption. The principal leaders and officials of the Communist regime have been indicted, individually or collectively on charges of genocide, crimes against humanity, summary or arbitrary executions, detention, disappearances and forcible resettlement before a national court. The first sentence was pronounced on 10 November 1999: Colonel Getachew Terba was condemned to death in absentia for crimes against humanity: he was found guilty of having ordered the jailing, torture and murder of five persons.

While the new non-Communist regime has been accused of various violations of human rights, bringing public officials before a court of law for crimes committed against their own citizens is without precedent in Ethiopia and in most of Africa. It is also, up to now, the only example of Communist leaders being actually prosecuted and liable to be sanctioned for crimes committed during their tenure of power, except for the possible trial of Khmer Rouge leaders (see Chapter 6). However, Mengistu himself fled to Harare on 21 May 1991 where Robert Mugabe granted him political asylum. In the Autumn of 1994, Zimbabwe refused to extradite him to Ethiopia, where Mengistu was to be presented to the Ethiopian court.[36]

International Justice

The first international criminal tribunals have been created at the end of World War II. A first attempt at international justice, at the end of World War I, aborted: a few criminal cases were dealt with by German courts. In both instances, only the vanquished were to be tried. International criminal justice started as 'victors' justice'.

World War I (1914–1918)

The large-scale massacres of World War I, a traditional war of nationalistic pride and conflict over territories were made worse by a long equilibrium of forces and the insane and criminal offensives decided by generals under government and public opinion pressure in order to gain vain glory and a few metres of ground at the

[36] Beigbeder (1999), pp. 129–132; Courtois, pp. 968–981; <myweb.worldnet.net/~gbforhan/execute/ethiopia.html>, 11 March 2001.

expense of recurrent slaughters of their own troops: in five days of the 1917 offensive directed by French General Nivelle, 100 000 were killed in the Allies' camp.

The war was carried out by both camps – essentially France and Britain on one side, and Germany on the other – as a crusade: as noted by Soutou,[37] hate of the enemy surpassed all ancient limits since the wars of religion in Europe. A crusade of virtue against evil, the fight of civilization against barbarity, based on real or invented tales of atrocities committed by the enemy. For the first time in history, war became total, covering vast expenses of territories, including civilians as victims of the Allies' economic blockade, the sinking of passenger ships, the first air bombing of urban centres and the use of chemical weapons. War extended to the economy and propaganda mobilized all human, economic and moral resources of the nations at war. Winning was not enough: the enemy was to be destroyed. No serious negotiations took place for a compromise settlement: the French wanted Alsace-Lorraine back, the Germans refused to return these provinces to France. The final victory was due to the American intervention: the USA had declared war on the side of the Allies in April 1917.

Human losses caused by the 1914–1918 war were larger than in any previous wars. For the whole of Europe, an estimated 10 million were killed, plus the disabling of millions of soldiers. Besides enormous financial and economic losses for the European countries, the dominant remaining impression of the combatants was the horror of the war. A pacifist movement developed, with the illusion that the Great War would be the last: never again ...

However, a feeble and one-sided, albeit innovative, attempt was made to identify and sanction the authors of the war. The Paris Peace Conference, which started on 18 January 1919, established a Commission on the Responsibility of the Authors of the War and the Enforcement of Penalties.[38] The Commission's report submitted in March 1919 charged Germany and her allies with extensive violations of the laws of the war. The Commission recommended that '[A]ll persons belonging to enemy countries, however high their position may have been, without distinction of rank, including Chiefs of State, who have been guilty of offences against the laws and customs of war or the laws of humanity, are liable to criminal prosecution'. The US opposed the recommendation to submit Chiefs of State to criminal prosecution: In their view, heads of state are agents of the people and only responsible politically to the people. A compromise was reached. Under Article 227 of the Treaty of Versailles, signed on 28 June 1919, the former German Emperor was to be tried by an international tribunal of five judges, one each from the USA, Great Britain, France, Italy and Japan. He was to be charged with a 'supreme offence against international morality and the sanctity of treaties'. The charge did not refer to

[37] G.-H. Soutou, 'La Première Guerre mondiale: une rupture dans l'évolution de l'ordre européen' in *Politique étrangère*, No. 3–4, Autumn–Winter 2000. See also Pierre Miquel, *Histoire de la France, de Vercingétorix à Charles de Gaulle* (Marabout, Librairie Arthème Fayard, 1976), p. 503.

[38] See Beigbeder (1999), pp. 27–28.

violations of the laws of war nor to a criminal responsibility: it was therefore to be a political trial, and not a judiciary process based on alleged violations of humanitarian conventions. Having taken refuge in the Netherlands, whose government refused his extradition, the Emperor was never tried by an international tribunal.

Possible criminal prosecution was only addressed to 'enemy countries': there was no suggestion that the Allies might have committed similar offences. The aborted prosecution was a first example of potential 'Victors' Justice'.

World War II (1939–1945)

The killings, devastations, losses and suffering caused by World War II were larger than in World War I – 10 million deaths in World War I, over 50 million in World War II – and they became world wide by their extension to Asia. It was in part a traditional war of territorial and economic expansion, but it took another dimension in Europe as a result of the racist ideology of the Nazis, which caused the persecution of the Jews followed by their systematic extermination. It is estimated that 5 100 000 persons were murdered between 1941 and 1945 at the instigation of the Nazi authorities for the only reason that they were Jews. As from the end of 1942, the Gypsies joined the Jews as victims of the Nazi racist theories and cruelty: the number of deaths caused by this other genocide ranges from 200 000 to 500 000. The harassment and mass murder of millions of Soviet prisoners of war, another class of 'sub-humans', was in part due to the racist theories of Aryan superiority over the Slavs, and in part to the political and military struggle between Nazism and Communism.

Much of Asia was devastated by World War II: there were approximately 20 million victims in the Asian theatre. A total of 2.5 million Japanese military died in the war and nearly 1 million civilians perished in air raids. It is estimated that 10 million Chinese died as a result of the Japanese invasion, most of them civilians. Between 300 000 and 1 million Indonesians were mobilized as forced labour by the Japanese: of these, estimates of deaths range from tens of thousands to half a million. Japanese atrocities include massacres of non-combatants, the maltreatment and killing of prisoners of war, torture, forced labour and institutional torture and murder in the form of lethal medical experiments. Sixty thousand Allied soldiers died during the Asian war.

The repulsion felt when the Nazi and Japanese atrocities were known encouraged the Allied governments, supported by public opinion, to create international military tribunals to judge and punish the major German and Japanese war criminals.

The First Two International Criminal Tribunals

The Nuremberg International Military Tribunal was established by the London Agreement signed on 8 August 1945 by the UK, the USA, France and the USSR, to which was annexed the Nuremberg Charter.[39] Nineteen other governments later adhered to the Agreement, thus reinforcing its international credentials. The Tribunal was set up 'for the just and prompt trial and punishment of the major war criminals of the European Axis'. One judge and one alternate were appointed by each of the four powers, who also appointed a Chief Prosecutor. The jurisdiction of the Tribunal was based on a definition of the following crimes, 'for which there shall be individual responsibility': crimes against peace – namely, planning or waging a war of aggression, or a war in violation of international treaties; war crimes – namely, violations of the laws or customs of war; crimes against humanity – namely, murder, extermination, enslavement, deportation and other inhumane acts committed against any civilian populations. Leaders, organisers, instigators and accomplices participating in the formulation or execution of a common plan or conspiracy to commit any of these crimes were to be responsible for all acts performed by any persons in execution of such plan.

The trial lasted from 14 November 1945 to 1 October 1946. Twenty-four individual defendants were indicted, including political and military leaders, high nazi officials. Twelve were sentenced to death by hanging, three to life imprisonment, two to 20 years imprisonment, one to 15 years and one to 10 years, three were found not guilty and released. One had committed suicide in his cell before the trial and a senior industrialist was not tried on account of his senility. Among the indicted organisations, the Leadership Corps of the Nazi Party, the Gestapo and the SD, and the SS were declared criminal.

One basic criticism was that the creation of the Tribunal by a quadripartite agreement, even if later confirmed by 19 other countries, did not conform with the norms of customary international law which would require the negotiation and approval of an international treaty in a diplomatic conference and ratification by states' signatories. This would have been a long process without assurance that a sufficient number of states would support the creation of an international court to judge the Nazi violators of international humanitarian law. This was the 'original sin' of the Nuremberg Trial, in the opinion of a number of international law specialists. However, the need for urgent action and the concurrent claims for revenge did not allow this lengthy process: expediency prevailed.

The historical origin of the Tribunal, its purpose, the nationality of its judges and prosecutors leave no doubt that the victorious nations had decided that the leaders of the defeated nation should be judged and punished for their responsibility in the commitment of crimes. Only German criminals were judged in Nuremberg and any charges that the Allies had also committed crimes against peace or war crimes were rejected by the Tribunal as outside the terms of its Charter and therefore outside its mandate. A few samples of Allied Crimes follow: crimes against peace: the joint German/Soviet aggression against Poland of August 1939; the Soviet aggression

[39] See Beigbeder (1999), Chapters 2 and 3 for a detailed account of the creation and performance of the Nuremberg and Tokyo Tribunals.

against Finland and the Baltic States between November 1939 and June 1940. War crimes: the Katyn massacre of Polish officers of September 1941 by Soviet troops on Stalin's orders; the British and American strategic air bombing of Hamburg, Dresden and other German cities.

A serious legal wart of the Nuremberg trial was ex post facto legislation: the defendants' counsels argued that the proceedings concerning Crimes against Peace were pursuant to a new penal law enacted only after the crime. This would also apply to the new concept of crimes against humanity. As to war crimes, none of the Hague or Geneva Conventions provided for a judgement of senior officials by an international criminal court, nor did they prescribe a scale of sanctions. Another judiciary deficiency was that there was no court of appeal: the Nuremberg judgements were final.

On the positive side, the trial played an important political role in reducing the tensions between victors and the vanquished, by substituting a judiciary process for the victims' urge for revenge. It also focused the charges on high officials, in an effort to avoid long-term collective guilt on all the German people.

Even if it were an imperfect, one-sided political justice, Nuremberg made a significant contribution to international criminal law and justice. It established the principle and set the precedent that individuals at the highest levels of government and armed forces could be prosecuted and tried by an international tribunal for grave violations of international humanitarian law. It thus established individual responsibility for crimes against peace, war crimes and crimes against humanity. Even the limited application of the charge of 'crimes against humanity' by the Tribunal served as a basis and an inspiration for the Genocide and Apartheid Conventions and the extension of protection to civilian populations in the 1949 Geneva Conventions and the 1977 Protocols. 'Nuremberg Law' complemented the Hague and Geneva Laws. It has provided an essential historical, legal and judiciary basis for the later creation of the Tribunals for the Former Yugoslavia and Rwanda, and for the formulation of the Rome Statute of the future International Criminal Court.

On 26 July 1946, China, the UK and the USA, later joined by the USSR, issued the Potsdam Declaration announcing their intention to prosecute high-level Japanese officials for the same crimes committed by the Germans in the European War. On 19 January 1946, General MacArthur, the Supreme Commander for the Allied Powers in Japan, issued a Proclamation establishing an 'International Military Tribunal for the Far East for the trial of those persons charged individually, or as members of organisations, or in both capacities, with offences which include crimes against peace'. The Tribunal's Charter, dated 26 April 1946, confirmed the creation of the Tribunal 'for the just and prompt trial and punishment of the major war criminals in the Far East'. The supremacy of the USA was asserted by the authority granted to the Supreme Commander. The Tribunal's 11 members (judges) were appointed by MacArthur from names submitted by the Signatories to the Instrument of Surrender of Japan, e.g. the UK, Australia, China, the USSR, France,

Canada, the Netherlands, New Zealand and the USA. India and the Philippines were added although they were not yet independent states. The President of the Tribunal (an Australian) was also appointed by the Supreme Commander. The Prosecutor (Chief of Counsel) was an American, assisted by 10 associate counsels, each having the nationality of one of the 10 countries other than the USA. The crimes coming within the jurisdiction of the Tribunal were the same as those of the Nuremberg Charter: crimes against peace, war crimes and crimes against humanity, including the participation in a common plan or conspiracy to commit those crimes. No provision was made for the trial of allegedly criminal groups or organisations.

The Tokyo Trial opened on 3 May 1946 and the Tribunal delivered its majority judgement in November 1948, followed by four separate or dissenting Opinions and one concurring Opinion. Seven defendants were condemned to death by hanging, the others were given jail sentences ranging from life to seven years. None was acquitted.

In addition to the flaws affecting the Nuremberg Trial, the Tokyo suffered from its own weaknesses: the excessive American domination and control of the Trial, serious differences among the judges resulting in several dissenting opinions. Tu quoque arguments also applied to the Asian theatre. The USSR declared war against Japan on 8 August 1945 thus committing a 'crime against peace'. Strategic air bombing of Japan's major cities and the atomic bombing of Hiroshima and Nagasaki in August 1945 by US forces were deemed by one judge and a number of jurists to constitute war crimes, as terror warfare on civilian populations forbidden by the laws of the war. The later discovery that the USA had secretly bargained with and granted immunity to the leaders of Unit 731, made the USA a belated accomplice to a particularly odious war crime and crime against humanity. This Unit was a Japanese army's bacteriological warfare research and experimentation organisation which carried out medical experiments on prisoners of war, experiments similar to those carried out in Nazi concentration camps under the direction of Josef Mengele. These experiments were not divulged to the Tribunal.

Finally, the decision to grant immunity to Emperor Hirohito, taken for political reasons, faulted the equity of the trial. There was evidence that the Emperor had approved the decision to declare war in the Pacific. The fiction of the Emperor's 'innocence' has been a factor in maintaining the amnesia of the Japanese people concerning their country's aggressions and their armed forces' abuses. Perhaps the Tokyo Tribunal has succeeded too well in sanctioning a few political and military leaders and avoiding to lay collective criminal responsibility on the Japanese people.

In spite of its faults, the Tokyo Trial confirmed the Nuremberg precedent in recognising the individual criminal responsibility of high-level officials for launching an aggressive war, for conventional war crimes and for crimes against humanity.

Crimes in the Former Yugoslavia (1991–1999)

The wars in the Former Yugoslavia, which started in 1991, first internal then international, broke up the country through wars of independence carried out in the name of the right of populations to self-determination associated with ethnic cleansing and religious separation. Encouraged by their leaders, old hatreds were revived, territorial claims legitimized and atrocities committed to a degree unknown in Western Europe since the end of World War II. It is estimated that more than 200 000 deaths have been caused by the Balkan wars, to which should be added the streams of refugees, and physical destruction.

On 25 May 1993, the UN Security Council confirmed its previous decision of 22 February 1993 to establish an International Tribunal for the Prosecution of Persons Responsible for Serious Violations of International Humanitarian Law Committed in the Territory of the Former Yugoslavia since 1991.

The creation, achievements and problems faced by this Tribunal are reviewed in Chapter 2.

The Rwanda Genocide (1994)

The Rwanda genocide took place between April and July 1994, causing the violent death of between 500 000 and 800 000 Rwandans, mostly Tutsi. It also created about 2 million displaced persons and another 2 million refugees.[40]

On 8 November 1994, the UN Security Council created a second *ad hoc* international criminal court, the International Tribunal for the Persons Responsible for Genocide or other Serious Violations of International Humanitarian Law Committed in the Territory of Rwanda and Rwandan Citizens Responsible for Genocide and other Such Violations Committed in the Territory of Neighbouring States, between 1 January 1994 and 31 December 1994. The creation, achievements and problems faced by this Tribunal are reviewed in Chapter 3.

Mixed National/International Tribunals

As a new and recent phenomenon, mixed national/international tribunals are being considered for both Cambodia and Sierra Leone. International efforts to create such tribunals are reviewed in Chapter 6.

CONCLUSION

The 20th century, the century of hope and progress, which should have brought peace and happiness to humanity – at least to the privileged humanity of the 'civilized nations' – this century showed in fact a succession of international wars and civil wars, with their inevitable retinue of killings and atrocities, torture and rape, forced expulsions of populations and floods of refugees, famine, and their consequences, immense suffering, irrecuperable human losses, the loss of homes and ancestral villages, the dispersion of families, the break-up of countries, the

[40] Beigbeder (1999), pp. 169–170.

breakdown of state institutions, the exacerbation of violence, hatreds and claims for revenge, ethnic or religious divisions, without omitting the economic losses, increased poverty, lower birth-rates and poor health.

The 20th century has the infamous record of having witnessed two World Wars, of having initiated several genocides, and of having carried out massacres in all parts of the world. The long litany of massacres and genocides in this Chapter do not unfortunately exhaust the subject: they are only short reports on a selection of collective atrocities. The list of cases given shows that roots of conflicts erupting into massacres are diverse: abusive nationalism, intolerant ideology or religion, territorial disputes, ethnic strife, economic and social grievances, or simply rivalry for political and economic power. Many of these crimes have been ordered and carried out by leaders and their accomplices of all origins, of all nations, of all creeds, of all ethnic groups, whatever their level of education. Perpetrators have included men and women, adult and children.

The main purpose of this Chapter is to show that most of the major perpetrators of these war crimes, crimes against humanity and genocides, even if they have been identified, have not been prosecuted nor judged. Many have been conveniently protected by amnesties or pardons. Many of these crimes are still wilfully hidden from school books and collective memory, some are covered with false glory, some are forgotten, their origin is, for some, attributed to the wrong actors. The accountability of leaders has only been imposed, and only selectively, in the second half of the century, with the creation of international criminal tribunals.

This review of the collective crimes committed during the 20th century could lead to a deep pessimistic feeling that man's inhumanity to man has no limit, although its expression may be subject to certain conditions and circumstances:

- Official wars legitimize the murder of the military enemy, but civilians are more and more taken as targets or hostages;
- Governments leaders or officials, religious authorities, rebel chiefs may ignore, support or even organise massacres or genocides for political, territorial, economic, religious or ethnic reasons, by first dehumanizing the target victims;
- Leaders may encourage brutal revenge for real or imagined grievances;
- Political authorities, police, army commanders, judges may lack the authority or the willingness to prevent or sanction those responsible for serious violations of humanitarian law;
- Authoritarian governments holding all powers – executive, legislative, judiciary – may prevent the fourth power, the media from exercising an independent monitoring, verifying and publicizing the violations, which may 'shame' the perpetrators, if not prevent or stop their violence.

Mary Robinson, the UN High Commissioner for Human Rights, said on 13 March 2001 in a conference in Geneva: 'You have to be an optimist if you deal with human rights'.

Among the reasons to remain a cautious optimist is the hope that the 21st century may improve the human rights record of the 20th, in spite of periodical tragedies and unending wars. Rays of hope may come from the increasing number of democracies in the world, the surge of an activist and courageous generation of judges and prosecutors, the ever-increasing, world-wide impact of the media, the increasing pressure of citizens and human rights NGOs to see that justice is done, the creation and performance of the two international criminal tribunals, the creation of national tribunals with international participation and the probable creation of an International Criminal Court.

CHAPTER 2

THE INTERNATIONAL CRIMINAL TRIBUNAL FOR THE FORMER YUGOSLAVIA

The spirit of Nuremberg found a new life with the creation of the International Criminal Tribunal for the Former Yugoslavia in 1993 (ICTY), and of the International Criminal Tribunal for Rwanda (ICTR) in 1994.

Similarly to the Nuremberg Tribunal, these new, temporary Tribunals are judging individuals for war crimes and crimes against humanity. As in Nuremberg, the official position of any accused person, whether as Head of State or Government or as a responsible government official, does not relieve that person of criminal responsibility, nor mitigate punishment.

Nuremberg and the new Tribunals were created by an exception to the norms of customary international law, which would have required the negotiation and approval of an international treaty in a conference and ratification by states' signatories, e.g. the process adopted for the creation of the International Criminal Court. Nuremberg was established by an international agreement of the four victors of World War II, while the two new Tribunals have been created by the UN Security Council.

However, the differences are many. The new Tribunals are not military Tribunals. Nuremberg was created in the aftermath of World War II to try and 'punish' the German major war criminals, then in allied detention. The ICTY was set up in the midst of the Yugoslav wars, to prosecute those responsible for serious violations of international humanitarian law in the Former Yugoslavia since 1991. The ICTR was created to try those responsible for the then completed Rwanda genocide. None of those to be tried were in detention when these two Tribunals were created.

The new Tribunals have an international composition, a significant progress over Nuremberg, whose judges and prosecutors were only citizens of the victorious countries.

Nuremberg judged individuals and organisations: the new Tribunals only judge individuals. Nuremberg had jurisdiction over crimes against peace, war crimes and crimes against humanity, insofar as the latter were related to crimes against peace. The new Tribunals have no jurisdiction over crimes against peace. The ICTY has jurisdiction over grave breaches of the Geneva Conventions of 1949, violations of the laws or customs of war, genocide (a newly-recognised crime based on the Genocide

Convention of 1948) and crimes against humanity. The ICTR has jurisdiction over genocide, crimes against humanity and violations of article 3 common to the Geneva Conventions and of Additional Protocol II, specifically applicable to armed conflict not of an international character. There is no reference to 'violations of the laws or customs of war', in view of the internal nature of the Rwanda conflict.

Contrary to Nuremberg, an accused person may not be tried in absentia. While the Nuremberg judgements were final and not subject to judiciary review, the new Tribunals have Trial and Appeal Chambers. They may impose a prison sentence, but not the death penalty as in Nuremberg.

This Chapter deals essentially with the International Criminal Tribunal for the Former Yugoslavia, although a few references are made to the Tribunal for Rwanda, in view of their structural links: Members of the Appeals Chamber of the Tribunal for the Former Yugoslavia also serve as members of the Appeals Chamber of the Rwanda Tribunal, and the Prosecutor of the Yugoslavia Tribunal also serves as Prosecutor of the Rwanda Tribunal. Chapter 3 deals with the Rwanda Tribunal.

THE RETICENT FOUNDERS

On 25 May 1993, the UN Security Council unanimously confirmed its decision of 22 February 1993 to establish an International Tribunal for the Prosecution of Persons Responsible for Serious Violations of International Humanitarian Law Committed in the Territory of the Former Yugoslavia since 1991.[1]

This decision was taken as a result of public opinion pressures, moved by the reports in the media of atrocities committed mainly by the Serbs, more as a substitute for an effective political or military intervention by the Security Council than by a genuine belief in the virtues of international justice.

In July 1992, Human Rights Watch, an NGO, called for the establishment at the highest level of an international tribunal responsible for the prosecution, judgement and punishment without discrimination of those responsible for war crimes on the territory of ex-Yugoslavia.[2]

The Bush Administration was originally hostile to intervening in the Balkan conflict and to the creation of an international tribunal: Secretary of State James Baker had said "We don't have a dog in this fight".[3] The US felt that the conflict should be dealt with by the Europeans. The Europeans were divided. Only Germany called for an intervention. France and the UK supported and participated in the UN humanitarian activities and in the UN Protection Force but resisted calls for a forceful, well armed intervention to stop ethnic cleansing and its attendant massacres, torture and streams of refugees. Roland Dumas, then French Minister

1 Security Council res. No. 808 and 827.

2 Quoted by P. Hazan, *La justice face à la guerre, De Nuremberg à La Haye* (Stock, Paris, 2000), p. 36. Information on the French attitude is also based on this book, pp. 36–40.

3 R. Holbrooke, *To End a War* (Random House, New York, 1998), p. 27.

of Foreign Affairs, proposed to President Mitterrand in 1992 the creation of an ad hoc tribunal, on the grounds that it would calm French public opinion and that it would be a political assurance against possible later charges of French complicity with the Serb nationalists. Mitterrand was very reticent, he wanted a political solution, but finally agreed. In August 1992, at the London Conference, the German minister of Foreign Affairs Klaus Kinkel proposed the creation of a tribunal, but no decision was taken by the Conference. Basically, the UK and France believed that the prosecution of war criminals would damage prospects for a peace settlement.

By resolution 780 of 6 October 1992, the Security Council established a Commission of Experts to investigate and collect evidence on 'grave breaches of the Geneva Conventions and other violations of international humanitarian law' in the conflict in former Yugoslavia. When the Commission first met in December 1992, US Secretary of State Lawrence Eagleburger gave his 'naming names speech': he announced that the US had identified 10 suspected war criminals who should be brought to trial – among other actors, Slobovan Milosevic, President of the Federal Republic of Yugoslavia, Radovan Karadzic, leader of the self-proclaimed Serbian Republic of Bosnia and Herzegovina, and General Ratko Mladic, commander of the Bosnian Serb military forces

However, the priority for the Western Powers and the UN was a political settlement, and they felt that an activist Commission might be an impediment to this aim. In September 1993, the Commission's Chairman, Frits Kalshoven, resigned his post in protest. He said in an interview that the real problem was the lack of support by important UN member States such as France and Britain and also 'bureaucratic entanglements at the UN'.[4] In spite of these obstacles, the Commission's Final Report of May 1994 stated that out of a population of 6 million, 1.5–2 million were refugees abroad after being deported or forced to flee their homes. Civilian and military casualties exceeded 200 000. Violations included murder, rape, torture, kidnapping, hostage-taking, forced eviction and imprisonment.[5] The reality of the atrocities was confirmed in another, separate investigation carried out by Tadeusz Mazowiecki, former Polish Prime Minister, appointed by the UN Human Rights Commission in August 1992 as a Special Rapporteur. Mazowiecki's requests to undertake missions to the Federal Republic of Yugoslavia in order to collect first-hand information and to investigate allegations of human rights abuses had been rejected. On 27 July 1995, he resigned from his position in protest for the UN having allowed the Srebrenica and Zepa 'safe areas' to fall to abusive forces. He deplored the lack of consistency and courage displayed by the international community and its leaders: 'Crimes have been committed with swiftness and brutality and by contrast the response of the international community has been slow and ineffectual'.[6]

4 *IHT*, 13–14 November 1993.

5 UN Doc. S/1994/674.

6 Human Rights Watch, 'Bosnia-Herzegovina, The Fall of Srebrenica and the Failure of UN Peacekeeping', Vol. 7, No. 13, October 1995.

By the time the Clinton Administration took over from the Bush Administration (on 26 January 1993), the US had come around to support the proposed creation of a tribunal. Based on French and Italian draft resolutions, the Security Council approved resolution 808 on 22 February 1993 and 827 of 25 May 1993, including the Statute of the Tribunal in the latter's Annex. Roland Dumas told a French journalist later: 'The tribunal was a political weapon to threaten Karadzic and Mladic. I also hoped that it could play a dissuasive role'.[7] The Chinese were reticent but were told that Tibet would not be involved. Russia had its own internal problems and Boris Yeltsin needed American support. Islamic countries, including Pakistan, a non-permanent member of the Security Council at the time, supported the resolutions.

Mandate and Structure

Under its Statute, the Tribunal has the power to prosecute persons who have committed, or have ordered to be committed, grave breaches of the Geneva Conventions of 1949 (the Law of Geneva); persons who have violated the laws or customs of war (the Law of The Hague); persons who have committed genocide (the 1948 Genocide Convention); persons responsible for crimes against humanity (in part, the Law of Nuremberg), crimes committed in armed conflicts, whether international or internal in character, and directed against any civilian population. The Tribunal has primacy over national courts (Art. 1–5, 9).

The Tribunal, whose seat is in The Hague, consists of three organs (Art. 11).

The first organ, the Chambers were originally composed of 11 independent judges of different nationalities. Three serve in each of the Trial Chambers, five serve in the Appeals Chamber. High judicial qualifications are required of the judges. They are elected by the UN General Assembly from a list submitted by the Security Council. The judges elect their President (Art. 12–14). The revised Statute of 30 November 2000 has increased the composition of the Chambers: 16 permanent independent judges and a maximum at any one time of nine *ad litem* independent judges (see section on 'Reform'[8]).

The second organ is that of the independent Prosecutor, who is appointed by the Security Council on nomination by the Secretary-General. The third organ is the Registry, responsible for the administration and servicing of the Tribunal (Art. 16–17).

The Prosecutor initiates investigations ex-officio or on the basis of information obtained from any source, particularly from governments, UN organs, intergovernmental and non-governmental organisations. Upon determination that a prima facie case exists, the Prosecutor prepares an indictment containing a concise statement of the facts and crime or crimes with which the accused is charged under the Statute

[7] Hazan, p. 68.

[8] Statute of the International Tribunal, 30 November 2000, as amended by Security Council resolutions 1166 and 1329, <www.ur.org/icty/basic/statut/stat2000.htm, 23 May 2001.

(Art. 18). The indictment is transmitted to a judge of the Trial Chamber who may either confirm it, if satisfied that a prima facie case has been established, or dismiss it if he is not so satisfied. Upon confirmation of an indictment, the judge may, at the request of the Prosecutor, issue orders and warrants for the arrest, detention, surrender or transfer of indicted persons (Art. 19). In the best circumstances, the indicted person is taken into custody, informed of the charges against him/her and transferred to the Tribunal. Hearings are public and the rights of the accused are protected, as well as those of victims and witnesses. Judgements are rendered by a majority of the Trial judges and delivered in public. Separate or dissenting opinions may be appended (Art. 20–23). Penalties are limited to imprisonment whose terms should be related to the general practice regarding prison sentences in the courts of the former Yugoslavia. In imposing the sentences, the Trial Chambers should take into account such factors as the gravity of the offence and the individual circumstances of the convicted person. The Chambers may order the return of any property and proceeds acquired by criminal conduct to their rightful owners (Art. 24).

The Appeals Chamber hears appeals from persons convicted by the Trial Chambers or from the Prosecutor on the grounds of an error on a question of law invalidating the decision or an error of fact which has occasioned a miscarriage of justice. The Appeals Chamber may affirm, reverse or revise the decisions taken by the Trial Chambers (Art. 25). Imprisonment is served in a state designated by the Tribunal from a list of states which have indicated to the Security Council their willingness to accept convicted persons (Art. 27). By August 1999, Austria, Finland, Italy, Norway, Spain and Sweden had signed or initialed an agreement with the UN on the Enforcement of Sentences.[9]

States 'shall' cooperate with the Tribunal in the investigation and prosecution of persons accused of committing serious violations of international humanitarian law. They 'shall' comply without undue delay with any request for assistance or an order issued by a Trial Chamber including the identification and location of persons, the taking of testimony and the production of evidence, the service of documents, the arrest or detention of persons, the surrender or the transfer of the accused to the Tribunal (art. 29).

---

[9] Bosnia and Herzegovina, Croatia, Denmark, Germany, Iran and Pakistan have indicated their willingness to enforce the Tribunal's sentences, although no agreement had yet been concluded. The President of the Tribunal has adopted two Practice Directions relating to enforcement: see UN Doc. A/54/187-S/1998/846, Sixth Report of the ICTY, 25 August 1999, VII. In 2001, two defendants were serving their sentence in Finland, one in Germany and one in Norway.

The Tribunal's expenses are funded by the UN regular budget (Art. 32). A few governments and organisations have made additional voluntary contributions and provided free legal assistance through gratis personnel.[10]

Initial Financial and Staffing Problems

At the first plenary session of the Tribunal, on 17 November 1993, the judges found that they had no locale, no furniture, no funds, no jails, no accused in detention, no police at their disposal, no prosecutor. The few computers had been rented, four secretaries had three month contracts. The Tribunal's budget had not yet been approved by the UN.

The Western powers and the UN wanted to keep the Tribunal under control, still giving precedence to diplomacy, sanctions and threats of military intervention over international justice.

In mid-September 1993, the General Assembly elected 11 judges, nine men and two women, from a list of 23 candidates submitted by the Security Council. They were from both civil and common law countries: three from Asia, two from Europe, two from Africa, two from North America and one each from Latin America and Australia.

On 17 November 1993, the judges elected Antonio Cassese (Italy) as their president. A respected international jurist and professor, he had been instrumental in the creation of Permanent People's Tribunals in the 1960s and 1970s.[11] An activist lawyer and internationalist, he considers law as a weapon to transform the world and hoped that the Tribunal would serve as a laboratory for a future international criminal court.

On 11 February 1994, the Tribunal adopted its Rules of Procedure and Evidence, based on a largely adversarial approach.[12] In an attempt to compensate for the lack of in absentia trials – generally admitted by civil law countries but rejected by common law states – when the Tribunal is unable to obtain custody of an accused, Rule 61 provides for a mini-trial, at which the accused is not present nor represented, to enable the prosecutor to introduce in open court testimony of witnesses, documentation, physical evidence and video recordings of witness interviews. If the Trial Chamber is satisfied that there are reasonable grounds for believing that the accused has committed all or any of the crimes charged in the indictment, the Chamber will have the relevant parts of the indictment read out by the Prosecutor. The Trial Chamber will also issue an international arrest warrant in respect of the

---

[10] In its Resolution 47/235 of September 1993, the General Assembly invited Member States and other interested parties to make voluntary contributions to the Tribunal in cash and in other form of services and supplies acceptable to the Secretary-General: see UN Doc. A/54/187-S/1998/846, Sixth Annual Report of the ICTY, 25 August 1999, VIII.

[11] Hazan, pp. 81–107 – on International Peoples' Tribunals, see Beigbeder (1999), pp. 137–145.

[12] UN Doc. IT/32/REV.19 – the latest amendments were dated 1 and 13 December 2000.

accused which will be transmitted to all states. Indictments against Radovan Karadzic and Ratco Mladic are among those confirmed under Rule 61.

In the same spirit, but with the specific purpose of facilitating the arrest of accused unaware of being indicted by the Tribunal, Rule 53 allows a Judge or a Trial Chamber, in exceptional circumstances and in the interests of justice, to order that there be no public disclosure of an indictment until it is served on the accused.

By late 1993, feeling the benefit that the Tribunal's prosecutions and judgements could give it, the US decided to send to The Hague 22 high-level officials, military analysts from the Pentagon, information specialists from the CIA, legal specialists for an initial period of two years. They were 'gratis' personnel, entirely paid by the US, but 'baptized' as UN officials by signing the oath of office. This American input to the investigation work of the Prosecutor's office was widely criticised by authorities in France, Italy, Germany, states which, however, did not offer the same assistance. The UK sent five gratis personnel, Sweden and the Netherlands each sent three, and two each were sent from Denmark and Norway.

Richard Goldstone (South Africa), appointed as Chief Prosecutor on 8 July 1994 by the Security Council, had promoted the loans of gratis personnel and also obtained voluntary contributions of $8.3 million from 13 countries.[13]

The Tribunal's budget increased regularly from $10 800 000 in 1994, $25 300 000 in 1995, $64 775 300 in 1998 to $96 443 900 in 2001. As of September 2001, the Tribunal employed 1188 staff members from 77 countries.[14]

The current staffing and budgets of the Tribunal are shown in Table 2.1.

The Role of the Prosecutors

Richard Goldstone is credited for having saved the Tribunal from an expected, and for some countries, hoped-for failure, or at least from paralysis. Goldstone, a judge on the Constitutional Court of South Africa, had previously, at the end of apartheid, been the chairperson of the Commission of Inquiry Regarding Public Violence and Intimidation, known as the Goldstone Commission, which preceded the Truth and Reconciliation Commission.

As the Tribunal was unable to obtain custody of the main actors of the Yugoslav conflict, Goldstone adopted a strategy of investigating 'lower-level persons directly involved in carrying out the crimes in order to build effective cases against the military and civilian leaders who were party to the overall planning and organisation of those crimes'.[15] The first tranche of indictments named 22 suspects, including Dusko Tadic. The first prosecution was that of Tadic, tried for the murder of 13 persons and the torture of 19 others. Tadic was a direct perpetrator of crimes, an

[13] M. P. Scharf, *Balkan Justice, The Story Behind the First International War Crimes Trial Since Nuremberg* (Carolina Academic Press, Durham, 1997), p. 82.

[14] 'ICTY Key Figures' in <www.un.org/icty/glance/keyfig-e.htm, 13 April 2001.

[15] Scharf, p. 85.

Table 2.1. Staffing of the International Criminal Tribunal for the former Yugoslavia (ICTY) as of September 2001

Judges:
President: Claude Jorda (France), *Vice-President*: Mohamed Shahabuddeen (Guyana)
Presiding Judges: Richard George May (United Kingdom), Wolfgang Schomburg (Germany), Liu Daqun (China).
Judges: Florence Ndepele Mwachande Mumba (Zambia). David Anthony Hunt (Australia), Patrick Lipton Robinson (Jamaica), Mehmet Güney (Turkey), Asoka de Zoysa Gunawardana (Sri Lanka), Fausto Pocar (Italy), Theodor Meron (USA), Amin El Mahdi (Egypt, Carmel A. Agius (Malta), Alphonsus Martinus Maria Orie (Netherland), O-gon Kwon (Korea).

***Ad Litem* Judges**
Amarjeet Singh (Singapore), Maureen Harding Clark (Ireland), Ivana Janu (Czech Republic), Chikako Taya (Japan), Fatoumata Diarra (Mali), Sharon A. Williams (Canada), Rafael Nieto-Navia (Columbia).

Prosecutor:
Chief Prosecutor: Carla Del Ponte (Switzerland), since 15 September 1999.
Deputy Prosecutor: Graham Blewitt (Australia), since 15 February 1994.

Registrar:
Hans Holthuis (Netherlands), since 1 January 2001.

Deputy Registrar: Bruno Cathala (France), since 18 May 2001.

ICTY PERSONNEL:
1188 staff members from 77 countries.

	Yearly budgets (from the UN regular budget)	
1993: $276 000	1994: $10 800 000	1995: $25 300 000
1996: $35 430 622	1997: $48 587 000	1998: $64 775 300
1999: $94 103 800	2000: $95 942 600	2001: $96 443 900

Source: 'The ICTY at a glance', as of 12 December 2001. <www.un.org/icty/glance/index.htm>

'ordinary' killer and torturer, not a high level leader. However, Tadic was available – he had been arrested in Germany in 1994 – his trial gave evidence of the numerous crimes committed during the conflict and it allowed the Tribunal to test and improve its procedures. In April 1995, Goldstone gave notice that indictments were likely against such major figures as Radovan Karadzic and Ratko Mladic, a political inconvenience for the diplomats. Karadzic, as the political leader of Bosnian Serbs, directed the campaign of ethnic cleansing of Bosnian Muslims during the Bosnian war. General Ratko Mladic was the military commander accused of the worst atrocities committed in Europe since the end of World War II, including the massacres of Srebrenica. On 8 May 1995, Goldstone gave notice that the Tribunal was considering indictments against Croats suspected of mass killings in Central Bosnia. On 11 July 1996, the first anniversary of the massacres in Srebrenica, the Tribunal issued an international warrant for the arrest of Karadzic and Mladic. Goldstone resigned in October 1996 to assume his functions in the newly created

South African Constitutional Court.[16] Before leaving his post. Goldstone upbraided Western leaders for their failure to back up the work of the Tribunal with substantial arrests, such as those of Karadzic and Mladic. On a more positive note, Goldstone pointed out that the prohibition against applying international humanitarian law to civil wars has almost been obliterated. Secondly, both the Tribunal's Statute and the indictments confirmed the international criminalization of rape, as a war crime.

Scharf[17] praised Goldstone's personality and performance:

> A compact, quietly charismatic man with a resonant voice, the 56-year-old Goldstone effused a sense of deep commitment and had a nose for international politics. Through his unwavering persistence during his two years in the post of prosecutor, Goldstone would expertly navigate the minefields of the UN bureaucracy and lead the Yugoslavia Tribunal to international recognition and influence.

Goldstone was replaced in 1997 by a respected Canadian jurist, Louise Arbour, a judge of the Ontario Court of Appeals and an expert in criminal law.

By June 1997, the total of those indicted by the Tribunal stood at 76, but only 9 were in custody.

Arbour changed Goldstone's strategy. Leaving aside the 'small fish', her team focused on the military hierarchy and political leaders who planned the crimes and also on all those who were personally responsible for exceptionally brutal acts. She also introduced with success the use of sealed indictments, in accordance with Rule 53 of the revised Rules of Procedures and Evidence. As one example, Tribunal judges issued a sealed indictment against Slavko Dokmanovic on 26 March 1996: he was arrested by the Tribunal's investigators with the assistance of peacekeepers of the UN Transitional Administration for Eastern Slavonia (UNTAES) on 27 June 1997 in the Serb-held Croatian region of Eastern Slavonia without the knowledge or cooperation of the Serbs. He was invited by UNTAES to visit Vukovar and then taken into custody. The accused had served as the Serb mayor of Vukovar and was implicated in the killing of 260 Croats and other non-Serbs removed from the city's hospital in November 1991. Discussing the arrest, Arbour defended the practice: 'There is nothing tricky about arresting people without giving them advance warning. That's the way police forces operate all over the world'. She added that the Tribunal would continue to issue sealed indictments and pursue individuals so indicted until receiving 'a signal from the international community that the member states will carry out their obligations'.[18]

---

[16] Facts in this section are in part based on J. Tessitore and S. Woolfson (Eds), *A Global Agenda: Issues Before the 51st, 52nd, 53rd, 54th, 55th General Assembly, Legal Issues* (Rowman New York/Boulder/Oxford, 1996, 1997, 1998, 1999, 2000).

[17] Scharf, p. 79.

[18] Tessitore and Woolfson, *Issues Before the 53rd General Assembly*, p. 272.

In March 1999, the Tribunal's investigators concluded that the Croatian Army had carried out summary executions, indiscriminate shelling of civilian populations and ethnic cleansing during an August 1995 military offensive called Operation Storm.

Also in March, Arbour warned the Federal Republic of Yugoslavia leadership of its accountability for the commission of serious violations of international humanitarian law in Kosovo. This warning was followed by the historic joint indictment of President Slobodan Milosevic and four other leading Serb officials on 27 May 1999. This indictment was issued without concertation with the Western powers, showing the Tribunal's independence to the chagrin of Western foreign affairs officials who still considered Milosevic as a necessary and useful negotiator.

Arbour's determination and her achievements have significantly increased the credibility of the Tribunal. Arbour only served three out of her four-year term: she accepted an appointment to the Supreme Court of Canada, effective 15 September 1999. By the time of her departure, 66 indictments had been issued publicly, 33 accused were in custody.

On 11 August 1999, the Security Council appointed unanimously Carla Del Ponte, a former attorney-general of Switzerland since 1994, for a four-year term. Another determined and courageous judge, she was well-known and not always appreciated for her inquiries and prosecutions against organised crime and corruption, notably against the Russian mafia and its connections with Swiss Banks and other firms, and the Italian mafia. In December 1999, she identified the arrest of at-large indictees as her top priority.

On 2 June 2000, Del Ponte reported to the Security Council that there was no basis to investigate allegations of crimes committed by personnel and leaders of the North Atlantic Treaty Organisation (NATO) during its 1999 bombing campaign against the FRY. Although NATO had made mistakes, it had not deliberately targeted civilians (see below).

The Judges and Their President

In accordance with Articles 11 to 14 of the Tribunal Statute, the Chambers, initially composed of 11 judges, are one of the three organs of the Tribunal. Three judges serve in each of the two Trial Chambers and five judges in the Appeals Chamber. The judges are independent, in parallel to the independence of the Prosecutor. They are nationals of different states. They should be persons of high moral character, impartiality and integrity possessing the qualifications required in their respective countries for appointment to the highest judicial offices. They are elected by the General Assembly from a list submitted by the Security Council. The judges elect a President, who is a member of the Appeals Chamber and presides over its proceedings. After consultation with the judges, the President assigns them to the Appeals or Trial Chambers.

As noted above, the judges elected Antonio Cassese (Italy) as the first President of the Tribunal at their first meeting in The Hague on 17 November 1993.

Besides their judicial role, the Tribunal's Presidents have often addressed publicly the Security Council, the creator of the Tribunal, and/or the General Assembly, and the media in order to press the Western Powers and NATO to effectively arrest indicted persons, and to apply pressure on the non-cooperating FRY and, initially, Croatia.

In May 1996, Cassese called for the re-imposition of sanctions against the FRY for failing to execute arrest warrants. He threatened that the Tribunal judges would resign en masse in the Fall of 1997 if top and mid-level indicted leaders had not been arrested and brought before the Tribunal by then.[19]

In November 1997, the judges selected Gabrielle Kirk McDonald to succeed Cassese as President. She had been a judge on the Tribunal since its creation in 1993 and had presided over the Dusko Tadic trial. McDonald made a name for herself as a civil rights lawyer in the 1960s and 1970s. At the age of 37, she was appointed by President Jimmy Carter as federal district judge. Under her leadership, the Tribunal significantly increased its caseload and applied pressure, through the Security Council, on the FRY, the Republika Srpska and Croatia to extradite indicted war criminals and, when these efforts failed, to encourage NATO forces to apprehend them. McDonald addressed the Security Council twice about this issue and wrote four letters to the Council about the FRY lack of cooperation. She deplored that the Council did not apply sanctions against the FRY and Croatia for their lack of cooperation.

McDonald left the Tribunal in November 1999. A few days before her departure, she addressed the General Assembly in clear terms.

> It is simply unacceptable that territories have become safe havens for individuals indicted for the most serious offenses against humanity. It must be made absolutely clear to such states that this illegal and immoral behaviour will not be tolerated.

In a news briefing, she said that the majority of suspected war criminals indicted by the Tribunal were walking free in the FRY and the Serbian enclave in Bosnia, patrolled by French troops in the NATO force. She said that the French force must arrest Karadzic and Mladic, both indicted for war crimes: 'What does it take ? It takes action'.[20]

On 13 May 1998, a Third Trial Chamber was created by resolution 1166 of the Security Council. As a result, the number of judges was raised by three to 14, thus amending articles 11 and 12 of the Tribunal's Statute.

On 17 November 1999, Claude Jorda (France), former general prosecutor in Bordeaux and Paris, Tribunal judge since January 1994, was elected President by his

[19] Scharf, p. 225.

[20] *IHT*, 10 November 1999.

peers. He was first designated to preside over a Trial Chamber and took an active part in the drafting and implementation of the Rules of Procedure.

As noted above, the composition of the Chambers was again increased by the revised Statute of 30 November 2000 (see later in section on Reform).

The Basic Custody Problem

The Statute of the Tribunal was approved on 25 May 1993 by the Security Council under Chapter VII of the UN Charter (Res. 827). Its implementation by all States was therefore a legal obligation under article 25 of the Charter. Alinea 4 of the preamble of the Council's resolutions was clear:

> [The Security Council] *Decides* that all states shall cooperate fully with the International Tribunal and its organs in accordance with the present resolution and the Statute of the International Tribunal and that consequently all states shall take any measures necessary under their domestic law to implement the provisions of the present resolution and the Statute, including the obligation of states to comply with requests for assistance or orders issued by a Trial Chamber under Article 29 of the Statute.

According to Article 29 of the Tribunal's Statute, '*Cooperation and judicial assistance*'

> (1) States shall cooperate with the International Tribunal in the investigation and prosecution of persons accused of committing serious violations of international humanitarian law.
>
> (2) States shall comply without undue delay with any request for assistance or an order issued by a Trial Chamber, including, but not limited to:
>
> (a) the identification and location of persons;
>
> (b) the taking of testimony and the production of evidence;
>
> (c) the service of documents;
>
> (d) the arrest and detention of persons;
>
> (e) the surrender or the transfer of the accused to the International Tribunal.

On the eve of the Dayton negotiations, Goldstone formally asked the United States to make the surrender of indicted suspects a condition for any peace agreement.[21] His stand was supported by Bosnian President Alija Izetbegovic. Finally, Milosevic agreed to the inclusion in the Peace Accord of December 1995 of

[21] *New York Times*, 3 November 1995.

five references to the obligations owed the war crimes Tribunal.[22] The first reference, contained in the General Framework Agreement, required the parties to 'cooperate in the investigation and prosecution of war crimes and other violations of international humanitarian law'. The second reference, contained in the Agreement on the Military Aspects of the Peace Settlement (Annex 1 of the Accord) stated that the parties 'shall cooperate fully with ... the International Tribunal for the Former Yugoslavia'. The same Agreement specifically obligated the parties to 'comply with any order or request of the International Tribunal for the Former Yugoslavia for the arrest, detention, [and] surrender of 'persons who the Tribunal has indicted'. The other two references were contained in the new Constitution of Bosnia (Annex 4 of the Dayton Accord). The first of these provided that 'all competent authorities in Bosnia and Herzegovina shall cooperate with and provide unrestricted access to ... the International Tribunal for the Former Yugoslavia'. The second stated that 'no person who is under indictment by the Tribunal and who has failed to comply with an order to appear before the Tribunal, may stand as a candidate or hold any appointive, elective, or other public office in the Territory of Bosnia and Herzegovina'.

The Attitude of Countries

The Attitude of NATO and NATO Countries

The Bosnia Constitution contained the authority of the NATO Implementation Force (IFOR) to arrest any indicted war criminals 'it encounters or who interfere with its mission', an authority which was interpreted restrictively as NATO troops, on several occasions, ignored identified top indicted war criminals which they could have arrested. However, the Pentagon was resolute in its position that the arrest of war criminals was not in NATO's mandate, in spite of its overwhelming presence and military capacity.

Edward N. Luttwak recalls 'Operation Amber Star', in which the objective was the capture and delivery for trial of Radovan Karadzic and Ratko Mladic, both indicted by the Tribunal. Following two years of detailed preparations with the support of the US National Security Agency, the Balkans Task Force of the CIA, Federal Bureau of Investigation agents and US marshals, in cooperation with the British director of Special Forces, and millions of dollars spent, the US Joint Chiefs of Staff allegedly refused to authorize the mission.[23] Karadzic and Mladic are still free.

The reasons for NATO's initial attitude of non-involvement are several: the US humiliation in Somalia in 1993 which led to a no-casualty policy; the (exaggerated) risks of an arrest operation; the fear of adverse political reactions of the FRY and

[22] Scharf, pp. 88–89.

[23] *IHT*, 7 February 2001.

the breakdown of the Dayton Accord; the concern that NATO troops could be labelled as anti-Serb, which could affect their safety; more urgent tasks were to be addressed in the early stages such as demilitarization, enforcing cease-fires and holding elections.

The attitude of the UK and France towards the Tribunal improved with a change in government in the UK and as a result of public denunciations and pressures by the Tribunal's prosecutors in the case of France.

Since Tony Blair's Labour Party won the elections in 1997, he pledged to track down suspected war criminals. In July 1997, NATO British troops tried to arrest Simo Drljaca, Prijedor Police Chief and a local warlord, but killed him when he fired on them. In July 1999, British troops arrested without incident Radoslav Brdjanin under a sealed indictment. He was a senior politician of the Bosnian Serb machinery of ethnic cleansing run by Karadzic against Bosnian Muslims and Croats. He was charged with planning, ordering and committing killings, beatings, detentions and deportations of Muslims and Croats from the Krajina region around Banja Luka during the first 9 months of the war. He was indicted as an individual and as a hierarchical superior. More than 100 000 Moslems or Croats of Bosnian origin were forced to leave the area. In December 1999, the British troops arrested another senior Serb official, Major General Stanislav Ganic, one of the senior military commanders who reported directly to Karadzic and Mladic. He was in charge of the Bosnian Serb Army's Sarajevo Romanija Corps when the city was under encirclement and bombardment, a period which symbolized the horror of the Bosnian ethnic conflict while it showed the incapacity or unwillingness of the Western powers to stop it. According to indictment, the military forces he commanded 'used shelling and sniping to kill, maim, wound and terrorize the civilian inhabitants of Sarajevo'. In June 2000, British troops arrested Dusko Sikirica, the former camp commander of Keraterm, where more than 3000 Bosnian Muslims and Croats were held: detainees 'were killed, sexually assaulted, tortured, beaten and otherwise subjected to cruel and inhuman treatment'. On 10 August 2001, British troops arrested, in Banja Luka, Bosnian Serb Colonel Vidosav Blagokevic and transferred him to The Hague. He was charged with abetment with genocide, war crimes, deportation and inhumane acts during the Srebrenica massacre in July 1995.[24]

Tony Blair's government lifted a ban on providing classified material to the Tribunal. London also offered to cover the entire cost of building a second courtroom for the Tribunal which was completed in May 1998.[25]

Although France approved the Statute of the Tribunal, it adopted unofficially a policy of non-cooperation with the Tribunal, initiated and carried out by its Ministry of Foreign Affairs with the full support of its senior military leaders. France and the UK tried unsuccessfully to find a political solution to the Former Yugoslavia wars,

---

[24] *IHT*, 7 July 1999, 21 December 1999, 26 June 2000; *Le Monde*, 12–13 August 2001.

[25] 'Tribunal Update' no. 37, 7/14–19/97.

and supported a humanitarian intervention in preference to a military expedition. France provided its soldiers to UNPROFOR, had some of them taken hostages by the Serbs and had 68 soldiers killed in Bosnia between 1992 and April 1997.[26] France had an historical link with the Serbs which allowed, in the French sector of Bosnia, a covert collusion between the Serbs and the French military, with the initial blessing of local French military authorities and of the French government under Mitterrand's presidency. France was the only Western country to prevent its former peace-keeping commanders from giving testimonies to the Tribunal as witnesses, in violation of its legal obligations: the French Parliament had approved a law of judicial cooperation with the Tribunal in 1995. This attitude was based on the fear of the French military authorities that these commanders could become accused, and not only witnesses, in view of their role during the Balkan wars, and particularly before and during the Srebrenika massacre.

The French non-cooperation policy was first revealed bluntly by Alain Richard, French Minister of Defence, during a lunch with the press in December 1997, when he accused the Tribunal of practising a 'show justice' ('justice spectacle') and declared that no French officer would ever testify before the Tribunal.

A few days later, Louise Arbour gave an interview in *Le Monde* (14–15 December 1997): she considered that these remarks reflected an unacceptable refusal to cooperate with the Tribunal's investigations and trials. The only arrest had, so far, been carried out in the British sector, while no action had been taken in the French sector where many war criminals resided who felt in absolute security.

In March 1998, Hubert Védrine, French Minister of Foreign Affairs, in a complete and welcome reversal, declared in The Hague that French officials and officers would now be allowed to testify to the Tribunal.

However, in February 2000, Carla Del Ponte had, again, to press France into greater action, as French troops were still seen as providing a de facto haven for key suspects in their sector.[27]

The first arrest made in June 1998 by French NATO troops, with the support of US troops, was that of Milorad Krnojelac, commander of a detention centre for women and children in Foca, in 1992–1993, publicly indicted for war crimes. Dragan Gagovic, a former police chief in the city of Foca, was killed in January 1999 by French troops at a French roadblock which he tried to force. In August 1999, French and German troops arrested Radomir Kovac, a former paramilitary leader and military policeman in Foca. He was accused of having enslaved and raped Muslim women in 1992 and 1993. In January 2000, Mitar Vasiljevic was arrested by French troops. A Bosnian Serb, he was indicted for having participated from May 1992 to October 1994 to the 'extermination and persecution' of the Moslem population of Visegrad.

---

[26] Hazan, p. 68.

[27] *Le Monde*, 18 March 1998, *IHT*, 11 April 2000.

The most important arrest by French-led NATO troops was that of Momcilo Krajisnik in April 2000, who had been the subject of a sealed indictment. He was considered as one of the masterminds of the genocide and ethnic cleansing in Bosnia, together with Karadzic. He was a signatory of the Dayton Peace Accords.[28]

In spite of this recent success, the French contingent has failed to arrest the most important indicted personalities, when such arrests were within their reach, those of Mladic and Karadzic.

The United States have been the best supporters of the Tribunal since its creation, in terms of financial, logistical, legal and manpower assistance. In 1993, the Clinton Administration had loaned to the Tribunal 22 senior 'gratis officials'. Among other contributions, the US announced on 12 March 1999 a pledge of $1 million to finance the Tribunal's investigators in Kosovo, and $100 000 in October 2000 to the ICTY Outreach Programme, a UN Trust Fund. The Programme aims at strengthening contacts between the Tribunal and communities across the Former Yugoslavia. Outreach offices have been opened in Banja Luka, Sarajevo and Zagreb. Denmark, The Netherlands, Finland, the UK and the John D. and Catherine T. MacArthur Foundation also support the Programme.[29]

The US record of arrests of indicted persons is however not impressive: only three indictees were arrested by US troops.

Bosnian Serb Major General Radislav Krstic was arrested in the US sector in December 1998 under a sealed indictment of 30 October 1998 and under protest of the Bosnian Serb authorities. The highest-ranking Serb to appear before the Tribunal so far, he was indicted for the massacres committed in Srebrenica in July 1995. Dragan Nikolic was arrested in April 2000, the first individual indicted by the Tribunal (on 4 November 1994). The initial indictment charged Nikolic with crimes against humanity, violations of the law or customs of war, and grave breaches of the Geneva Conventions committed against Muslims and non-Serb civilians at Susika prison camp in Bosnia-Herzegovina during 1992. Failing attempts to serve the indictment on Nikolic, the judges publicly confirmed the indictment and issued an international arrest warrant for the accused on 20 October 1995. It was the first time the judges had invoked Rule 61 of the Rules of Procedure and Evidence and had issued such a warrant. On 15 April 2001, Dragan Obremovic was arrested in Zvornic in the Bosnian Serb sector under another sealed indictment. He is charged with complicity in genocide and crimes against humanity in the persecution and murder of Muslims during the July 1995 attack on Srebrenica.[30]

In 1999, the US issued a poster in Bosnia-Herzegovina and Serbia offering a reward of 'up to $5 million for information leading to the arrest and/or conviction of

[28] *Libération*, 11 January 1999, *Le Monde*, 30 January 2000, *IHT*, 3 August 1999 and 4 April 2000.

[29] Hazan, pp. 94, 187; USIS Geneva Daily Bulletin, ESX501, 16 October 2000. A first $100,000 contribution had been provided by the US in 1999.

[30] *Le Monde*, 4 December 1998; Sean D. Murphy, 'International Criminal Law', *American Journal of International Law*, July 2000, Vol. 94, pp. 537–538; *IHT*, 17 April 2001.

persons indicted by the International Criminal Tribunal for the Former Yugoslavia'. Photos of Milosevic, Karadzic and Mladic are featured prominently on the poster which was re-issued in March 2000. Leaving aside the arrest of Milosevic and his transfer to The Hague on 29 June 2001, this approach has not produced any results so far.[31]

The Attitude of China and Russia

Although Resolution 827 approving the Secretary-General's statute for the Tribunal was adopted by an unanimous vote of the 15 members of the Security Council, China, a permanent member, had told the Council that it had serious reservations and that it believed that the approach envisaged in the Secretary-General's report 'is not in compliance with the principle of state judicial sovereignty'. In spite of the reaffirmation of its traditional position of principle to protect its own sovereignty, China has participated in the Tribunal's activities through the appointment of a Chinese judge to the Tribunal.

The pro-Serb position of Russia, another permanent member of the Council, has often been expressed by its authorities, as well as its opposition to the Tribunal. Although Russia should arrest war crimes suspects on its territory, it gave a warm welcome, for five days in May 2000, to the then Yugoslav defense minister, General Dragoljub Ojdanic. Ojdanic had been indicted on 27 May 1999, together with Milosevic and three other senior Serb officials, for the persecution and deportation of Kosovar Albanians as from January 1999. Foreign Minister Igor Ivanov blamed a 'technical hitch' for this incident and told NATO foreign ministers that 'measures' were being taken to see that it would not happen again. However, on 20 November 2000, the Russian representative made sharp criticisms of the Tribunal in the General Assembly. He criticised the Tribunal, accusing it of being a political institution; of being anti-Serb; of being over-resourced; of improperly issuing sealed indictments; of being less than vigilant in the Prosecutor's examination of NATO following the bombing campaign; of entering an illegal agreement with NATO; and finally, that the Tribunal was a threat to the unity of accepted international law and that by making new legal interpretations, the Tribunal was thereby creating anarchy in the international law.

Carla Del Ponte found these allegations offensive and without foundation in her statement to the Security Council delivered on 21 November 2000. She felt that, unless these allegations were maliciously or politically motivated, they were based on misunderstandings, which could have been clarified had the Russian government responded to her many requests to visit Moscow to discuss the work of the Tribunal.[32]

---

31 USIS Geneva Daily Bulletin, EUR422, 2 March 2000.

32 *IHT*, 26 May 2000; ICTY *Press Release*, 24 November 2000.

The Attitude of Former Yugoslavia States

None of the three parties involved in the wars which divided Former Yugoslavia is wholly innocent of war crimes and crimes against humanity. However, it can be estimated that most victims are found among the Muslims and most perpetrators of violence among mainly the Serbs, and to a lesser degree the Croats.

In consequence, the Moslems had most to gain from international criminal justice, while the Serbs and the Croats had more to fear from the Tribunal's investigations and judgements. In turn, the Bosnian Muslim government showed most cooperation with the Tribunal, while the FRY government has consistently rejected the authority of the Tribunal and refused its cooperation. The Croat government has been pressured by the US to exert a degree of cooperation with the Tribunal, a cooperation which increased following the death of Franjo Tudjman in 1999 and the election of a new, more democratic President, Stjcpan Mesic, in February 2000.

In January 1996, the Muslim-led government arrested eight Bosnian Serbs, including a general (Djordje Djukic) and a colonel (Aleska Krsmanovic), suspected of war crimes, who were then transferred to The Hague. In March 1996, Bosnian Muslim Zejnil Delalic, was arrested in Munich and transferred to The Hague. He was charged with directing crimes committed by subordinates in the Celibici camp. In June 1996, the Bosnian government sent to The Hague two Muslim prison camp officials accused of murdering and raping Bosnian Serb inmates, Hasim Delic and Esad Landzo. It was the first time that a signatory to the Dayton Accords had extradited nationals already indicted for war crimes.[33]

Croat 'cooperation', generally obtained under intense pressure by Western governments, and especially more credible US pressures, on President Tudjman, started with voluntary surrenders to the Tribunal. In April 1996, Bosnian Croat General Tihomir Blaskic gave himself up. Former Chief of Staff of the headquarters of the Croatian Defense Council, he was wanted for his alleged role in atrocities committed by his soldiers in the Lasva Valley in 1992–1993. His surrender – in reality, his extradition – was due mainly to strong US pressures and the threat of UN Security Council sanctions. In October 1996, seven other Bosnian Croats suspected of involvement in the same atrocities (Dario Kordic, Mario Cerkez, Zoran Kupreskic, Mirjan Kupreskic, Vladimir Santic, Drago Josipovic and Dragan Papic) also surrendered to the Tribunal. In April 1997, the Croat authorities allowed Zlatko Aleksovski, first jailed in Croatia in June 1996, to be sent to The Hague. He was suspected of mistreating Muslim prisoners while commander of a detention camp at Kaonik. The pressure behind this decision was the US threat to block International Monetary Fund approval of some $500 million in loans to Croatia and to oppose Zagreb's efforts to join NATO and other international organisations.

---

33 Tessitore and Woolfson, *Issues Before the 51st General Assembly*, p. 286.

In March 1996, another Bosnian Croat, Zdravko Mucik, was arrested in Vienna and transferred to the Tribunal one month later.

In March 1999, Tribunal's investigators concluded that the Croatian Army had carried out summary executions, indiscriminate shelling of civilian populations and ethnic cleansing during an August 1995 military offensive called 'Operation Storm'. They recommended indicting three Croatian generals, Mirko Norac, Ante Gotovina and Ivan Cermak

On 9 August 1999, Vinko Martinovic, a Bosnian Croat, was transferred from a Croat jail where he was serving an eight-year sentence for the murder of a woman, to The Hague. He was indicted for his active participation in ethnic cleansing in the Mostar region, between 1992 and 1995. The Croat government authorized his transfer to The Hague when threatened by the Tribunal of a referral to the Security Council. His co-indictee, Mladen Naletilic, was transferred to The Hague in March 2000. In September 2000, the Croat police arrested a dozen persons suspected of war crimes. Among them, Croat Generals Ivan Andabak and Ignac Kostroman, for their participation in the massacre of Muslims during the Bosnian war. As another sign of increasing Croat determination in the prosecution of alleged Croat war criminals, retired General Mirko Norac was indicted on 7 February 2001 by the Rijeka Tribunal for the massacre of 40 Serb civilians in 1991 in the Gospic region. He surrendered on 21 February to the Croat Tribunal. He had been assured that he would not be extradited to The Hague, with the agreement of Carla Del Ponte, as his crimes had been committed on Croat territory and were therefore within the jurisdiction of the Croat judiciary authorities. Croat war crimes during World War II were also recognised, belatedly and symbolically, by the condemnation of Dinko Sakic, 78, by a Croat Tribunal in Zagreb to 20 years in prison. He was the last living concentration camp commander and was found guilty of carrying out or condoning the torture or slayings of inmates while in charge of the Jasenovac camp, where tens of thousands of Serbs, Jews, Gypsies and anti-fascist Croats died.[34]

In her address to the Security Council on 21 November 2000, Carla Del Ponte recognised that there had been an improvement in relations between Croatia and the Tribunal when compared with the previous policy of obstruction and delay adopted by the former government [under President Tudjman]. However, 'where Croatia perceives cooperation to be against its political or narrow security interests, a real difficulty still exists'. She referred to the long-standing, unresolved, problem of the provision of Croatian material for use as evidence in the Kordic trial, and Croatia's stubborn refusal to allow access to witnesses and documents related to the 1995 Croatian campaign against Serbs in Croatia, known as Operation Storm. She also deplored the leaks by the government to the media of details requested by the Tribunal, and a negative media campaign against the Tribunal.

---

[34] *Le Monde*, 6 March 1998, 11 and 25 August 1999, 14 September 2000, 23 February 2001; *IHT*, 5 October 1999, 22 March 2000, 27 February 2001, 13 March 2001. On the Fascist Independent State of Croatia, see *The New York Times International*, 12 April 1997.

Milosevic's Yugoslavia not unexpectedly rejected all cooperation with the Tribunal, which it considered illegitimate. As the main instigator of the wars which divided his country, caused massacres, the exodus of refugees, suffering and hates, the promoter of ethnic cleansing and of its attendant brutality and atrocities, Milosevic's regime and its satellite Republika Srpska protected their war criminals and ignored the Tribunal's warrants.

On 21 May 1993, the government of FRY sent a letter to the General Assembly and to the Security Council affirming that all perpetrators of war crimes committed in the territory of the Former Yugoslavia should be prosecuted and punished under national laws. FRY criticised the selective approach taken to establish a Tribunal only for the Former Yugoslavia and expressed doubts about the impartiality of the Tribunal, as a Tribunal for Serbs only. It challenged the Security Council's action: the Council has no mandate under the Charter to establish such a Tribunal. Its creation was politically motivated and without precedent in international legal practice. Finally, the Constitution of the FRY prohibits the extradition of Yugoslav nationals.[35]

The main reason for the Serb refusal to cooperate with the Tribunal was of a political nature. Serb public opinion largely held – and still holds – that the Tribunal was 'anti-Serbian'. On legal grounds, some of the Serb lawyers, experts on international and criminal law, took the stance that the Security Council exceeded its mandate by adopting resolution 827 (1993) and the Tribunal was therefore illegitimate. Sharing these views, the Yugoslav authorities supported this position for some time, emphasizing that the FRY did not 'recognise' the Tribunal and was not willing to cooperate with it. In an insulting and vulgar letter of 27 May 2000 to the 'whore Carla Del Ponte, self-proclaimed prosecutor of the criminal tribunal of The Hague', Petar Jojic, Serb Minister of Justice, wrote that the Tribunal was an illegal and perverse institution, not related to international justice. For the writer, the Tribunal is a nest of spies, impostors, fortune hunters and immoral persons. Graham Blewitt, Deputy Prosecutor, replied that this was a flagrant example of Belgrade's paranoia.[36]

In practice, the FRY and Republika Srpska refused consistently to arrest indictees. Dusko Tadic was the first indictee arrested outside Former Yugoslavia. He was extradited by Germany to The Hague on 24 April 1995, the sole occupant of the Tribunal's 21-cell detention centre. He had been arrested in Munich on 12 February 1994 on suspicion of 'murder, aiding and abetting genocide, and causing grievous bodily harm'. He was formally indicted by the Tribunal on 13 February 1995.

Other indicted Serbs were either arrested by the Bosnian Muslim authorities (Djordje Djukic and Aleska Krsmanovic, and six others, in January 1996). UN peacekeepers (Slavko Dokmanovic, in June 1997), or by NATO forces. Goran Jelisic, called the 'Serb Adolf of Bosnia', was arrested in January 1998 by the SFOR.

35 UN Doc. A/48/170-S/25801, 21 May 1993.

36 *Le Monde*, 27 May 2000.

In December 1998, the arrest of General Radislav Krstic by US NATO troops for crimes in connection with the fall of Srebrenica, was a major catch which raised strong protests from the Bosnian Serb authorities.

On the other hand, the number of voluntary surrenders of Serb indictees to the Tribunal confirmed the legitimacy of the Tribunal, showing trust in its impartiality. In February 1998, three Bosnian Serbs indicted for war crimes committed in Bosanski Samac (Milan Simic, Miroslav Tadic and Simo Zaric) surrendered to Western authorities. In March 1998, Dragoljub Kunarac surrendered to French NATO troops. Zoran Zigic followed his example in April 1998. The surrender of Biljana Plavsic, a former president of the Bosnian Serb Republic in January 2001, was an important victory for the Tribunal, as the highest-level politician yet to appear before the Tribunal. She was indicted for joining other high officials of the Bosnian Serb Republic's war presidency from July 1991 to December 1992 in plotting and provoking the campaign to purge Bosnia of its Muslim and Croat inhabitants.

As an exception to their non-cooperation policy, Bosnian Serb authorities transferred Zoran Zigic to the Tribunal in April 1998. He had been indicted concerning acts at the Omarska prison camp and had been detained at a military stockade for a murder unrelated to the indictment. Milomir Stacik, the former mayor of Prijedor, was arrested by the Serbian police and transferred from Belgrade to The Hague in March 2001, a first step in cooperation between the post-Milosevic FRY and the Tribunal.[37]

KOSOVO AND THE FALL OF MILOSEVIC

Following ten years of lost and brutal wars which reduced 'Greater Serbia' to a small country under the nationalistic leadership of Milosevic, the Kosovo war started his decline.

In March 1987, Milosevic as Chief of the Communist League of Yugoslavia imposed a new Constitution which reduced the autonomy of Kosovo. On 30 September 1991, in a clandestine referendum, the Republic of Kosovo was proclaimed. The Dayton Accords of 1995 did not refer to Kosovo. In 1996, the Kosovo Liberation Army (KLA) claimed for the first time that it was responsible for a series of bombing incidents. Since March 1998, the Serb forces fought against the KLA: the repression caused a first exodus of refugees. On 16 October 1998, an agreement was signed by the FRY and the Organisation for Security and Cooperation in Europe (OSCE) providing for the OSCE to establish a verification mission in Kosovo, including the undertaking of the FRY to comply with previous resolutions of the UN Security Council. Resolution 1203 adopted by the Council on

[37] On Tadic, see Scharf, pp. 97–101; on others, *Le Monde*, 6 March 1998, 2 December 1998, 27 May 2000; *IHT*, 12 January 2001, 24–25 March 2001; and Tessitore and Woolfson, *Issues before the 53rd General Assembly*, pp. 268–269.

24 October 1998 expressed deep alarm and concern at the continuing grave humanitarian situation throughout Kosovo and the impending humanitarian catastrophe. It also called for a prompt and complete investigation, including international supervision and participation, of all atrocities committed against civilians and full cooperation with the International Tribunal for the Former Yugoslavia, including compliance with its orders, requests for information and investigations.

In February 1999, the Rambouillet (France) negotiations failed: the peace plan proposed by the Contact Group – Germany, the UK, France and the USA – was rejected by the Yugoslav delegation. It included a substantial autonomy of Kosovo, the deployment of an international force, the demilitarization of Kosovo.

From 24 March to 10 June 1999, NATO conducted an air campaign against the FRY, codenamed Operation Allied Force. On 19 May, Milosevic indicated that the principles laid out by the Group of Seven nations and Russia would be acceptable but that 'details' had to be 'negotiated with the United Nations' [by-passed by NATO]. On 25 May, NATO decided to increase its presence in Macedonia to about 50 000 soldiers, a threat that a ground invasion had become a serious option.

On 27 May 1999, Milosevic and four other Serb leaders,[38] were indicted by the Tribunal. It charged each accused with three counts of crimes against humanity and one count of violating the laws or customs of war, as related to the persecution and deportation of Kosovar Albanians as of 1 January 1999. Unanimously acclaimed by the main Western leaders, Milosevic's indictment effectively blocked him from participating in any further negotiation and, no doubt, played a role in his final capitulation on 3 June, together with Russia' pressure. Russia had joined the Western allies in agreeing with the substance of NATO's demands.

NATO bombing operations ceased on 10 June, following a technical military agreement on the modalities of the withdrawal of Serb troops from Kosovo and the deployment of the NATO-led KFOR mission. Resolution 1244 adopted by the Security Council also on 10 June 1999 reintroduced the UN in the provisional settlement of the crisis. The UN was to provide an interim administration in Kosovo 'under which the people of Kosovo can enjoy substantial autonomy within the Federal Republic of Yugoslavia'. Again, the resolution demanded full cooperation by all concerned, including the international security presence [i.e. NATO forces] with the International Tribunal for the Former Yugoslavia.

On 24 September 2000, general elections in the FRY gave contested results: Milosevic's supporters claimed that he had won, while the opposition maintained that Vojislav Kostunica had obtained an absolute majority of 52% and asked for a recount. Facing a popular bloodless rebellion, Milosevic resigned on 5 October 2000.

---

[38] Milan Milutinovic (President of Serbia), Nikola Sainovic (FRY Deputy Prime Minister), Dragoljub Ojdanic (Chief of Staff of the FRY Army), and Vlajko Stojiljkoviv (Minister of Internal Affairs of Serbia): see Tessitore and Woolfson, *Issues before the 54th General Assembly*, p. 264.

Kostunica then declared that he was President of Yugoslavia since 24 September, date of the first round of the presidential election which he had won.[39]

On 21 March 2001, Carla Del Ponte announced that she considered herself competent for the events in Kosovo and in South Serbia since the intervention of NATO forces in June 1999, as well as in Macedonia, as these events are all part of one conflict. She then initiated two investigations for crimes against humanity; one on crimes allegedly committed against Serbs and other minorities by Albanian groups in Kosovo, the other one on crimes allegedly committed by the Liberation Army in South Serbia as from November 1999.[40]

On 1 April 2001, under US financial pressure, the FRY authorities decided to jail Milosevic in Belgrade and indicted him for abuse of power and corruption, then for inciting violence to prevent his arrest. President George W. Bush lauded the arrest and urged that he be sent for trial to The Hague. President Jacques Chirac was 'overjoyed' by the news. In his appeal to be released from custody, Milosevic admitted secret state funding for the wars in Croatia and Bosnia, an admission which might facilitate another indictment by the Hague Tribunal for war crimes and crimes against humanity.

Milosevic's Transfer to The Hague

On 5 April 2001, Hans Holthuis, registrar of The Hague Tribunal formally presented to the Serbian Justice Minister, Vladan Batic, the original indictment of former President Milosevic and a warrant for his arrest. On 3 May, a Belgrade court delivered the indictment to Milosevic in his jail cell: he refused to accept the document.

Under Article 29.2(e) of the Statute of the Tribunal, the FRY should comply without undue delay with the Tribunal's warrant and transfer the indictee to The Hague. On 3 April 2001, in a press conference, the Federal President Kostunica repeated that justice rendered in The Hague is a selective justice and that cooperation with the Tribunal did not necessarily include the transfer of the former President to The Hague: 'there will not be an automatic extradition'. During a chilly meeting with Carla Del Ponte in January 2001, Kostunica had questioned the legality and procedures of the Tribunal and said that his government would not cooperate with it in the apprehension of indicted war suspects for trial in The Hague. He also said that Milosevic's transfer to The Hague was not a priority for his government.

Without conceding this point, Kostunica had admitted, in an interview on a CBS News programme in October 2000, that the Yugoslav Army and special police forces had carried out widespread ethnic killings in the largely ethnic Albanian province of Kosovo in 1998 and 1999: 'For what Milosevic has done and, as a Serb, I will take responsibility for many of these crimes'. He also said that both Serbs and ethnic

---

39 *Le Monde*, 7 October 2000; *IHT*, 16 October 2000.

40 *Le Monde*, 23 March 2001.

Albanians had been killed. It was the first time that a Yugoslav leader had accepted responsibility for any of the ethnic conflicts in the Former Yugoslavia.

As a significant but limited gesture to break with the long-established policy of impunity for the Yugoslav Army's violations of the laws of the war and of international humanitarian law, the Army's General Staff announced on 24 April 2001 that investigations had been initiated against 245 officers and soldiers for 'killings and putting in danger the life, dignity, morals and property of citizens' in the period March 1998 to June 1999 in Kosovo. The Army Prosecutor has indicted 183 persons. Human Rights Watch (HRW) welcomed cautiously this announcement but said that the paramount obligation of the Yugoslav government was to transfer high-ranking state officials indicted by the Tribunal to The Hague. An HRW director had previously said: 'It's hard to imagine that a Serbian court could do justice for Croatian, Bosnian and Kosovar victims of Serb war-time abuses. Only an international forum can guarantee accountability in an even-handed way.[41]

President Bush told the Yugoslav President on 9 May 2001 during the latter's visit to Washington that US and international aid to his country depended on Belgrade's cooperation with the international Tribunal. Bush said quite clearly that Milosevic must face justice for his international crimes. He urged Kostunica to take 'concrete steps' to cooperate with the Tribunal.

However, Kostunica was urging the West to allow Yugoslavia to rebuild at its own pace. He said in New York on 8 May: 'As if Yugoslavia's problems are not enough, we have to cope with the West's reluctance to give us a chance to build our institutions and establish the rule of law by allowing our judiciaries to implement national laws and to try war crimes suspects'.

The European Union did not have such reluctance: the Union's security chief, Javier Solana said that the Union would not put pressure on Yugoslavia in the case. Robin Cook, the then British Foreign Secretary said in Belgrade in April 2001 that although Milosevic must face the war crimes charges, 'the people of Serbia are entitled to hear the full truth of his crimes against the Serb people in court'. Hubert Védrine, the French Minister for Foreign Affairs, was favourable to a 'friendly' pressure on Belgrade so that Milosevic would be delivered, in time, to The Hague.

Carla Del Ponte, in her address to the Security Council on 21 November 2000 did not appreciate Kostunica's statement that cooperation with the Tribunal was not a priority for him: she called it a clever line, a true politician's phrase. She said that Milosevic must be brought to trial before the International Tribunal. This clear position was reasserted in a Press Briefing on 4 April 2001 by the Chef de Cabinet of the President of the Tribunal, Stephane Bourgon: for both the President and the Prosecutor, the obligation rested on the authorities of the FRY to transfer Milosevic

[41] *IHT*, 25 October 2000, 6 and 25 April, 4 May 2001; *Le Monde*, 24 January and 5 April 2001; hrw-news@igc.topica.com 7 February and 26 April 2001.

at the earliest possible opportunity: Yugoslavia had an absolute, non-negotiable obligation to comply with his transfer to The Hague.[42]

On 29 June 2001, Milosevic was transferred to The Hague by the government of Serbia led by President Zoran Djindjic, overriding a constitutional court and without the approval of President Kostunica. This decision was motivated to a large extent by a financial pressure exercised by the US which had threatened not to attend an international donors' conference in Brussels scheduled for 30 June: Yugoslavia was to obtain $1.28 billion in aid.

Carla Del Ponte qualified Milosevic's transfer and detention as an important day for international criminal justice and a very positive development. For the first time, a former head of state was to be judged by an international tribunal for alleged crimes committed while in office.

On 3 July, Milosevic appeared before the Tribunal alone, without lawyers. In a defiant stance, he said: 'I consider this tribunal as a false tribunal and indictments false indictments' and that 'the trials' aim is to produce false justification for the war crimes NATO committed in Yugoslavia'. He refused to enter a plea of guilty or not guilty. The Tribunal then decided that he had entered a non-guilty plea.

Under an initial indictment of 24 May 1999 and an amended indictment confirmed on 29 June 2001, Milosevic faces charges of violations of the laws or customs of war and crimes against humanity committed during the Serb campaign of terror and violence directed at the Kosovo Albanian civilians by virtue of his position. In October 2001, in a second indictment, the Tribunal indicted Milosevic with war crimes and crimes against humanity committed during the 1991–1995 war in Croatia. Carla Del Ponte announced that a third indictment would be issued shortly for genocide committed during the war in Bosnia.[43]

On 31 August, a Dutch court rejected Milosevic's attempt to have his detention in The Hague declared illegal and 'a kidnapping'. The judge ruled that the ICTY was a legal court established by the Security Council and that the Dutch courts had no jurisdiction to rule in this case. The judge cited the ICTY's own appeals court, as well as another judgement from the European Court of Human Rights.[44]

As a consequence of Milosevic's transfer to The Hague, Croatia and Bosnia were compelled to improve their cooperation with the ICTY. On 25 July 2001, Croatian General Rahim Ademi surrendered to the Tribunal. Target of a sealed indictment, he was charged with persecution on political, racial or religious grounds, murder and plunder of public or private property committed during a Croatian assault in September 1993 in the Medak pocket in Central Croatia, during which Serbian civilians and soldiers who surrendered to the Croats were killed. A second suspect,

[42] *Le Monde*, 11 April 2001; *IHT*, 5 April and 10 May 2001; ICTY *Press Release*, 24 November 2000, www.un.org/icty/briefing/PB040401.htm, 4 April 2001.

[43] *IHT*, 10 October 2001.

[44] *IHT*, 25 June, 30 June, 4 July, 31 August, 1–2 September 2001; ICTY *Press Release* C.C./P.I.S./597-e, 29 June 2001,

General Ante Gotovina, who led the 1995 Operation Storm, refused to surrender to the Tribunal. On 3 August 2001, Mehmed Alagic and Enver Hadzihasanovic, both retired Bosnian Muslim generals and Colonel Amir Kubura surrendered to the Tribunal. They were charged with war crimes against Serbs and Croats committed in 1993.[45]

Milosevic's transfer to The Hague was a major victory for the Tribunal's credibility. However, by January 2002, neither Karadzic nor Mladic had been arrested nor transferred to The Hague.

THE TRIBUNAL'S ACHIEVEMENTS

These achievements, as of January 2002 are summarised in Table 2.2.

Judgements and Issues

A selection of important issues arising from judgements of the Tribunal follows.

The Legality of the Establishment of the Tribunal

In a motion filed with the Trial Chamber in June 1995, Dusko Tadic's counsels challenged the jurisdiction of the Tribunal first on the grounds that it had not been established in a valid manner, because the Security Council lacked the power to do so.[46]

The Prosecutor took the position that the Tribunal did not have authority to decide the issue. Goldstone said: 'This International Tribunal is not a constitutional court set up to scrutinize the actions of organs of the United Nations. It is, on the contrary, a criminal tribunal with clearly defined powers, involving a quite specific and limited criminal jurisdiction'. The Trial Chamber agreed, holding that the question was 'pre-eminently a matter for the Security Council and for it alone and no judicial body, certainly not this Trial Chamber, can or should review that step': for the Chamber, the question was political and therefore 'non-justiciable'. On 2 October 1995, the Appeals Chamber rejected this conclusion, finding instead that its inherent 'incidental' power to determine the propriety of its own jurisdiction (*compétence de la compétence)* permitted review of the legality of the Council's action in establishing the Tribunal. This finding ran contrary to the caselaw of the International Court of Justice, who had declared in several judgements that it lacked the power to review the legality of Security Council's decisions. Legal specialists objected to the finding on the grounds that a subsidiary court (the Tribunal) could not, or should not deviate from the jurisprudence of the International Court of Justice, the principal judicial organ of the UN.

[45] *IHT*, 26 July, 4–5 August 2001.

[46] Beigbeder (1999), pp. 156–157; Scharf, pp. 104–106.

Table 2.2. The Tribunal's Achievements as of January 2002

Individuals publicly indicted since the inception of the ICTY

(pursuant to Rule 53 of the Rules of Procedure and Evidence, additional undisclosed indictments may also have been confirmed).

- **43** Accused currently in custody at Detention Unit
- **6** Accused provisionally released
- **31** Arrest warrants issued to particular States have been issued against all accused and are currently outstanding (as listed)
- **11** Accused transferred/released

  2 accused acquitted, proceedings completed
  3 accused found not guilty, proceedings completed
  3 accused transferred to serve sentence
  3 sentences served

- **26** Completed cases

  17 indictments withdrawn
  9 accused died including three after commencement of proceedings (see below 'Closed cases')

66 accused have appeared in proceedings before the Tribunal

- **20** Accused at pre-trial stage
- **8** Accused currently at trial
- **1** Accused awaiting Trial Chamber Judgement
- **31** Accused tried

  15 accused at appeal
  11 accused received their final sentence
  5 accused found not guilty

6 Closed cases

  3 Indictments withdrawn
  3 Deaths

Source: 'Fact Sheet on ICTY Proceedings', 4 January 2002 (Excerpts) <www.un.org/icty/glance/procfact-e.htm>

The second argument of Tadic's counsels was that 'to be duly established by law, the International Tribunal should have been established by treaty ... not by resolution of the Security Council'. This argument is similar to a criticism raised at the creation of the Nuremberg Tribunal by a four-nation Agreement, rather than by an international treaty. In both cases, the reason was a political one of expediency and urgency, due to the fact, in the case of the ICTY, that it had been determined that the situation constituted a threat to international peace and security.

Their key argument was that the Security Council lacked authority to establish a subsidiary organ with judicial powers over criminal matters. Another argument was that the Tribunal was not 'established by law' in accordance with Article 14(1) of the

International Covenant on Civil and Political Rights. That provision states. '[i]n the determination of any criminal charge against him or of his rights and obligations in a suit of law, everyone shall be entitled to a fair and public hearing by a competent, independent and impartial tribunal established by law'.

Again, the Appeals Chamber rejected these arguments. It found that 'the International Tribunal has been established in accordance with the appropriate procedures under the United Nations Charter and provides all the necessary safeguards of a fair trial. It is thus 'established by law'. The Chamber found that it was a legitimate measure aimed at the restoration of peace and security: the Council is a body which has the power to make binding legislative decisions under Chapter VII of the UN Charter.

Legal critics have challenged the notion that an international Tribunal could play a role in restoring peace and security, e.g. that the judicial process can serve a political goal. In another formulation, can the Security Council, a political organ, create an independent Tribunal?

An International or National Conflict

Under Article 2 of its Statute, the Tribunal has the power to prosecute persons committing or ordering to be committed 'grave breaches' of the Geneva Conventions of 1949. According to the text and the system of the Geneva Conventions and Protocols, the concept of grave breaches does not apply to violations of the law of non-international armed conflicts.[47]

Tadic's counsels challenged the legality of his indictment under Articles 2 and 3 of the Statute, on the ground that, according to international humanitarian law as it stands today, the notion of war crimes is limited to situations of international armed conflict. In a controversial interpretation, the Appeals Chamber ruled (on a four to one vote) that, although Article 2 of the Statute applied only in international armed conflicts, Article 3 (violations of the laws or customs of war) applied to war crimes 'regardless of whether they were committed in internal or international armed conflicts'. The Chamber assumed that the Security Council had intended that the Tribunal would punish serious violations of international humanitarian law 'without reference to whether the conflicts in Former Yugoslavia were international or national' and concluded that both types of conflicts had existed in those territories.

In order to try Dusko Tadic for grave breaches under Article 2, the Tribunal had to qualify the conflict in which he committed his crimes as international, e.g. a conflict between two or more High Contracting Parties. Concerning the conflict in the Prijedor region, in which Tadic was involved, the Appeals Chamber determined in its 1995 decision on jurisdiction that 'since it cannot be contended that the Bosnian Serbs constitute a State' it could only be classified as international based on the assumption that the Bosnian Serbs are organs or agents of the FRY. This meant

47 M. Sassoli and L. M. Olson, 'The judgment of the ICTY Appeals Chamber on the merits in the Tadic case', *International Review of the Red Cross*, September 2000, Vol. 82, No. 839, pp. 733–769.

that civilians may be protected by the 1949 Geneva Conventions and Protocols, and therefore the commission of atrocities against civilians can be prosecuted and sanctioned under Article 2 of the Tribunal's Statute.

On 15 July 1999, the Appeals Chamber set out an 'overall control test' in the continuing *Tadic* case, in order to determine whether the armed conflict in a specific case is international. The Appeals Chamber confirmed the applicability of this test in the case of Zlatko Aleksovski delivered on 24 March 2000. For the Chamber, the test provides greater protection for civilian victims of armed conflicts and is wholly consistent with the fundamental purpose of Geneva Convention IV, e.g. to ensure protection of civilians to the maximum extent possible.[48]

On 3 March 2000, the Trial Chamber issued two decisions regarding activities by the Croatian Defense Council (HVO) in the ethnic cleansing campaign waged against Bosnian Muslims in Central Bosnia. In the decision concerning Tihomir Blaskic, the Chamber found that the conflict between the HVO and Bosnian Muslims was international in nature. Supporting factors included: (1) the involvement of the Croatian Army as well as the control by Croatia over Bosnian Croat forces; (2) the nationalistic and expansionist political views of the former President of Croatia, Franjo Tudjman; and (3) the amount of financial assistance flowing to Bosnian Croats from Croatia.[49]

On 20 February 2001, the Appeals Chamber, in the *Celebici* case, recalled that in the Tribunal's jurisprudence, the Prosecution must prove the existence of an international armed conflict in relation to any offences charged under Article 2 of the Statute. The Trial Chamber found that the armed conflict in Bosnia and Herzegovina at the relevant time was international, as the Bosnian Serb forces fighting in Bosnia and Herzegovina were under the control of the FRY. The Appeals Chamber reaffirmed its *Tadic* Conviction Appeal Judgement, which had been followed in its *Aleksovski* Appeal Judgement, which held that what must be established by the prosecution is that the foreign intervening party was in '*overall* control' of the local forces.[50]

Elements of Crimes Against Humanity

Again in the *Tadic* case, the Appeals Chamber refined, in its 1999 judgement, the definition of crimes against humanity. Overturning the Trial Chamber's holding, the Appeals Chamber clarified that a discriminatory intent is necessary only for 'persecution type' crimes against humanity, not for all crimes against humanity listed in Article 5 of the Statute. On 14 January 2000, the Trial Chamber issued convictions in the *Kupreskic et al.* trial. According to Judge Cassese, the phenomenon of ethnic

[48] ICTY 'Summary of Appeals Chamber Judgement, The Prosecutor v. Zlatko Aleksovski, 24 March 2000'. See also M. Cherif Bassiouni, *Crimes Against Humanity in International Criminal Law* (Kluwer Law International, The Hague/London/Boston/New York, 1999).

[49] ICTY *Press Release* JL/P.I.S./474-e, 3 March 2000.

[50] ICTY *Press Release* JL/P.I.S./564-e, 20 February 2001.

cleansing can be punishable as persecution: he placed persecution on a continuum with genocide:

> Both persecution and genocide are crimes perpetrated against persons that belong to a particular group and who are targeted because of such belonging. In both cases, what matters is the intent to discriminate: to attack persons on account of their ethnic, racial, or religious characteristics.

He however stressed the most important differences between the two crimes:

> [I]n the case of persecution the discriminatory intent can take multifarious inhumane forms and manifest itself in a plurality of actions including murder, in the case of genocide that intent must be accompanied by the intent to destroy, in whole or in part, the group to which the victims of the genocide belong.

Also in the *Tadic*'s appeal case, the Appeal Chamber overturned the Trial Chamber's finding that a crime against humanity was a more serious offence than a war crime and, all other things being equal, thereby required a stricter sentence. On this point, the Appeal Chamber held that 'there is in law no distinction between the seriousness of a crime against humanity and ... a war crime'.[51]

Rape as Crime Against Humanity

In the Bosnian conflicts, it is estimated that thousands of women, mostly Muslim, were rape victims. Rape is one of the crimes against humanity listed under Article 5 of the Tribunal's Statute.

An important contribution of the *Celibici* judgement was that it was the first conviction for rape as torture. The Tribunal declared: 'There can be no question that acts of rape may constitute torture under customary law'. In the *Furundzija* judgement delivered on 12 November 1998, the Trial Chamber affirmed and applied the *Celibici*'s findings that rape may amount to torture. It also defined the elements constituting the offence of rape. Furundzija was a commander of the Jokers, a Croatian paramilitary unit which took part in a campaign to drive Muslims out of Central Bosnia. A witness testified that she had been locked up in a house in May 1993, where she was regularly beaten and raped by a soldier. Furundzija failed to intervene and continued to interrogate her. He was found guilty of two counts of violating the laws or customs of war. On 10 December 1998, he was sentenced concurrently to ten years' imprisonment.

The *Foca* trial was the first to focus exclusively on charges of organised sexual slavery. The Trial Chamber judgement, delivered on 22 February 2001, was deemed historical: for the first time, the rape of civilians in wartime was qualified as a crime against humanity. Dragoljub Kunarac was found guilty of sexually assaulting and

[51] Sassoli and Olson, pp. 761–762; ICTY *Press Release* JL/P.I.S./474-e, 3 March 2000; Tessitore and Woolfson, *Issues before the 55th General Assembly*, p. 237.

torturing Muslim women. Radomir Kovac was found guilty of war crimes and crimes against humanity by rape. Zoran Vukovic was convicted of raping and torturing a girl of 15. Kunarac was sentenced to 28 years, Kovac to 20 years and Vukovic to 12 years. Although these Bosnian Serbs were not high-level commanders, the Chamber said that 'lawless opportunists should expect no mercy, no matter how low their position in the chain of command may be'. The rapes were used by members of the Bosnian armed forces as an instrument of terror. The dozens of rape victims forced into quasi-brothels included girls as young as 12 and 13. Kunarac commanded a reconnaissance unit of the Bosnian Serb Army, Kovac and Vukovic were paramilitary leaders.[52]

Nationality of Protected Persons

In the *Tadic* Conviction Appeal Judgement of 1999, the Appeals Chamber held that 'a person may be accorded protected person status, notwithstanding the fact that he is of the same nationality as his captors', a ruling subsequently endorsed by the Appeals Chamber in *Aleksovski.*[53]

Command Responsibility

In the *Celibici* Case, the Trial Chamber found Zdravko Mucic (one of the four accused) to be Commander of the Celibici camp and declared guilty under the principle of superior responsibility for crimes committed by his subordinates, including murder, torture and inhuman treatment, under Article 7.1 of the Statute.[54] He was also found guilty of personal responsibility for the unlawful confinement of civilians. He was given a total sentence of seven years.

Mucic argued that command responsibility is limited to de jure commanders, or those superiors with control over subordinates equivalent to such de jure authority. On 20 February 2001, the Appeals Chamber rejected this argument, accepting that a position of de facto command may be sufficient to establish the necessary superior-subordinate relationship, as long as the relevant degree of control over subordinates is established. This is established where the superior has effective control over the persons committing the violations of international humanitarian law, in the sense of having the material ability to prevent or punish the commission of these offences. The Appeals Chamber found no basis to review the Trial Chamber's finding that there was sufficient evidence to establish that Mucic was a de facto commander.

Zejnil Delalic was alleged to have coordinated the activities of the Bosnian Muslim and Bosnian Croat forces in the area and later to have been the Commander

52 Tessitore and Woolfson, *Issues before the 54th General Assembly*, pp. 268–270; *IHT*, 23 February 2001; *Le Monde*, 24 February 2001.

53 ICTY *Press Release* JL/P.I.S./564-e, 20 February 2001.

54 Article 7 deals with 'Individual criminal responsibility'. Article 7.1: 'A person who planned, instigated, ordered, committed or otherwise aided and abetted in the planning, preparation or execution of a crime referred to in Articles 2 to 5 of the present Statute, shall be individually responsible for the crime'.

of the First Tactical Group of the Bosnian Army. He was alleged in that capacity to have had authority over the Celibici camp. The Trial Chamber found him not guilty on all counts, on the basis that he did not have sufficient command and control over the Celebici camp and its guards to found his criminal responsibility as a superior for the crimes which they committed in the camp.

The prosecution had appealed against the Trial Chamber's interpretation of the requirement, in Article 7.3, that a superior 'knew or had reason to know' that a subordinate is about to commit crimes or had done so. The Appeals Chamber concluded that the phrase 'reason to know' in Article 7.3 means that a superior will be charged with knowledge of subordinates' offences if information of a general nature was available to him which would have put him on notice of those offences. The Appeals Chamber was satisfied that the Trial Chamber's conclusions on this issue were consistent with that interpretation.

The prosecution also contended that the ability of an accused to exercise forms of influence should suffice to establish the relevant superior–subordinate relationship. The Appeals Chamber concluded that, whilst indirect as well as direct relationships of subordination will suffice, the relevant standard of effective control over subordinates must be established, and that any forms of influence which fall short of such control would not suffice. The Appeals Chamber was satisfied that, on the evidence before the Trial Chamber, it was open to a reasonable tribunal of fact to acquit Delalic on the basis that he was not a superior in relation to the Celibici camp and those working there.[55]

Sentences

Sentences by Trial and Appeals Chambers have ranged from a maximum of 46 years to acquittal. A few examples of sentences follow.

On 2 August 2001, Radislav Krstic, former Bosnian Serb General, was found guilty of genocide for his role in the massacre of thousands of Bosnian Muslims in Srebrenica between 10 and 19 July 1995. He was sentenced to 46 years in jail. It was the first sentence for genocide rendered by the ICTY. Some legal observers felt that a life sentence should have sanctioned a genocide conviction.[56]

General Tihomir Blaskic, the most senior military leader in the Tribunal's custody, was sentenced to 45 years' imprisonment on 3 March 2000. The charges against him related to his activities as Colonel in the armed forces of the Croatian Defense Council (HVO) and as commander of the HVO in Central Bosnia. From May 1992 to January 1994, the armed forces of HVO committed serious violations of international humanitarian law against Bosnian Muslims in Bosnia and Herzegovina. The specific charges against Blaskic involved grave breaches of the 1949 Geneva Conventions, violating the laws or customs of war, and crimes against

[55] ICTY *Press Release* JL/P.I.S./564-e, 20 February 2001.
[56] *IHT*, 3 August 2001; *Le Monde*, 4 August 2001.

humanity. Charges related to mass atrocities in the Lasva Valley where, in mid-April 1993, Bosnian Muslim villages were destroyed, civilians killed and beaten, women raped, and homes razed. Although Blaskic did not commit personally any of these atrocities, he was accused of having 'ordered, planned, instigated or otherwise aided and abetted' their perpetration. He was also charged with command responsibility over those subordinates who committed these crimes.[57]

On 14 December 1999, the Trial Chamber sentenced Goran Jelisic to 40 years' imprisonment. Jelisic held a position of authority at the Luka camp, where Bosnian Serb forces confined, under inhumane conditions, hundreds of Muslim and Croat men and a few women. He was condemned for crimes against humanity and violations of the laws or customs of war, but the charge of genocide was not retained. The Chamber considered that his 'scornful attitude towards [his] victims, [his] enthusiasm for committing the crimes, the inhumanity of the crimes and [his] dangerous nature' amounted to 'especially aggravating circumstances'.

On 14 January 2000, five Bosnian Croats were condemned for crimes against humanity to sentences ranging from six to 25 years: Vladimir Santic was sentenced to 25 years, Drago Josipovic to 15 years, Zoran Kupreskic to 10 years, Mirjan Kupreskic to 8 years and Vlatko Kupreskic to six years. The accused were found guilty of persecution for helping to organise or participating in the murder of only Muslim inhabitants, the burning of houses and mosques in the Lasva Valley from January to May 1993.

On 26 February 2001, the Trial Chamber sentenced Dario Kordic, a close ally of former President Franjo Tudjman, to 25 years' imprisonment for helping to plan and instigate a ruthless campaign against Muslim civilians which led to the persecution, killing and imprisonment of hundreds of people. It also convicted Mario Cerkez, a former brigade commander of Croatian troops in Bosnia of similar crimes: he was sentenced to 15 years.[58]

Review of Sentences by the Appeals Chamber

One question in *Aleksovski* was whether the Appeals Chamber was bound by its previous decision in another case, *Tadic*. The Chamber recognised that in both the common law and civil law systems, the highest courts, whether as a matter of doctrine or of practice, will normally follow their previous decisions and will only depart from them in exceptional circumstances. This is to preserve the principles of consistency, certainty and predictability. The need to preserve these principles is particularly great in criminal law where the liberty of the individual is implicated. The same principles apply in International Tribunals. The Chamber concluded that it should follow its previous decisions, but that it should be free to depart from them for cogent reasons in the interest of justice, such departure remaining the exception.

---

[57] *Le Monde*, 5–6 March 2000.

[58] *IHT*, 15 December 1999, 15–16 January 2000, 23 and 27 February 2001.

In the *Aleksovski* case, the Appeal Chamber noted that appellate review of sentencing is available in the major legal systems, but is usually exercised sparingly. In *Tadic*, the Appeals Chamber held that it should not intervene in the exercise of the Trial Chamber's discretion with regard to sentence unless there is a 'discernible error'.

Tadic had originally been sentenced to 20 years' imprisonment; On 11 November 1999, his sentence was raised to 25 years' imprisonment in light of additional convictions. On 26 January 2000, the Appeals Chamber reduced Tadic's sentence to 20 years on the grounds that 'although [Tadic's] conduct ... was incontestably heinous, his level in the command structure, when compared to that of his superiors, e.g. Commanders, or the very architects of the strategy of ethnic cleansing, was low'.[59]

In *Aleksovski*, the Appeals Chamber found that there was a discernible error in the Trial Chamber's exercise of discretion in imposing sentence. That error consisted of giving insufficient weight to the gravity of the conduct of the Appellant and failing to treat his position as commander as an aggravating feature in relation to his responsibility under Article 7(1) of the Statute. The Appeals Chamber then raised the sentence from two-and-a-half years to seven years.

In the *Celibici* Case, the Prosecution had challenged the sentences imposed on Mucic of seven years, to be served concurrently, as 'manifestly inadequate'. Mucic challenged his sentence as too long in all the circumstances. The Appeals Chamber concluded that the Trial Chamber failed to take adequate account of the gravity of offences for which Mucic was convicted and that, in a number of respects, it failed to take into account, or gave inadequate weight to, various matters in aggravation. The Appeals Chamber then remitted the matter of the imposition of an appropriate revised sentence for Mucic to the Reconstituted Trial Chamber, with the indication that, had it not been necessary to take into account a possible adjustment in sentence because of the dismissal of the counts referred to, it would have imposed a sentence of around ten years.[60]

Conduct of a Judge

In the *Celibici* case, Esad Landzo challenged the fairness of the trial on the basis that the Presiding Judge, Judge Karibi-Whyte, had been 'asleep during substantial portions of the trial'. The Appeals Chamber stated, firmly, that Judge Karibi-Whyte's conduct could not be accepted as appropriate conduct for a judge. If a judge suffers from some condition which prevents him or her from giving full attention during the trial, then it is the duty of that judge to seek medical assistance, and, if that does not help, to withdraw from the case. In the case, the Appeals Chamber did

[59] *Prosecutor v. Tadic*, Judgement in sentencing appeals, 26 January 2000, para. 56.

[60] ICTY 'Summary of Appeals Chamber Judgement – The prosecutor v. Zlatko Aleksovski, 24 March 2000; ICTY *Press Release*, 20 February 2001.

not find that any specific prejudice had been suffered by Landzo or the other appellants: it rejected this ground of appeal.[61]

Conduct of a Lawyer

On 31 January 2000, the Appeals Chamber issued another important judgement on matters relating to the professional responsibility of lawyers appearing before the Tribunal. It found one of Dusko Tadic's attorneys, Milan Vujin, in contempt of court for his conduct in representing Tadic from 30 March 1999 to 18 November 1999. The Chamber found that Vujin had put forward evidence which was known to him to be false. Vujin had also manipulated two unnamed witnesses. The Chamber ordered Vujin to pay a fine of 15 000 Dutch guilders to the Registry of the Tribunal. It also requested the Registrar to 'consider striking' Vujin off the list of assigned counsel and 'report' Vujin's conduct to the professional legal body to which he belongs.[62]

REFORMS

On 30 November 2000, the Security Council approved unanimously resolution 1329 establishing a pool of ad litem judges in the International Tribunal for the Former Yugoslavia and enlarging the membership of the Appeals Chambers of the Tribunals for the Former Yugoslavia and for Rwanda. Henceforth, the Chambers would be composed of 16 permanent independent judges and a maximum at any one time of nine ad litem independent judges.[63]

This decision came as a result of several reports submitted to the General Assembly and to the Security Council. One basic reason for setting inquiries in the operation and functioning of the International Criminal Tribunals was the duration of their trials, considered excessive, the limited number of completed trials in relation to the number of indictees, questions about the time needed to complete all trials and, in consequence questions about the date on which the Tribunals would complete their mandate and then be terminated.

In 1998, the General Assembly asked the Secretary-General to conduct a review of the operation and functioning of the International Tribunals. The Secretary-General appointed a five-member expert group. The experts focused primarily on judicial management but they also examined the organisational structure of the Tribunals. After soliciting input from states and interested NGOs and reviewing material provided by both Tribunals, the experts interviewed the judges, registrar,

---

61 ICTY *Press Release*, 20 February 2001.

62 ICTY Trial Information Sheet, Tadic Case (IT-94-1-A), 2 February 2000. See also 'The Code of Professional Conduct for Defence Counsel appearing before the International Tribunal, Decision IT/125, 12 June 1997.

63 Articles 12, 13 and 14 of the Statute of the Former Yugoslavia Tribunal, and Articles 11, 12 and 13 of the Rwanda Tribunal were amended under Annexes I and II of resolution 1329.

prosecutor and senior staff of both Tribunals, and several defense counsels. The group first met in April 1999 and submitted its report to the Secretary-General on 22 November 1999.[64]

The group formulated 46 recommendations for improving the operation and functioning of the Tribunals. Of these, 16 were put into practice between the time when the group started work and the submission of Comments on the Experts' Report.[65] The intent of these recommendations was essentially to reduce the length of trials while fulfilling the statutory right of the accused to a fair and expeditious trial.

On trials in absentia, the group recommended that the judges consider whether the 'right of an accused who had voluntarily surrendered to be tried in person is waivable by the accused following his initial appearance'. The prosecutor objected to this recommendation and asserted that, although trials in absentia may be permissible in some national systems, they are inappropriate in the context of the International Tribunals and 'tantamount to an admission of defeat by the Tribunal as a judicial institution'.

The experts encouraged the judges to assume greater control over proceedings through the more active use of existing rules and the adoption of new rules. For instance, rules should be adopted that explicitly permit the judges to question counsel and witnesses, halt irrelevant or repetitive testimony, and exclude witnesses whose testimony is cumulative or of no material value with respect to disputed issues. They asserted that a liberal judicial policy regarding adjournments significantly contributes to the length of trials.

In addition to many other technical recommendations, the group recommended consideration of the use of temporary judges to reduce the backlog of cases, if that is the 'only practical solution for expediting completion of the missions of the Tribunal'.

The group also made recommendations concerning administrative matters. Among these:

- the adoption by the ICTY of a rule similar to ICTR Rule 44 bis, which establishes a roster of qualified-duty defense counsel to be assigned for limited purposes and of limited durations when the accused would otherwise lack an attorney owing to the unavailability of assigned counsel;

---

[64] 'Report of the Expert Group to Conduct a Review of the Effective Operation and Functioning of the International Tribunal for the Former Yugoslavia and the International Criminal Tribunal for Rwanda, UN Doc. A/54/634 (1999). See D.A. Mundis, 'Improving the Operation and Functioning of the International Criminal Tribunals' (2000), *The American Journal of International Law*, Vol. 94, pp. 759–773.

[65] 'Comments on the Report of the Expert Group to Conduct a Review of the Effective Operation and Functioning of the International Tribunal for the Former Yugoslavia and the International Criminal Tribunal for Rwanda', UN Doc. A/54/850 (2000).

- the adoption of more stringent standards for attorneys wishing to be included on the list of potential defense counsel; and
- oversight by the Chambers of the amount of fees paid to defense counsels to reduce their inclination to employ obstructive and dilatory tactics based solely on the expectation of additional fees.

Following the submission of the report of the expert group, President Jorda initiated consultations with the Tribunal's judges on its contents. The judges designed and adopted unanimously a plan at an extraordinary plenary meeting on 18 April 2000, which was then issued as the 'Jorda Report'. This was the first internal review of the state of the Tribunal in its seven years of operation, besides the Tribunal's annual reports which have a different purpose and rhythm. The Jorda Report includes proposals rejected by the judges, an analysis of the Tribunal's future prospects and recommendations. President Jorda submitted his Report to the UN Secretary-General by letter dated 12 May 2000, who transmitted it to the General Assembly and the Security Council on 14 September 2000. The Report had been communicated to the Office of the Prosecutor, which expressed general agreement with the assessment of the Tribunal's projected workload, support for a more dynamic pre-trial process and recognition of the need to increase the Tribunal's capacity to try cases.[66]

The first rejected proposal was to transfer cases to the national court systems of certain states. In the view of the judges, the adoption of this proposal would result in a two-tiered justice system, potentially leading to unequal treatment of the accused and inconsistent caselaw. It would also detract from the development of a unified international criminal justice system and 'would go against all the efforts expended to establish an International Criminal Court'.

A second proposal to create a second tribunal to hear cases involving 'minor' perpetrators was also dismissed, in part because of the prosecutor's policy of focusing on trying senior-level perpetrators: anticipated gains in efficiency would be minimal. The third proposal was to transfer the ICTY caseload to the International Criminal Court when established. For the judges, [E]ven if this solution is tempting in the long-term, the judges consider that it constitutes no more than the simple transferral of ICTY problems to another international court'.

The fourth proposal was to hold ICTY trials outside The Hague. While this would increase the Tribunal's visibility, the judges considered that it would not contribute to shortening trials and could actually exacerbate the situation. It would raise security and financial problems. The fifth proposal was to conduct trials before a single judge. While this would triple the number of cases that could be heard simultaneously, this proposal was rejected because the 'credibility of international justice would be too seriously affected'. The sixth proposal considered trials in

66 'Report on the Operation of the International Tribunal for the Former Yugoslavia, Submitted by Judge Claude Jorda, President on Behalf of the Judges of the Tribunal', UN Doc. A/55/382-S/2000/865, Annex I, UN Doc. A/55/382-S/2000/865, 14 September 2000.

absentia, a proposal already discussed by the expert group. The last rejected proposal was to create an additional trial chamber: the judges determined that it was unsatisfactory, although President Jorda indicated that it would contribute to a solution for a limited period.

The report includes a detailed analysis of the Tribunal's projected lifespan. On the basis of estimates and projections, the judges predicted that the Tribunal would not fulfill its mandate until at least 2016, not including the time taken for appeals. In presenting a draft reform of the operations and structure of the Tribunal to the Security Council in June 2000, the judges drew the attention of the Council that this state of affairs could well compromise the accomplishment of their mission, a temporary one which must make possible a lasting return to peace in the Balkans. They also highlighted the risk that the fundamental right of the accused to be tried without undue delay might be jeopardized, a risk already proven by the amount of time the accused currently spent on remand. Lastly, they stressed the financial cost to the UN of such a situation and, more fundamentally the dangers it represents to the credibility of international justice, a credibility which is more than necessary to ensure when states are due to ratify the Statute of the International Criminal Court.

The Jorda Report then submitted a two-part plan based on three principles: (1) the need for more active pretrial management; (2) the reduction of the time allowed for hearings to the absolute minimum so as to reduce the length of trials; and (3) the use of flexibility to adjust to the 'ebb and flow' of the caseload.

To expedite the pretrial management, the judges proposed delegating part of the pretrial judicial administration to the senior legal officers of the Chambers. The delegated authority would extend, inter alia, to setting deadlines, preparing a procedural summary of the pretrial activitiy, and taking depositions. A full bench of the Trial Chamber would retain the ability to render any decisions regarding jurisdictional matters.

However, this 'solution would have a true impact only if combined with a substantial increase in the trial capacity of the Trial Chambers'. The judges reached a consensus on the creation of a pool of ad litem judges. In practice, if none of the Trial Chambers were available to hear a case as soon as the pretrial process had been completed, three judges from the pool of ad litem judges would be called on to serve in one of the Trial Chambers for a given case. In a later clarification, a Tribunal's representative stated that the concept of ad litem judges was based on the fact that 'a Judge is a Judge is a Judge': the ad litem judges had all the same powers and privileges and the same status as permanent judges. However, ad litem judges would only sit on trials, not on appeals. Internal reforms would also be needed, not requiring additional resources. Rules for administering and presenting evidence must be amended to make them more effective. The judges' powers of control over the conduct of the proceedings must be bolstered for the purposes of expediting trials, avoiding all stonewalling tactics, with due regard to the demands of fairness. One issue was to regulate the number of witnesses that either party could call, in order to avoid endless lists of witnesses who might all be testifying to the same facts. The judges will also propose to the Registrar and the Prosecutor new measures enabling the three organs of the Tribunal to set in concert their longer-term judicial priorities and to cooperate more closely in meeting them within as short a time as possible.

In his speech to the Security Council of 21 November 2000, President Jorda reminded the Council that the highest-ranking political and military officers indicted by the Tribunal were still at large. He appealed to the Council to use all its influence over the Member States, and especially the Successor States of the Former Yugoslavia, so that they arrest and bring before the Tribunal the accused in their territory.

On 13 December 2000, at a Plenary meeting, the judges approved the establishment of two new bodies: a Coordinating Council, composed of the President, the Prosecutor and the Registrar, which will meet once a month in order to discuss the coordination between the three organs – a Management Committee, composed of the President, the Vice-President, one further judge, the Registrar, his Deputy and the Chief of Administration – which will meet twice a month to discuss matters pertaining to the on-going administrative management of the Tribunal, with the exception of those matters relating to the Office of the Prosecutor.[67]

NATO'S 'WAR CRIMES' IN KOSOVO

The Charges

As noted above, NATO conducted a bombing campaign against the FRY from 24 March 1999 to 10 June 1999. During and since that period, the Prosecutor received numerous requests from individuals and NGOs that she investigate allegations that senior political and military figures from NATO countries committed serious violations of international humanitarian law during the campaign and that she prepare indictments pursuant to Article 18(1) and (4) of the Statute. As a separate and distinct legal initiative, the FRY instituted proceedings before the International Court of Justice based, in part, on a compilation prepared by its Ministry of Foreign Affairs entitled 'NATO Crimes in Yugoslavia' (White Book): this Book and other documentation were submitted to the Prosecutor. The legitimacy of the recourse to force by NATO members against the FRY is a subject before the Court, for which the ICTY is not competent.

In May 1999, a group of American and Canadian international affairs experts and lawyers, supported by anti-war law professors in Britain, France, Greece and Norway, submitted a proposal to the Prosecutor to bring charges against the US, Britain and the other alliance countries, as well as the leaders of NATO itself, on the basis of 'overwhelming evidence' of specified violations of international humanitarian

[67] ICTY *Press Release*, JD/P.I.S./541-e, 21 November 2000; ICTY Weekly Press Briefing, 6 December 2000, 5 January 2001, 11 April 2001.

law.[68] Human Rights Watch (HRW) sent various documents to the Tribunal: a letter to the Secretary-General of NATO during the bombing campaign, a paper on *NATO's Use of Cluster Munitions*, and a report on *Civilian Deaths in the NATO Air Campaign*, issued in February 2000. Kenneth Roth, Executive Director of HRW, said in an interview in June 2000 that, of the approximately 500 Yugoslav civilians killed in Serbia and Kosovo by NATO bombs, half died unnecessarily because of NATO violations of international humanitarian law and practice. He criticised NATO in four areas: the use of cluster bombs, 'inherently indiscriminate weapons', near civilian areas; the deliberate bombing of targets with little or no military significance, including the television station, Belgrade's heating plant, bridges, some factories and other infrastructures; the bombing of targets, like the Varvarin bridge, during the daytime, when civilians would be nearby at a market, and the failure to take sufficient precautions to identify mobile targets before bombing.[69]

On 7 June 2000, Amnesty International (AI) issued a report entitled 'Collateral Damage or Unlawful Killings? Violations of the Laws of War by NATO during Operation Allied Force.[70] Extracts from the conclusion of the report follow:

> Amnesty International believes that in the course of Operation Allied Force, civilian deaths could have been significantly reduced if NATO forces had fully adhered to the laws of war. NATO did not always meet its legal obligations in selecting targets and in choosing means and methods of attack. In one instance, the attack on the headquarters of the Serbian state radio and television (RTS), NATO launched a direct attack on a civilian object, killing 16 civilians. Such attack breached article 52(I) of Protocol I[71] and therefore constitutes a war crime. In other attacks, including the Grdelica railroad bridge, the automobile bridge in Luzane, and Varvarin bridge, NATO failed to suspend their attack after it was evident that they had struck civilians, in contravention of Article 57(2)(b) of Protocol I. In other cases, including the attacks on displaced civilians in Djakovica and Korisa, insufficient precautions were taken to minimise civilian casualties.
>
> ... Also, aspects of the Rules of Engagement, specifically the requirements that NATO aircraft fly above 15,000 feet, made full adherence to international humanitarian law virtually impossible.
>
> ... NATO was under a legal obligation to implement fundamental precautions from the start of the campaign, rather than prioritizing the safety of its aircraft

68 *IHT*, 20 January 2000.

69 *IHT*, 8 June 2000.

70 Amnesty International, www.amnesty.or/ailib/aipub/2000/EUR/47001800.htm. The report's findings are similar to those in a Human Rights Watch report of February 2000: 'Human Rights Watch, Civilian Deaths in the NATO Air Campaign', www.hrw.org/reports/2000/nato/.

71 Protocol Additional to the Geneva Conventions of August 12, 1949, and Relating to the Protection of Victims of International Armed Conflicts (Protocol I), June 8, 1977, 1125 UNTS 3. The US is not a party to this Protocol.

> and pilots over protecting civilians, including those civilians on whose behalf it said it was intervening.
>
> ... The confidential nature of any investigations and the reported absence of measures against any NATO personnel cast doubt on NATO's commitment to getting to the bottom of specific incidents in accordance with international law. In one case only, the bombing of the Chinese Embassy in Belgrade, were the results of an investigation disclosed, compensation paid and disciplinary measures taken against those found to be responsible. The impression that these measures were taken in that instance primarily because of political reasons is inescapable.

AI urged NATO to establish a body to investigate credible allegations of violations of international humanitarian law and ensure that victims of violations receive adequate redress. 'NATO member states must bring to justice any of their nationals suspected of being responsible for serious violations under international humanitarian law, in particular grave breaches of Protocol I'.

NATO's Response

NATO's Secretary General, Lord Robertson, rejected AI's allegations as baseless and ill-founded, in a statement issued on 7 June 2000.[72]

> NATO scrupulously adhered to international law, including the law of war, throughout the conflict and made every effort to minimise civilian casualties, Unfortunately, as we have always acknowledged, among over ten thousand bombing missions, in a few cases mistakes were made, or weapons malfunctioned, leading to civilian deaths or injuries. We deeply regret such incidents. But such incidents must be weighed against the atrocities that NATO's action stopped.
>
> NATO's air campaign put an end to the most brutal ethnic violence seen in Europe since World War II. Extensive documentation by the OSCE, Human Rights Watch and the media show that Serbian military and police forces engaged in a deliberate, massive, and prolonged campaign of violence against Kosovar Albanian civilians in gross violation of international law and civilized norms of behaviour. The clear priority now is to bring to justice the war criminals that perpetrated this violence against the people of Kosovo.

The Tribunal's Position

On 2 June 2000, Carla Del Ponte told the Security Council that there was no basis to investigate allegations of crimes committed by personnel and leaders of NATO

[72] Geneva US Mission Daily Bulletin, EUR205, NATO Press Release, 7 June 2000.

during its bombing campaign against the FRY. Although NATO had made some mistakes, it had not deliberately targeted civilians.[73]

On 14 May 1999, the previous Prosecutor, Louise Arbour, had established a Committee to assess the allegations and accompanying material, and advise the Prosecutor and Deputy Prosecutor whether or not there was a sufficient basis to proceed with an investigation into some or all of the allegations or into other incidents related to the NATO bombing. The 'Final Report to the Prosecutor by the Committee Established to Review the NATO Bombing Campaign Against the Federal Republic of Yugoslavia' was submitted on 13 June 2000.[74]

The Committee applied the same criteria to its review as those applied by the Office of the Prosecutor (OTP) to the activities of other actors in the Former Yugoslavia. Its report listed the documentation at its disposal, and the key incidents and target categories. It reviewed charges of damage to the environment, the use of depleted uranium projectiles, the use of cluster bombs and gave an overview of applicable law. It reviewed five specific incidents. As a mild criticism, the Committee noted that when the OTP requested NATO to answer specific questions about specific incidents, the NATO reply was couched in general terms and failed to address the specific incidents. Its conclusion was that, if one accepts the figures in the FRY compilation *NATO Crimes in Yugoslavia* of approximately 495 civilians killed and 820 civilians wounded in documented instances,

> [t]here is simply no evidence of the necessary crime base for charges of genocide or crimes against humanity. Further, in the particular incidents reviewed by the committee with particular care (see paras. 9, and 48–76) the committee has not assessed any particular incidents as justifying the commencement of an investigation by the OTP. NATO has admitted that mistakes did occur during the bombing campaign; errors of judgment may also have occurred. Selection of certain objectives for attack may be subject to legal debate. On the basis of the information reviewed, however, the committee is of the opinion that neither an in-depth investigation related to the bombing campaign as a whole nor investigations related to specific incidents are justified. In all cases, either the law is not sufficiently clear or investigations are unlikely to result in the acquisition of sufficient evidence to substantiate charges against high level accused or against lower accused for particularly heinous offences.
>
> On the basis of information available, the committee recommends that no investigation be commenced by the OTP in relation to the NATO bombing campaign or incidents occurring during the campaign.
>
> This recommendation was accepted by the Prosecutor.

---

[73] UN *Press Release* SC/6870, 2 June 2000.

[74] See www.un.org/icty/pressreal/nato061300.htm. The Committee's Recommendations are in paras. 90 and 91. Its members were not identified by name and nationality in the report: they were military lawyers, military analysts, prosecuting attorneys and other experts.

The Kosovo Report

This report was prepared by the Independent International Commission on Kosovo, created at the initiative of the Prime Minister of Sweden, Mr Göran Persson, who was concerned by the absence of independent analysis of the conflict in Kosovo and any real attempt to research the lessons to be learned from the conflict. It was presented to UN Secretary General on 23 October 2000.[75]

Among its conclusions:

- the NATO intervention was illegal but legitimate;
- NATO falsely believed that a short bombing campaign would be enough to achieve an agreement and totally underestimated the risk that the Serbian government would attack the Kosovo Albanians. Air power was incapable of stopping expulsions and murder. NATO had to expand the air campaign to strategic targets in Serbia proper, which increased the risk of Serbian casualties. In spite of the fact that NATO made substantial efforts to avoid civilian casualties some serious mistakes were made;
- There is no evidence of deliberate targeting of civilians, but there is reason to question the selection of targets relating to the infrastructure of the FRY in which the probability of civilians being present and killed was quite high;
- The Commission was critical of the use of cluster bombs, the environmental damage caused by the use of depleted-uranium tipped armor-piercing shells and missiles and by toxic leaks caused by the bombing of industrial and petroleum complexes in several cities, and the attack on Serbian television on 17 April 1999.

The Commission accepted the view of the Final Report of the ICTY that there is no basis in the available evidence for charging specific individuals with criminal violations of the Laws of War during the NATO campaign. 'Nevertheless some practices do seem vulnerable to the allegation that violations might have occurred and depend, for final assessment, on the availability of further evidence'.

A Legal Critique of the Final Report

In an article published in December 2000 by the International Review of the Red Cross,[76] Professor Natalino Ronzitti first showed that any violation of international humanitarian law committed during the NATO air campaign against the FRY is

---

[75] Justice Richard Goldstone (South Africa) and Mr Carl Tham, Secretary-General of the Olof Palme International centre in Stockholm were co-chairmen. The other nine members were from Benin, Canada, Czech Republic, France, Japan, the UK, and two from the USA. The Report was published by Oxford University Press in 2000. See also *Press Release* from the Commission, 23 October 2000 and www.kosovocommission.org.

[76] N. Ronzitti, 'Is the *non liquet* of the Final Report by the Committee Established to Review the NATO Bombing Campaign Against the Federal Republic of Yugoslavia acceptable?', *International Review of the Red Cross*, December 2000, Vol. 82, No. 840, pp. 1017–1027.

clearly within the competence of the Tribunal. He then identified two main flaws in the report of the Committee established by the Prosecutor in the reasons why the Committee did not recommend an investigation by the Office of the Prosecutor: the law if not sufficiently clear – investigations are unlikely to result in the acquisition of sufficient evidence to substantiate charges against high level accused or against lower accused for particular heinous offences.

On the first point, the author said that difficulties in interpretation of the law are not a good excuse for not starting an investigation. It is precisely the task of the Tribunal to interpret and 'clarify' the law. The *non liquet* is not part of the Tribunal's jurisprudence or that of any other tribunal.

On the second point, the author also finds that the difficulty to obtain sufficient evidence is no excuse for not commencing an investigation. The Tribunal's Prosecutor enjoys substantial powers for collecting evidence and the Committee's conclusion is unduly pessimistic.

The author then reviews the lawfulness of depleted uranium weapons, which, in his view, cannot be considered as prohibited by contemporary international law. On the attack on the Serbian radio and TV station in Belgrade, he agrees with the Report's conclusion: the view that media, including installations of broadcasting and television stations, are a legitimate military objective, or may become one, is supported by the compilation of military objectives made by the International Committee of the Red Cross in the context of its 1956 Draft Rules for the Limitations of the Dangers incurred by the Civilian Population in Time of War.

In the case of the attack on the Leskovac railway bridge, the author finds that the Report is 'completely insufficient. The Committee should have assessed more thoroughly the incident related to the second bomb. Since several people were killed or injured, the rule of proportionality should have been looked into'. In this respect, the Report seems to have adopted a broad interpretation of that rule, in repudiation of the doctrine established by the Tribunal in the *Kupreskic* judgement.

Finally, the author finds that the Report of the Committee cannot be considered entirely satisfactory: 'The Committee, instead of saying that the law is vague, should have squarely admitted that the alleged facts, even if proven, were not considered as amounting to a war crime.

Because of its deficiencies, the Report does not constitute the definite and conclusive element on which a decision not to proceed may be grounded. This is even more true if the statement by a former judge and President of the Tribunal that the NATO air campaign deserved an investigation by the Tribunal is taken into account.[77]

---

[77] A. Cassese, in *La Re pubblica*, 26 March 2000, p. 17. Frederick Bonnart, editorial director of NATO's *Nations*, an independent military journal, supported the same view: 'An investigation into these various accusations and a determination of the degree of responsibility of different individuals should certainly take place if the alliance wishes to remain on the moral high ground that is the present reason for its existence': *IHT*, 20 June 2000.

CONCLUSION

Security Council resolution 827 of 25 May 1993 created the Tribunal. The basis for its decision was its 'grave alarm' at continuing reports of widespread and flagrant violations of international humanitarian law within the territory of Former Yugoslavia, the continuation of this situation deemed to constitute a threat to international peace and security. This reasoning allowed the Council to create the Tribunal under Chapter VII of the UN Charter.

However, the list of measures not involving the use of armed forces which may be employed by the Council under Article 41 of the Charter to give effect to its decisions does not include the creation of an international tribunal: they refer to the interruption of economic relations, of means of communications and the severance of diplomatic relations. The authors of the Charter did not envisage that the Council could take upon itself to create other international tribunals, besides the International Court of Justice, the principal judicial organ of the UN.

The creation of international criminal tribunals by the Council is a considerable innovation, which has been criticised by legal experts on the basis that legitimate international tribunals should only be created through diplomatic negotiations, the approval of a statute and ratification by a set number of states, as in the case of the International Criminal Court.

The Security Council is a political organ and the creation of the ICTY was a political decision, motivated by the disarray of the Council's members faced with continuing mass killings, organised detention and rape of women and ethnic cleansing, and the inability or unwillingness of the main powers to put an end to the conflicts through effective negotiations or military intervention. Creating a tribunal was an alibi, a visible gesture to counteract widespread criticisms aroused by the mediatized atrocities. There was no time to go through the long and uncertain process of a negotiated international treaty: expediency prevailed. At the same time, most of the tribunal's creators did not expect that their 'creature' would survive and become effective, in terms of judging and sanctioning a number of perpetrators of the atrocities, including a former head of state. The Tribunal, with the support of a few countries (mainly the USA, the UK and the Netherlands), and the political and judicial skills of its judges and prosecutors, exercised the independence which had been granted to it by its Statute, fought against the resistance and non-cooperation of mainly France and Russia, and successor states to the Former Yugoslavia (Serbia and Croatia), obtained funds and staff from an obstructing UN secretariat and achieved results: 106 individuals publicly indicted since the inception of the ICTY, 12 judgements on Trial and 14 on Appeal. The accused and judged now include the former president of the FRY, the former president of the Bosnian Serb Republic and seven generals or former generals, Serbs, Croats and Muslims.

The Tribunal has confirmed the Nuremberg precedent in affirming the individual criminal responsibility of persons at the highest political and military levels. As stated by the newly appointed Registrar of the Tribunal, Mr. Hans Holthuis, on 22 May 2001,[78]

> By focusing on individual responsibility, the founders of the Tribunal wished to prevent the stigmatization of a whole national, ethnic or religious group and to neutralize those persons who sustain the climate of hatred and nationalism which caused the terrible chaos. By making *individuals* responsible, the international community hoped to deter others from taking that same road.

It has strengthened international humanitarian law by including as charges grave breaches of the Geneva Conventions of 1949, violations of the laws or customs of war, genocide and crimes against humanity. It has sanctioned rape and sexual slavery as crimes against humanity. It has further eroded the distinction between the rules governing international conflicts and those governing the more frequent internal conflicts. It has created, tested and applied its internal judicial and administrative procedures, with due respect to the provisions of Articles 9, 10, 14 and 15 of the 1966 International Covenant on Civil and Political Rights.It has given hope to those who promote the creation of the International Criminal Court.

Is the ICTY independent? It is independent insofar as the Statute provides the judges with all the guarantees of independence and impartiality that the exercise of their functions requires. The Statute also recognises the Prosecutor's independence as a separate organ of the Tribunal, with the power to determine unfettered the penal policy to be pursued. He or she is not to seek or receive instructions from any government or from any other source.

In practice, the Tribunal depends on the cooperation of states for the arrest of indicted persons, their transfer to The Hague, the taking of testimony and the gathering of evidence. The Tribunal has no police force to enforce its summons and decisions: it is without the 'secular arm' which all national court systems possess. The inadequacy of cooperation and judicial assistance required of states under Article 29 of the Tribunal's Statute has, and still is, a major obstacle to the Tribunal's work. It is however fair to note that the recent progress of democracy in both Serbia and Croatia has resulted in better cooperation with the Tribunal. The arrest of former president Milosevic and his spectacular transfer to The Hague was made possible by the progressive democratization of Serbia together with the decisive pressure of the US. A significant and long-awaited outcome for the Tribunal, it also showed its dependence on governments' cooperation.

The Serbs and others have cast in doubt the political independence and the impartiality of the Tribunal, labelled as anti-Serb. The Tribunal has succeeded in extending its prosecutions to Croats and Muslim Bosnians, which has deflated the impact of this claim. In fact, while the Serbs have been the main perpetrators of violations of international humanitarian law, Croats and Muslims have their share of guilt.

---

[78] ICTY *Press Release* CC/P.I.S./592-e, 22 May 2001.

What about NATO? Are Western countries' political and military leaders immune from prosecution? Are Western armies not subject to international humanitarian law?

The Tribunal has essentially been created by Western countries, with the active or passive approval of others. The Tribunal is dependent on NATO and SFOR for the arrest and transfer of indictees. The charges of 'war crimes' allegedly committed by NATO during its bombing campaign in Kosovo raised, for the first time, a major challenge to the Prosecutor. Accepting an investigation of alleged NATO war crimes would undoubtedly have aroused severe criticisms on the part of Western political and military leaders, and NATO officials. The mere suggestion of an investigation, demanded by Human Rights Watch, Amnesty International and a few legal experts, not necessarily followed by prosecutions, was enough to set all Western parties against the Tribunal. It would have given ammunition to those, particularly in the USA, who are trying to prevent countries from ratifying the Rome Statute of the International Criminal Court.

It is more than probable that the decision of the Prosecutor to reject an investigation, a decision based on recommendations from the Final Report of the Committee established by Louise Arbour, has been influenced by such non-judiciary constraints.

In the preamble of resolution 827, the Security Council declared itself 'convinced' that the establishment of the Tribunal and the prosecution of persons responsible for serious violations of international humanitarian law '... would contribute to the restoration and maintenance of peace', in line with the Council's primary responsibility for the maintenance of international peace and security under Article 24 of the UN Charter.

So far, there is no evidence that the existence and work of the Tribunal has contributed to the restoration and maintenance of peace. The Srebrenica massacre took place in July 1995, when the Tribunal was fully operational. Political and military means have contributed to the Dayton Peace Agreement of December 1995, not the Tribunal. Fighting between Albanian rebels and Macedonian troops in 2001 is not deterred by the Tribunal. Justice cannot replace politics and power: real peace in the Balkans will come when all countries in the region have working democratic institutions, democratic leaders, free media and when objective facts of their recent history have been objectively researched, published and inscribed in history books. Even after the fall of Milosevic, an opinion poll revealed in May 2001 that the Serbs have not become aware of crimes committed in their name in the Former Yugoslavia.[79]

The slow pace of the ICTY – and of the ICTR – have been criticised, triggering the creation of an expert group with the objective of enhancing the efficient use of the resources allocated to the Tribunals. Some of the recommendations submitted by the group in its report to the UN Secretary-General in November 1999 were designed to

[79] *Le Monde*, 22 May 2001.

reduce the length of the trials. The Jorda Report, completed in May 2000, contained several proposals and a two-part plan. On the basis of these two reports, the Security Council established on 30 November 2000 a pool of ad litem judges in the ICTY and enlarged the membership of the Appeals Chamber of the ICTY and ICTR.

Besides this well-needed increase in judicial resources, a proposal in the Jorda report was to transfer cases to the national court systems of certain states. This proposal was dismissed by the judges on several legal and political grounds, including the need to amend the ICTY Statute and obtain the consent of the prosecutor not to make a deferral request. The judges feared that the adoption of this system would result in a two-tiered justice system, potentially leading to unequal treatment of the accused and inconsistent caselaw. It might detract from the development of a unified international criminal system and 'would go against all the efforts expended to establish and International Criminal Court'.

Whatever the validity of some of these arguments, the rejected proposal has merits, not only as a means to lighten the caseload of the Tribunals, but also as a means to link the International Tribunals to national justice systems. Both the ICTY and the ICTR are struggling with a heavy schedule of cases, at pre-trial, trial and appeals stages under a strict corset of lengthy procedural requirements. Completion of all present cases – more are still coming in – may extend the life of the Tribunals beyond set dates. It would therefore be reasonable to use a two-tiered system, the International Tribunals retaining only the cases of persons who bear the greatest responsibility for the most serious crimes of concern to the international community as a whole. The Statute of the ICC has established a two-tiered system, based on the principle of complementarity between national courts which retain primacy of jurisdiction, and the ICC. A direct link is established between the ICC and national courts through Article 93.10.(a), whereby 'The Court may, upon request, cooperate with and provide assistance to a State Party conducting an investigation into or trial in respect of conduct which constitutes a crime within the jurisdiction of the Court or which constitutes a serious crime under the national law of the requesting State'. Amending the Statute of the Tribunals should not constitute an obstacle.

CHAPTER 3

THE INTERNATIONAL CRIMINAL TRIBUNAL FOR RWANDA

At first sight, the Tribunal for the Former Yugoslavia (ICTY) and the Tribunal for Rwanda (ICTR) would appear to be Siamese twins.

They were both created as ad hoc international criminal tribunals by a decision of the UN Security Council, acting under Chapter VII of the UN Charter. They are both time-limited subsidiary bodies of the Security Council. In both cases, the Council determined that the reported widespread and flagrant violations of international humanitarian law constituted a threat to international peace and security. They both focus on a specific country or countries. They both have jurisdiction over 'natural persons', e.g. individuals. They both have primacy over national courts. Their internal structure is identical: The Chambers, comprising Trial Chambers and an Appeals Chamber, the Prosecutor and a Registry. The 'siamese' link is materialized by organs common to the two Tribunals: the members of the Appeals Chamber of the ICTY also serve as members of the Appeals Chamber of the ICTR – the Prosecutor of the ICTY also serves as Prosecutor for the ICTR, assisted by a Deputy Prosecutor to assist with prosecutions before the ICTR. In both Tribunals, judges are elected by the General Assembly from a list submitted by the Security Council. The rights of the accused and the penalties are identical in both Tribunals. States have the same obligations of cooperation with both Tribunals.

There are a few differences with regard to the jurisdiction of each Tribunal.

Ratione materiae, both Tribunals may prosecute persons responsible for crimes against humanity and persons having committed genocide; only the ICTY may prosecute persons having violated the laws or customs of war, as the ICTR is not dealing with an international war, but with an internal conflict; the ICTY has jurisdiction over grave breaches of the Geneva Conventions of 1949 which apply to international armed conflict, while the ICTR has jurisdiction over serious violations of Article 3 common to the Geneva Conventions of 12 August 1949 for the protection of victims of war, and of Additional Protocol II thereto of 8 June 1977: the latter relate to the protection of victims of non-international conflicts.[1]

[1] Common Article 3 states, in part: 'In the case of armed conflict not of an international character occurring in the territory of one of the High Contracting Parties, each Party to the conflict shall be

Ratione tempore, the ICTR's jurisdiction is limited to crimes committed between 1 January and 31 December 1994, while the ICTY has a starting date – violations committed since 1991 – but no ending date.

Ratione personae et ratione loci, the ICTY's jurisdiction is limited to persons responsible for serious violations of international humanitarian law committed in the Territory of the Former Yugoslavia, while the ICTR's jurisdiction extends to persons responsible for such violations committed in the territory of Rwanda and Rwandan citizens responsible for such violations committed in the territory of neighbouring states.

Other differences concern the functioning of each Tribunal: they relate to the circumstances motivating their creation, the different nature of the crimes and different political, geographical and administrative constraints.

A Predictable Genocide

The Killers

The genocide, the mass elimination of the Tutsi minority in Rwanda together with the killing of moderate Hutu, started on 12 April 1994. It had been triggered on 6 April by the crash of the jet plane carrying the President of Rwanda, Juvénal Habyarimana and his colleague, President Cyprien Ntariyamira of Burundi. All aboard were killed, including several senior members of Habyarimana's staff and the French air crew. The genocide ended on 18 July with the victory of the Rwandan Patriotic Front (RPF), originally based in Uganda and grouping together exiled

---

bound to apply, as a minimum, the following provisions:

(1) Persons taking no active part in the hostilities, including members of armed forces who have laid down their arms and those placed *hors de combat* by sickness, wounds, detention, or any other cause, shall in all circumstances be treated humanely, without adverse distinction founded on race, colour, religion or faith, sex, birth or wealth, or any other similar criteria.
To this end, the following acts are and shall remain prohibited at any time and in any place whatsoever with respect to the above-mentioned persons:

(a) violence to life and person, in particular murder of all kinds, mutilation, cruel treatment and torture;
(b) taking of hostages;
(c) outrages upon personal dignity, in particular humiliating and degrading treatment;
(d) the passing of sentences and the carrying out of executions without previous judgment pronounced by a regularly constituted court, affording all the judicial guarantees which are recognised as indispensable by civilized peoples.

(2) The wounded and sick shall be collected and cared for.

. . . .

Tutsi and dissident Hutu and the formation of a new government, replacing the interim Hutu government.[2]

In a population of 7 million before the genocide, the genocide has caused the violent death of between 500 000 and 800 000 Rwandans – women, children and men – mostly Tutsi: over three-quarters of the population registered as Tutsi were killed. Victims were treated with sadistic cruelty and suffered long unbearable agony. Thousands more were raped, tortured, and maimed for life. About 2 million, mostly Hutu, were displaced internally and another 2 million fled as refugees to neighbouring countries. In the words of a US NGO: 'Rwandans have been through a national nightmare that almost defies comprehension. Theirs is a post-genocide society that has also experienced civil war, massive refugee displacement, a ruthless [post-genocide] insurgency, deep physical and psychological scars that are likely to linger for decades ... and economic ruin so extensive that it is now one of the two least-developed countries in the world'.[3]

Without recalling colonial German, then Belgian, responsibility for differentiating Tutsi from Hutu,[4] periodical killings of Tutsi by Hutu and of Hutu by Tutsi in Rwanda and Burundi preceded the genocide. In 1959, a bloody Hutu revolt in Rwanda caused the massacre of 20 000 Tutsi and a first exodus, mainly to Uganda. In 1972, the government of Burundi, controlled by the Tutsi, tried to eliminate the educated class of the Hutu. Out of a population of 3.5 million inhabitants, from 100 000 to 200 000 Hutu were killed. In 1973, in Rwanda, the head of the armed forces, General Habyarimana, a Hutu, seized power. In October 1990, the RPF attacked on the north-east of Rwanda from Uganda, causing the arrest and massacres of Tutsi, accused of being RPF accomplices. A guerrilla war followed the RPF retreat back into Uganda. In February 1993, an RPF offensive in the north of the country provoked the exodus of a million Hutu. The RPF carried out summary executions. In March 1993, an International Commission of Inquiry set up by four human rights NGOs published a report condemning human rights violations in Rwanda, some of which qualified as genocide.[5] The Rwandan government denied

2 The information and assessments in this section are based on the report entitled *Rwanda: The Preventable Genocide*, called *OAU Report* hereunder, submitted on 29 May 2000 by an International Panel of Eminent Personalities mandated by the Organisation of African Unity, supplemented by other references. The Panel's mandate was 'to investigate the 1994 genocide in Rwanda and the surrounding events in the Great Lakes Region ... as part of efforts aimed at averting and preventing further wide-scale conflicts in the ... Region'. Panel Members were the former Presidents of Botswana and Mali, the Chairperson of the Swedish Committee for UNICEF, a former Liberian Government Minister, a former Chief Justice of the Supreme Court of India, a former Algerian Ambassador, a former Canadian Ambassador and Permanent Representative of Canada to the UN. See www.oau-oua.org/Document/ipep/ipep/ipep.htm.

3 US Committee for Refugees, 'Life After Death', quoted in para. 17.1 of *OAU Report*.

4 See Beigbeder (1999), p. 170; A. Destexhe, *Rwanda and Genocide in the Twentieth Century* (Pluto Press, London/East Haven, CT, 1995), with a Chronology in Appendix 2.

5 *Rapport de la commission internationale d'enquête sur les violations des droits de l'homme au Rwanda depuis le 1er octobre 1990 (7–21 Janvier 1993), Rapport final*, March 1993, p. 96.

the existence of 'death squads' and that some of the incidents were planned in advance.

Following the plane crash of 6 April 1994, Hutu Power took control in Rwanda. Colonel Theoneste Bagosora, head of administration at the Ministry of Defence, is deemed to have been the leader of the genocide: he has been detained by the Tribunal since January 1997. Jean Kambanda, the Prime Minister during the genocide, accepted his responsibility at his trial four years later when he pleaded guilty to genocide. Not only had the genocide been planned in advance, he admitted that 'there was in Rwanda in 1994 a widespread and systematic attack against the civilian population of Tutsi, the purpose of which was to exterminate them. Mass killings of hundreds of thousands occurred in Rwanda, including women and children, old and new, who were pursued and killed at places where they sought refuge: prefectures, commune offices, schools, churches, and stadiums.[6]

All Hutu authorities were involved in the genocide. First, the Akazu, the special inner circle of advisors to Habyarimana, most of whom came from the northwestern prefecture or were relatives of his wife. They were the centre of political, economic, social and military power in Rwanda. They bankrolled the interahamwe (the youth militia recruited and trained by the late President's party) and death squads. Then, the newly formed interim government, the military and the politicians worked as one. The elaborate governing structure in Rwanda implemented the genocide with remarkable efficiency, assisted by the Rwandan tradition of passive acceptance of authority.

The Role of Organisations, Institutions and Governments

At the United Nations, neither the secretariat nor the Security Council took any effective action to prevent or stop the genocide. The cable sent by General Romeo Dallaire (Canada) on 11 January 1994 to the UN peacekeeping department was a clear warning of events to come: an informant in the Hutu government had warned that the President's party was training militia, stockpiling weapons, planning to kill Belgian troops and registering members of the Tutsi minority. 'He suspects it is for their extermination'. Dallaire, Commander of the UN peacekeeping force in Rwanda (UNAMIR) recommended that UN troops seize weapon caches. UN headquarters' answer was to stop him from taking any initiatives, give this information to the President of Rwanda (the key planner of the future genocide) and inform various embassies. The Security Council's incredible and irresponsible decision, during the genocide, was to reduce the size of the UN Mission from 2500 soldiers to 270.[7] The UN secretariat's insistence of being 'neutral' between the killers and their victims amounted to appeasement, as in Bosnia.

[6] ICTR Judgement 97-23-S, quoted by the *OAU Report*, para. 14.4.

[7] Security Council res. 872 of 5 October 1993 and 912 of 21 April 1994.

On 14 April 2000, members of the Security Council recognised the UN responsibility for its inability to stop the genocide. They agreed with a finding of the *Report of the Independent Inquiry into the Actions of the United Nations during the 1994 Genocide in Rwanda* (or *Carlsson Report*) issued on 15 December 1999 according to which:

> The failure of the United Nations to prevent, and subsequently, to stop the genocide in Rwanda was a failure by the United Nations system as a whole. The fundamental failure was the lack of resources and political commitment devoted to developments in Rwanda and to the United Nations presence there. There was a persistent lack of political will by Member States to act, or to act with enough assertiveness. This lack of political will by Member States affected the response by the Secretariat and decision-making by the Security Council, but was also evident in the recurrent difficulties to get the necessary troops for the United Nations Assistance Mission for Rwanda (UNAMIR). Finally, although UNAMIR suffered from a chronic lack of resources and political priority, it must also be said that serious mistakes were made with those resources which were at the disposal of the United Nations.[8]

Secretary-General Kofi Annan acknowledged in his response to the Report dated 16 December 1999: 'I fully accept their conclusions, including those which reflect on officials of the UN Secretariat, of whom I myself was one'. He emphasized the peacekeepers' lack of power: 'All of us must bitterly regret that we did not do more to prevent it. There was a United Nations force at the time, but it was neither mandated nor equipped for the kind of forceful action which would have been needed to prevent or halt the genocide. On behalf of the United Nations, I acknowledge this failure and express my deep remorse'.[9] Annan had earlier travelled to Kigali and recognised that 'in their greatest hour of need, the world failed the people of Rwanda ... All of us who cared about Rwanda, who witnessed its suffering, fervently wish that we could have prevented the genocide'.

The US led the Security Council in its inaction. After losing 18 soldiers in Somalia in October 1993, the US opposed any attempt by the Council to intervene effectively to stop the killings in Rwanda, which were not to be called genocide. While other institutions and countries are also to blame, the *OAU Report* of May 2000 affirms that 'it is indisputably true that no nation did more than the US to undermine the effectiveness of UNAMIR'.[10]

---

8 The Security Council approved the initiative of the Secretary-General to set up the Inquiry. Members were Ingvar Carlsson (former Prime Minister of Sweden), Professor Han Sung-Joo (former Foreign Minister of the Republic of Korea) and Lieutenant-General Rufus M. Kupolati (rtd)(Nigeria). See www.un.org/News/ossg/rwanda_report.htm.

9 UN Secretary-General, 'Statement on Receiving the Report of the Independent Inquiry into the Actions of the United Nations during the 1994 Genocide in Rwanda', *Press Release* SG/SM/7263-AFR/196, 16 December 1999.

10 *OAU Report*, para. 12.41 (see Note ii above).

On 25 March 1998, President Clinton came to Kigali 'to pay the respects of my nation to all those who have suffered and perished in the Rwandan genocide'. Without apologizing for the US role, he said that the international community must 'bear its share of responsibility for this tragedy as well'. He also acknowledged, in an understatement, that 'we did not act quickly enough after the killing began. We should not have allowed the refugee camps to become safe havens for the killers. We did not immediately call these crimes by their rightful name: genocide'.[11]

When UNAMIR was formed in October 1993, Belgian troops constituted the largest single western contingent. For the next several months, responding to steady warning of imminent slaughter, Belgium pressed at the UN for greater freedom of action for UNAMIR and for a broadened mandate. The US refused any measures involving greater expense or any risk. On the day after the plane crash on 6 April 1994, ten Belgian Blue Helmets were murdered by government soldiers, as forewarned in Dallaire's cable. Belgium then withdrew all its military personnel from UNAMIR, a terrible blow for the mission. Also afflicted with the 'Somali' syndrome, the Belgians then lobbied vigorously at the UN for the entire UNAMIR mission to be cancelled. On 29 October 1998, three Belgian officers were sanctioned by the disciplinary commission of the army for 'passivity', 'lack of initiative' in Rwanda.[12]

From April through to July 1994, the OAU, like the UN, failed to call genocide by its rightful name and refused to take sides between the *genocidaires* and the RPF. The *OAU Report* found that the silence of the Organisation and a large majority of African Heads of State constituted a shocking moral failure.[13]

In a recent article,[14] Stephen Lewis, the Canadian member of the International Panel which produced the *OAU Report*, condemned France's action in Rwanda:

> We repudiate the position of the government of France, the position that asserts that they had no responsibility. They were closer in every way to the Habyarimana regime than any other government; they could have stopped the genocide before it began. They knew exactly what was happening.
>
> Worse, under the cover of Opération Turquoise, which had a limited humanitarian dimension, they facilitated the exodus of a huge number of *génocidaires*, thereby ushering in the larger Great Lakes catastrophe.
>
> They even engaged in the shipment of arms throughout the genocide and after. There is almost no redemptive feature to the conduct of the government of France.

[11] Geneva US Mission Daily Bulletin, 25 March 1998.

[12] *Le Monde*, 1–2 November 1998: the officers were to be deprived of any future commanding duties.

[13] *OAU Report*, para. 15.87.

[14] S. Lewis, 'After Rwanda, the World Doesn't Look the Same', *IHT*, 10 July 2000.

A French parliamentary report issued in 1998[15] concluded that France bore not the slightest responsibility for any aspect of the genocide. Paul Quilès, the President of the inquiry mission declared: 'France is neither responsible nor guilty'. On the other hand, the report blamed the 'international community' – meaning the US and Belgium above all – for the scale of the genocide. Within Rwanda itself, the report found that even the Catholic church was more culpable than France.

France's involvement with Rwanda and its Hutu government was decided upon by President Mitterrand, who was friendly with President Habyarimana. France's aberrant blindness to the Hutu genocidal plans and action was due to a large extent to its policy of supporting *francophonie*, and suspect the Tutsi, supported by English-speaking Uganda, to take over what France considered as part of its zone of influence.

Over 60% of Rwandans, both Hutu and Tutsi, belonged to the Catholic church. However, many churches became graveyards, and Christians killed Christians. As many as one-third of the Catholic clergy died in the genocide. The leadership of the Catholic and Anglican churches maintained their traditional close relationship with the Hutu establishment. Church leaders remained silent during the genocide. Many priests and pastors were involved in the killings, some under coercion, others not.

The voice of the Catholic hierarchy did not denounce, nor try to stop the massacres. High church dignitaries encouraged the killings, and some even participated in them. The murdered archbishop of Kigali, Mgr Vincent Nsengiyumva, was a member of the political bureau of the Hutu party. The Vatican has long hesitated to pronounce the word 'genocide' to qualify the Rwanda events of 1994. Some in the Catholic hierarchy continue to deny the genocide and crimes against humanity committed in Rwanda – some support the revisionist thesis of a 'double genocide', e.g. that Rwandans killed Rwandans and that the task is one of reconciliation. Finally, in March 1996, the Pope wrote to Mgr Thaddée Ntihimyurwa, president of the episcopal conference of Rwanda: 'All members of the Church who have sinned during the genocide must have the courage to bear the consequences of the acts which they have committed against God and against their fellow man'. However, he added that the Catholic Church 'cannot be held, as a church, responsible for the faults of its members'.[16]

In recent years, the leaders of the UN, the US, Belgium and the Anglican Church[17] have acknowledged their share of responsibility, or apologized for their failure to stop the genocide. No apology has yet come from the French government or the Catholic church.

---

15 Assemblée nationale de France, Mission d'information commune (Paul Quilès, Président), 'Enquête sur la tragédie rwandaise (1990–1994), 15 décembre 1998.

16 *Le Monde*, 23 March 1996.

17 The Archbishop of Canterbury apologized on behalf of the Anglican church.

Chapter 3

Rwanda and the International Tribunal

The Security Council created on 8 November 1994, by resolution 955, a second ad hoc international criminal court, the International Tribunal for the Prosecution of Persons Responsible for Genocide or other Serious Violations Committed in the Territory of Rwanda and Rwandan Citizens Responsible for Genocide and other Such Violations Committed in the Territory of Neighbouring States, Between 1 January 1994 and 31 December 1994 – in short the Rwanda Tribunal, or the ICTR. The Council created this Tribunal, as the ICTY, as an enforcement measure under Chapter VII of the UN Charter. The seat of the ICTR is Arusha, Tanzania.

While Yugoslavia had opposed the creation of the ICTY, the Tutsi-dominated Rwandan government proposed the creation of an international tribunal by letter to the President of the Security Council dated 24 September 1994. On 6 October, the President of Rwanda, Pasteur Bizimungu, urged the UN to establish an international tribunal in his country quickly to bring those responsible for genocide to justice. An international presence would ensure an exemplary justice which would be seen to be completely impartial and fair. The government believed that it was impossible to build a state of law and arrive at true national reconciliation without eradicating the culture of impunity which had characterised Rwandan society. However, Rwanda voted against resolution 955. Its main objection was that the Tribunal's Statute ruled out capital punishment, which is provided for in the Rwandan penal code. As a consequence, leaders who designed, planned and implemented the genocide would escape the death penalty, while lower-rank perpetrators 'would be subjected to the harshness of [the death] sentence'. Other objections related to the temporal jurisdiction of the Tribunal, considered too restrictive, and to its composition and structure.[18]

When the Office of the Prosecutor, based in Kigali, Rwanda, started its work, it was confronted with a climate of general hostility towards the UN, because of its inaction during the genocide. In 1997, the Rwandan government criticised firmly the Tribunal, requesting the dismissal of Prosecutor Louise Arbour and the designation of a Prosecutor exclusively in charge of Rwanda. The Deputy Prosecutor, Bernard Muna, attempted to improve the relations with the authorities. In July 1998, Vice-President Kagame finally declared that his government and the Tribunal were 'partners'. He congratulated the Tribunal for the important progress accomplished in difficult circumstances and promised to give it all necessary assistance. However, when the first sentence was pronounced by the ICTR in September 1998 – Jean Kambanda, sentenced to life imprisonment – Gérald Gahima, Secretary-General of the Ministry of Justice declared that if Rwanda had received one-twentieth of the sums given to the Tribunal, Rwanda 'would have much advanced towards the solution of its problems'.

[18] Beigbeder (1999), p. 174.

The Tribunal's geographical site in Arusha and its fair, but slow and complex procedures have not helped the Rwandans to understand and appreciate its work.[19]

Mandate and Structure

As noted above, according to its Statute, the jurisdiction of the Tribunal extends to genocide, crimes against humanity, violations of Article 3 common to the Geneva Conventions and of Additional Protocol II (Art. 2–4).

As for the ICTY, the organs of the ICTR are the Chambers, the Prosecutor and the Registry. The original Statute established two Trial Chambers and an Appeals Chamber, composed of 11 judges: three served in each of the Trial Chambers, five served in the Appeals Chamber (Art. 11, 12). On 30 April 1998, a Third Trial Chamber was created by resolution 1165 of the Security Council. As a result, the number of judges was increased from 11 to 14. Three judges sit in each of the Trial Chambers and five judges sit in the Appeals Chamber which is shared with the ICTY. On 30 November 2000, the Security Council decided unanimously to increase the number of judges of the Appeals Chamber common to the two Tribunals from five to seven by the election of two additional judges to the ICTR. Thereafter, the President of the ICTR will assign two of the 11 judges to sit in the Appeals Chamber. This decision should enable the two Tribunals to expedite the conclusion of their work at the earliest possible date. It was also intended to redress the absence of representation by ICTR judges in the Appeals Chamber. The ICTR judges did not request the provision of ad litem judges for their Tribunal, as they were confident that they could complete a substantial number of the 36 outstanding cases by 2003.[20]

The Tribunal's budget increased regularly from $29.4 million in 1996, to $43.2 million in 1997, $59 million in 1998, $75 million in 1999 and $79.7 million in 2000. As of January 2002, the Tribunal employed 810 staff members from more than 80 nationalities.[21]

The current staffing and budgets of the ICTR are shown in Table 3.1.

A Mixed Performance

On the positive side, the list of ICTR detainees as of August 2001 is impressive in terms of level of responsibility of the accused.[22] From a total of 51 detainees, the 14 political leaders include the former Prime Minister, the former Ministers of Foreign Affairs, of Health, for Culture and Education, of Interior, Commerce, Civil Service,

[19] A. Des Forges, *Aucun témoin ne doit survivre, Le génocide au Rwanda* (Ed. Karthala, Paris, 1999), pp. 865–867.

[20] Doc. ICTR/INFO-9-2-253.EN, 5 December 2000 and res. 1329.

[21] ICTR, General Information: www.ictr.org/ENGLISH/geninfo/ictrlaw.htm.

[22] 'ICTR Detainees – Status on 21 August 2001', www.ictr.org/ENGLISH/factsheets/detainee.htm.

Finance, Information, Transport, Family and Women Affairs, Education of the Interim Hutu Government formed after the plane crash of President Habyarimana, the President of the National Assembly and Secretary-General of the MRND,[23] the Director General of the Ministry for Foreign Affairs and President of the MRND. The 10 military leaders include the Director of Cabinet, Ministry of Defence and nine senior officers of the armed forces or of the Gendarmerie nationale. The four media leaders include the Director of Political Affairs in the Ministry of Foreign Affairs, the Director and a journalist of the 'Radio Libre des Mille Collines' (the voice of the genocide) and the Chief Editor, Kangura Newspaper. Another mixed list of 23 accused includes senior government administrators, e.g. 'prefects' and 'bourgmestres', an Anglican bishop, a Seventh Day Adventist Pastor, three businessmen and a medical doctor.

On the negative side, only a few accused have been judged by the Tribunal at the appeal or trial stages. By August 2001, only eight sentencing judgements on appeal (final judgements) had been rendered by the ICTR, and the Tribunal had only completed two trial cases. Sixteen trials were in process, ten cases had been assigned to a Trial Chamber but no date had been set, and ten cases had not been assigned to a Chamber.

What explains, but does not justify, this slow justice?

As for the ICTY, there were initial financial and staffing shortages. The first courtroom was only completed in November 1996. In contrast with the ICTY, the ICTR's location in a small, poor and remote African country added to staffing and material problems. The difficulties of calling witnesses and obtaining evidence also slowed the judicial process. Judges were blamed for taking extended holidays: according to a 1998 study by Amnesty International, the Tribunal had suspended its work during four months over a one-year period.[24] The ICTR also suffered from the initial priority given by the Prosecutors to the ICTY. The first Prosecutor had encouraged the Deputy Prosecutor to focus on national figures, a strategy which was not properly applied by the latter. The strategy of focusing on the architects and leaders of the genocide – the 'big fish' as opposed to relatively 'small fry', has been applied since 1997. Prosecutor Carla Del Ponte recently adopted the strategy of joint trials of individuals accused of involvement in conspiracy for the genocide. This should accelerate the Tribunal's judiciary processes by avoiding lengthy trials of single individuals and potential repetition of the same events.

Mismanagement has been a serious problem for the ICTR, not shared by the ICTY. A report by the UN Office of Internal Oversight Services (OIOS) issued on 6 February 1997 found that the Tribunal was suffering from serious operational deficiencies which developed from its inception. In the Registry, not a single administrative area functioned effectively. The Registrar had abusively asserted that

[23] 'Mouvement républicain national pour le développement et la démocratie', former 'parti unique'.

[24] Amnesty International, 'International Criminal Tribunal for Rwanda, Trials and Tribulations', April 1998.

Table 3.1. Current staffing of the International Criminal Tribunal for Rwanda (ICTR) as of January 2002

Trial Chamber I:
Judge Navanethem Pillay (South Africa), President of the Tribunal and of Trial Chamber I; Judge Erik Mose (Norway), Vice President of the Tribunal; Judge Andrésia Vaz (Senegal).

Trial Chamber II:
Judge William H. Sekule (Tanzania), Presiding; Judge Winston C.M. Maqutu (Lesotho); Judge Arlette Ramarason (Madagascar).

Trial Chamber III:
Judge Lloyd G. Williams (Saint Kitts and Nevis), Presiding; Judge Pavel Dolenc (Slovenia); Judge Yakov A. Ostrovsky (Russia).

Appeals Chamber:
Judge Claude Jorda (France), President; Judge Mohamed Shahabuddeen (Guyana); Judge David Hunt (Australia); Judge Mehmet Güney (Turkey); Judge Asoka de Zoysa Gunawardana (Sri Lanka); Judge Fausto Pocar (Italy); Judge Theodor Meron (USA).

The Prosecutor
Chief Prosecutor: Carla Del Ponte (Switzerland), for both the ICTY and the ICTR. The Office of the Prosecutor is based in The Hague. The Office of the Deputy Prosecutor, Mr. Bernard Muna (Cameroon), is based in Kigali.
The Office is composed of two Sections: the Investigation Section, divided into teams for collecting evidence implicating individuals in crimes within the jurisdiction of the Tribunal; the Prosecution Section, composed of Trial Attorneys responsible for prosecuting all cases before the Tribunal and Legal Advisers for both the Investigations and the Prosecution. In addition, an Information and Evidence Unit reports directly to the Deputy Prosecutor.

The Registry
The Registry is responsible for the overall administration and management of the Tribunal. It provides judicial and legal support services for the work of the Trial Chambers and the Prosecution. The Registry also performs other legal functions assigned to it by the Tribunal's Rules of Procedure and Evidence, and is the Tribunal's channel of communication. The Registry comprises the Judicial and Legal Services Division and the Division of Administration. The Registry has established a Support Programme for Witnesses and Potential Witnesses. The Programme supports NGOs which provide legal, psychological, medical and limited rehabilitation assistance to Rwandan witnesses and potential witnesses. Since 1998, the ICTR has undertaken an Outreach Programme to Rwanda, run by the Registry, with the goal of increasing the impact of the Tribunal's work inside Rwanda and thus fostering national reconciliation through justice. The Tribunal has recently set up a full-time Information and Documentation Centre in Kigali. The Registry is headed by the Registrar, who is also the Representative of the Secretary-General of the United Nations. The present Registrar is Mr. Adam Dieng (Senegal) and the Deputy Registrar is Mr. Lovemore Green Munlo (Malawi).

ICTR PERSONNEL
As of January 2002: 810 staff members from more than 80 nationalities.

Yearly budgets – in $ million (from the UN regular budget)

1996: $29.4	1997: $43.2	1998: $56.7
1999: $75.0	2000: $79.7	

Source: ICTR, General Information: The Organs of ICTR:
www.ictr.org/ENGLISH/geninfo/structure.htm, 15 January 2002, – Budget and staff, www.ictr.org/ENGLISH/geninfo/ictrlaw.htm, 15 January 2002.

his functions as Chief Administrative Officer gave him authority for all matters having administrative or financial implications. The Office of the Prosecutor had administrative, leadership and operational problems. Relationships between the Registry and the Office of the Prosecutor were often characterised by tension rather than by cooperation. These difficulties were caused or exacerbated by the recruitment of inexperienced or unqualified staff. Senior personnel in the UN headquarters' Department of Administration and Management and in the Office of Legal Affairs had failed to bear responsibility for the effectiveness of the Tribunal on the misperception of respect for the independence of the Tribunal. Rumors about chronic corruption, nepotism and systematic discrimination against non-Africans by the Tribunal's Deputy Prosecutor, Honoré Rakotomanana of Madagascar and its Registrar, Andronico Adede of Kenya were not confirmed in the report. However, on 26 February 1997, the Secretary-General accepted the resignation of both officials. Bernard Muna (Cameroon) was appointed as Deputy Prosecutor, and Agwu Okali (Nigeria) as the new Registrar. The chiefs of personnel, finance and administration in the Registry were also replaced. A Deputy Registrar was appointed.[25]

A report of the OIOS issued on 23 September 1999 showed that the Tribunal had satisfactorily implemented a number of previous recommendations and made improvements in financial management and filling vacant positions. However, improvements were needed in various administrative areas. OIOS recommended that that the legal adviser to the Registrar should be reassigned because of his involvement in the exchange of private funds with defence counsel. The Chief Finance Officer had violated rules and personally interfered in the procurement process, with no evidence of personal benefit, in obtaining goods and services for the Tribunal. He should be 'advised' against future violations or other interference in the procurement process. Another finding was that the Tribunal had encountered problems in attracting sufficient qualified information technology staff.[26]

A UN report issued on 1st February 2001 concerning allegations of fee-splitting between some defence counsels and their clients pointed out that none of the defence investigators had ever visited Rwanda during the course of their work. In the light of that report, the Tribunal instituted a more rigorous screening process to ensure that legal aid given to the accused is not abused.[27]

The initial major management problems seem to have been solved, although further improvements are needed as well as regular oversight.

---

25 Beigbeder (1999), pp. 178–180.

26 UN Doc. A/52/784, 6 February 1998, p. 2; paras. 111 and 112; A/54/393, 23 September 1999, paras. 70, 71 and 89; A/C.5/54/SR.22, 1 February 2000, para. 26.

27 See *Press Release*, ICTR/INFO-9-2-266.EN, 21 May 2001.

Cooperation by Governments

In contrast with the lack of cooperation, or poor cooperation experienced by the ICTY from states of the Former Yugoslavia and NATO countries, the ICTR has received effective support in the arrest and surrender of accused persons, after some initial obstacles, mostly from African countries, a few from European countries, and one from the USA. All the Tribunal's detainees were arrested outside Rwanda.

The first transfers were effected in 1996: three from Zambia, two from Belgium, one from Côte d'Ivoire, one from Kenya. In 1997, nine more were transferred from Kenya, six from Cameroon, and one from Switzerland. All transfers carried out in 1998 and 1999 came from African countries: Benin (2), Burkino Faso (1), Cameroon (3), Côte d'Ivoire (1), Kenya (2), Mali (1), Namibia (1), South Africa (1), Tanzania (1), Togo (2). A few transfers came from Europe in 2000 as a result of pressures by Prosecutor Carla Del Ponte: Belgium (1), Denmark (1), France (1) and the UK (1), and one from the USA. In 2001, three accused were arrested in Tanzania, two in Belgium, one in Kenya, in The Netherlands and in Switzerland, to be transferred to Arusha.

After a long period of wilful neglect, French justice and authorities finally agreed to cooperate with the Tribunal. At least two Rwandans accused of genocidal activities, a Catholic priest and a gynecologist, had found refuge in France. Judicial inquiries were called off in one case, following political and church pressures, and were not initiated in the other. On 26 November 1999, Jean de Dieu Kamuhanda, Minister of Education of the Interim government, was arrested in France by the French police accompanied by Tribunal's investigators. In March 2000, a French Appeals Court ordered Xavier Nzuwonemeye to be sent to Tanzania. A former Rwandan military officer, he faces trial for allegedly taking part in crimes against humanity during the genocide.[28]

The only US case is that of Elizaphan Ntakirutimana, the President of the Seventh Day Adventist Church in Rwanda. On 26 September 1996, in response to a request from the Tribunal, the US provisionally arrested the accused, who had entered the US in 1994 and settled in Laredo, Texas. The indictment charged him with genocide and crimes against humanity based on his participation in the slaughter of many Tutsi who had taken refuge in his church compound in Mugonero, and subsequent genocidal attacks on Tutsi, including survivors of the Mugonero massacre in the Bisessero area. Following lengthy and complex judiciary proceedings in several courts, a Fifth Circuit court held, in part, that extradition pursuant to a congressional-executive agreement was constitutionally permissible. He was finally transferred to the Tribunal on 24 March 2000. In a legal review of the case,[29] Mary Coombs concluded that cases such as Ntakirutimana's,

---

[28] *Le Monde*, 10 February 2000; *IHT*, 7 March 2000.

[29] M. Coombs, 'Fifth Circuit decision on the constitutionality of and probable cause for extradition to the International Criminal Tribunal for Rwanda', *American Journal of International Law* (2000), Vol.

> [u]ndermine international confidence in the ability of the US to participate effectively in the prosecution of genocide and crimes against humanity. First, although it was ultimately decided that the executive could hand Ntakirutimana over to the Tribunal, nearly two years had already passed since the original request. This unconscionable delay suggests the need to redraft American extradition law to permit extradition decisions to be appealed. Second, as suggested earlier, throughout the proceedings there were recurrent indications of the need to sensitize US judges to the practices of the rest of the world, and to address the insularity that undermines US claims to global leadership.

In July 2001, three more Rwandans were arrested in raids in three European countries, to be then transferred to the Tribunal. They were Emmanuel Ndindabahizi, a former Finance Minister arrested in Brussels, Emmanuel Rukundo, a former army chaplain arrested in Geneva, Simon Bikindi, arrested in Leiden.[30]

Selected Judgements and Issues

The ICTR rendered its first judgement on 2 September 1998 in the case of Jean-Paul Akayesu, former bourgmestre (mayor) of Taba.[31] He was found guilty of Genocide, Direct and Public Incitement to Commit Genocide and Crimes against Humanity (Extermination, Murder, Torture, Rape, and Other Inhumane Acts). For the first time, the Genocide Convention of 1948 was interpreted by an international tribunal, which formally confirmed that the 1994 massacres were a genocide. The judgement held that the massacres 'had a specific objective, namely the extermination of the Tutsi, who were targeted especially because of their Tutsi origin' and that 'genocide was committed in Rwanda in 1994 against the Tutsi as a group'. The Trial Chamber stated that 'there was an intention to wipe out the Tutsi group in its entirety, since even newborn babies were not spared'. The Chamber established the individual responsibility of the accused for the crimes: as a bourgmestre, he was responsible for maintaining law and public order in his commune, and he had effective authority over the communal police.

The Tribunal held that incitement to genocide can be implicit as well as direct, and that public incitement to commit genocide can be punished even when such incitement was unsuccessful.

The Chamber defined the crime of rape

94, pp. 171–178. On the events and Ntakirutimana's alleged role therein, see P. Gourevitch, *We wish to inform you that tomorrow we will be killed with our families* (Picador USA, Farrar, Straus and Giroux/ New York, 1999), pp. 25–43.

30 *Le Monde*, 13 July 2001.

31 On the Status of ICTR Detainees, see <www.ictr.org/ENGLISH/factsheets/detainee.htm>

> [a]s a physical invasion of sexual nature, committed on a person under circumstances which are coercive. Sexual violence is not limited to physical invasion of the human body and may include acts which do not involve penetration or even physical contact ... Threats, intimidation, extortion and other forms of duress which prey on fear or desperation could be coercion.

The Court held that sexual violence was an 'integral' part of the process of destruction of the Tutsi ethnic group.

The Akayesu judgement also clarified the issue as to whether an individual can be convicted of genocide, crimes against humanity and war crimes arising out of the same set of facts. The Tribunal held that multiple convictions were indeed possible in one of three circumstances: (1) where the offences have different elements; (2) where the provisions creating the offences protect different interests; or (3) where it is necessary to record a conviction for both offences in order to fully describe what the accused did.

On 2 October 1998, the accused was given three life terms for genocide, incitement to commit genocide and crimes against humanity relating to extermination. He was also sentenced to 15 years each on four separate counts of crimes against humanity related to murder and rape and ten years for separate counts of crime against humanity related to torture and other inhumane acts. On 1 June 2001, the Appeals Chamber dismissed appeals by the defence and affirmed decisions of the Trial Chamber.[32]

A more important actor, Jean Kambanda, Rwanda's Prime Minister during the genocide, pleaded guilty on 1st May 1998 to charges of genocide and crimes against humanity. On 4 September 1998, he was sentenced to life imprisonment, although his lawyers had suggested a term of two years. The sentence was based in part because of his having abused a position of trust in a high ministerial post. This negated any mitigating circumstances, such as pleading guilty, cooperating with the Tribunal and expressing remorse. His appeal was dismissed on 19 October 2000.[33]

On 14 December 1998, Omar Serushago, a leader of the Hutu Interahamwe militia in northwest Rwanda, pleaded guilty – the second defendant to do so – to one count of genocide and three counts of crimes against humanity related to murder, extermination and torture. On 5 February 1999, he was sentenced to 15 years' imprisonment. Judge Laïty Kama held that Serushago deserved a degree of clemency – less than a life sentence – because he had surrendered voluntarily, had cooperated with the Tribunal and had expressed remorse for his crimes. A fifth charge of rape was withdrawn by the Prosecution when he agreed to plead guilty to the other charges. His appeal against the sentence was dismissed on 14 February 2000. He was the first person to be definitively sentenced by the ICTR.[34]

---

32 *Press Release* ICTR/INFO-9-2-138, 2 September 1998; *IHT*, 3–4 October 1998. See also 54th General Assembly, p. 274; *Press Release* ICTR/INFO-9-2-269.EN, 1 June 2001.

33 ICTR Case No. 97-23-S, 4 September 1998.

34 ICTR/INFO-0-2-221en, 14 February 2000.

The joint trial of Clément Kayishema (MD) and Obed Ruzindana ended on 21 May 1999 with a conviction of genocide for both accused: the former was sentenced to life imprisonment and the latter to 25 years. Both were acquitted of crimes against humanity: as the Tribunal found these charges to be based on the same conduct and evidence as the genocide charges, they were subsumed under the charge of genocide. Kayishema, a Préfet (District Administrator) of Kibuye and Ruzindana, a businessman, were accused of a number of crimes, including having directed Interahamwe and civilians to attack and kill Tutsi seeking refuge in Kibuye and having participated in these attacks themselves. Over half of the victims of the genocide were killed in the Kibuye préfecture. On 1 June 2001, the Appeal Chamber dismissed appeals by the defence and affirmed decisions of the Trial Chamber in the two cases.[35]

On 6 December 1999, Georges Rutaganda was sentenced to life imprisonment on one count of genocide and two counts of crimes against humanity. During the genocide, he was a businessman, a leading member of the governing Hutu Power party (the MRND) as well as second Vice-President of the National Committee of the Interahamwe militia. The Trial Chamber held that Rutaganda incurred individual criminal responsibility for having ordered, incited, and carried out murders and for causing serious bodily or mental harm to members of the Tutsi ethnic group. The Chamber held that the sentence was appropriate as Rutaganda had held a high position in the Interahamwe when the crimes were committed, had knowingly and consciously participated in these crimes, and had shown no remorse. The sentence is under appeal.[36]

The two judgements in the case of Jean Bosco Barayagwiza caused first a serious political crisis with the Rwanda government, and then questions concerning the independence of the ICTR judges.

On 3 November 1999, the Appeals Chamber quashed the indictment against the accused, a minister in the Hutu government who helped set up a radio station used to incite anti-Tutsi violence, and ordered his release. This decision was based on lengthy delays in bringing the accused to justice, found to have violated his human rights. This decision created a crisis in relations between the ICTR and the Rwandan government. The government temporarily suspended all cooperation and assistance to the Tribunal. Prosecutor Del Ponte then filed with the Appeals Chamber a notice to suspend the release, which was followed up on 1 December 1999 with a brief in support of a motion that the Appeals Chamber review its decision of 3 November. She underscored how any delays did not prejudice the case of the accused and that failing to prosecute him would be the true travesty of justice. The government of Rwanda, which intervened as an amicus curiae in the case, had argued that Barayagwiza should be tried by the ICTR but, if the ICTR did not, it should send

[35] *Press Releases* ICTR/INFO-9-2-183, 13 May 1999, ICTR/INFO-9-2-184, 21 May 1999, ICTR/INFO-9-2-269, 1 June 2001.

[36] *Press Release* ICTR/INFO-9-2-216en, 6 December 1999.

him to a jurisdiction that is willing and able to prosecute him, namely Rwanda. The Appeals Chamber's initial decision to release the accused back to the Cameroon authorities – which had extradited him to the ICTR in the first place – was unsatisfactory to the Rwandan government as Cameroon had not passed legislation to punish the crime of genocide. On 31 March 2000, the Appeals Chamber unanimously overturned its previous decision to quash Barayagwiza's indictment.

Drumbl remarked that this crisis demonstrated the extent to which criminal trials may create conflict between victims and due process for the accused. It also raised a deeper question: what is the primary purpose of the ICTR – to promote accountability for mass atrocity or to maximise its credibility in the eyes of the international community?[37]

The outcome of the crisis raises the issue of the independence of the Tribunal. The second decision of 31 March 2000, overturning its first decision of 3 November 1999, could be explained technically by the incompetence of the judges of the first decision. The sequence of events tend to show that the second decision was in fact taken under pressure from the Rwanda government: in this particular case, political expediency seems to have won over judiciary legality and independence.

On 1 June 2000, Georges Ruggiu was sentenced to 12 years in prison, a final judgement. On 15 May, Ruggiu pleaded guilty to two counts: directly and publicly inciting the killing of Tutsi with the intention of destroying the Tutsi ethnic group in whole or in part, and, secondly, crimes against humanity for the persecution of Tutsi and moderate Tutu, as well as Belgians. Ruggiu asked for forgiveness and pardon. He promised to cooperate with the Tribunal by testifying as to the horrors of the genocide. Ruggiu was a Belgian-born radio journalist, whose incendiary broadcasts at Radio Television Libre des Mille Collines justified and encouraged the killings of Tutsi. He was the only non-Rwandan charged in the genocide.[38]

On 7 June 2001, the Tribunal found Ignace Bagilishema, a former Rwandan mayor, not guilty, the first acquittal of the ICTR. The Tribunal held that the prosecution had failed to prove beyond a reasonable doubt that the accused had committed the alleged atrocities in the Kibuye province. He was liberated under conditions on 8 June.[39]

Enforcement of Sentences

The Tribunal's policy preference is that, to the extent possible, its sentences should be served in African countries. Its rationale is that this approach takes better cognizance of social and cultural factors and should reinforce the deterrent message

[37] M. Drumbl, 'Legal Issues', in J. Tessitore and S. Woolfson (eds), *A Global Agenda, Issues Before the 55th General Assembly of the United Nations* (Rowman & Littlefield Publishers, Inc., Lanham/New York/Boulder/Oxford, 2000), pp. 243–245.

[38] *Press Release* ICTR/INFO-9-2-232en, 15 May 2000; *IHT*, 2 June 2000.

[39] *IHT*, 8 June 2001; conditions for Bagilishema's release are in *Press Release*, ICTR/INFO/9-2-272.EN, 8 June 2001.

of the work of the ICTR in Africa. Agreements have been reached between the Tribunal and the governments of Benin, Mali and Swaziland for the incarceration of individuals convicted by the Tribunal.[40]

Prosecuting Tutsi

On 13 December 2000, Carla Del Ponte said that the Prosecution was actively investigating some Rwanda Patriotic Front (RPF) soldiers who are alleged to have committed crimes within the Tribunal's jurisdiction in 1994.

This was a response to criticisms of partial justice: The atrocities committed by the Tutsi-run RPF against Hutu civilians was not equivalent to an organised genocide, but they could well constitute crimes against humanity.

This effort is however limited by the jurisdiction of the ICTR, which only includes crimes committed between 1 January and 31 December 1994. It has been reported that the worst atrocities of the RPF were committed between 1995 and 1997, with an estimated killing of hundreds of thousands of Hutu refugees in the Congo.[41]

National Justice

In Rwanda

While the ICTR was to judge the main organisers and perpetrators of the genocide and other crimes, the Tutsi-dominated government which came into power after the genocide was faced with the awsome challenge of rendering fair justice to others who participated, at various levels, in the massacres. The genocide and ensuing exodus of part of the Hutu population had led to the breakdown of law and order and the near total destruction of the judiciary system. Although Rwanda was ill-prepared and equipped to fairly identify, prosecute and judge all the actors of the genocide, if only because of their numbers, the new authorities jailed approximately 125 000 suspects in overcrowded prisons, waiting to be judged.

Progress has been achieved over the years in strengthening the Rwandan justice system. In 1994, Rwanda had 244 judges, in January 2002, they number 841. Prosecutors were only 12, they are now 156. Court clerks were 59, they are now 325. There were only 22 investigators, compared to 895 now.

In 1996, the legal framework for the prosecution of the perpetrators of genocide was set up, with the promulgation of the organic law on the prosecution of offences constituting the crime of genocide, providing inter alia for:

- the classification of degrees of responsibility for the perpetrators of genocide into four categories, with only category one, which includes planners and

40 <www.ictr.org/ENGLISH/pressbrief191000.htm>

41 *Press Release* ICTR/INFO-9-2-254.EN, 13 December 2000; *The Economist*, 23 December 2000.

organisers of the genocide potentially liable for the death penalty if found guilty;

- the establishment of a confessions and guilty plea programme for which all defendants, except those in category 1, would be eligible, with marked reduction of sentences.

Trials started in 1996, and by January 2002, 1989 defendants had been brought to trial. From these, 294 were sentenced to capital punishment (including two priests), 586 given life sentences, 809 were given sentences for different lengths of time, 300 acquitted. A total of 17 122 have taken part in the confessions and guilty programme. The arrest and trial of a Catholic Bishop, Augustin Misago, a Hutu, raised a conflict with the Vatican, which called the arrest 'an extremely serious act which hurt not only the church in Rwanda, but the entire Roman Catholic Church'. Misago was charged with genocide, crimes against humanity, non-assistance to persons in danger, incitation to murder.[42]

It is however estimated that 150 years would be needed to complete the judicial processes, an absurd and unacceptable time lag. Rwandan tribunals are overwhelmed with cases, lack legal and material resources, judges and lawyers lack experience, they work under the pressures of the political-military power.[43]

It was then decided to add to the regular justice system the traditional, participatory form of justice known as the gacaca tribunals. Their aims are to establish the truth about what happened, with the participation of the communities that were witness to the crimes, and to return punishment of the crimes to the people. They should help to deal effectively and promptly with the high number of cases. The gacaca tribunals will have competence to hear witnesses, determine guilt, classify it and give appropriate sentence. They are not entitled to pronounce capital punishment.

The first gacaca tribunals are expected to start their work in May 2002. Some 260 000 gacaca judges were elected in October 2001. Each will be entitled to six days of training. Gacaca jurisdictions at cell level will judge Category Four suspects, people charged with looting or destroying victims' property during the genocide. Those found guilty will have to pay reparations only. Judgements at this level cannot be appealed. Sector level gacaca courts will judge Category Three suspects, defined as 'the person who has committed or became accomplice of serious attacks without the intention of causing death to victims'. District level gacaca courts will judge Category Two suspects, those alleged to have committed murder: these face a maximum sentence of life imprisonment. District level courts will also handle appeals from the sector level. Courts at the province levels will serve solely as appeals

[42] *Le Monde*, 22–23 August 1999; *IHT*, 1 October 1999. According to Des Forges, one estimate is that the FPR may have killed from 25 000 to 45 000 persons between April and August 1994. An FPR member's estimate is the slaughter of about 60 000 between August 1994 and August 1995. These estimates probably include both military personnel and civilians (p. 23).

[43] *Le Monde*, 13 April 1999, 6 April 2000.

courts to district courts' cases. Suspected genocide planners placed in Category One will continue to be tried by the ordinary courts. They may face the death penalty.

It is hoped that the innovative introduction of the gacaca court system may accomplish what neither the ICTR nor the regular judicial system can accomplish, e.g. to judge more effectively and promptly the thousands of suspects accused, at various levels, of participation in the genocide, within a popular, traditional justice system, which, however, remains to be tested.[44]

In Other Countries

A few Rwandans have been judged, in Switzerland and in Belgium, on the grounds of universal jurisdiction. Fulgence Niyonteze, a former mayor, was arrested in Switzerland in 1996 and condemned by a military tribunal in May 1999 first to life imprisonment for war crimes, a sentence then commuted to 14 years in appeal, a judgement confirmed on 27 April 2000. Not a major actor, Niyonteze was accused of incitement to the killing of Tutsi and moderate Hutu. In June 2001, a Belgian court sitting in Brussels sentenced four Rwandan Hutu to prison terms for their role in the genocide. This was the first trial in which a jury of citizens judged defendants for war crimes committed in another country. Consolata Mukangango (Sister Gertrude), a Benedictine nun, received a 15-year sentence for her role in the massacre of some 6000 people seeking refuge in her convent. Another nun, Julienne Mukabutera (Sister Maria Kisito), received a 12-year sentence, for her role in the same events. Alphonse Higaniro, a politician and businessman, received a 20-year sentence and Vincent Ntezimana, a university professor, 12 years, for inciting massacres of Tutsi. The trial was held under a 1993 Belgian law which gives local courts jurisdiction over violations of the Geneva Conventions on war crimes, wherever they were committed. In February 1999, another Belgian law affirmed the competence of its tribunals to prosecute the perpetrators of genocide and crimes against humanity.[45]

Conclusion

The International Crisis Group (ICG) issued a report on 7 June 2001 titled 'International Criminal Tribunal for Rwanda: Justice Delayed' in which the slow pace of the ICTR was sharply criticised.[46] It said that the Tribunal had judged only nine individuals. It suggested that not one of the alleged masterminds of the genocide had been brought to trial, including one in prison for five years. Former influential leaders freely travel between various countries, including the Democratic Republic of

---

[44] See www.rwandemb.org/updates1.html, and 'Fondation Hirondelle, Media for Peace and Human Dignity', www.hirondelle.org/hirond... /... Open Documenwww, 18 January 2002.

[45] *Le Monde*, 28 April 2000; *IHT*, 9–10 June 2001.

[46] See www.crisisweb.org/projects/showreport.cfm?reportid=304, 7 June 2001. The ICG is a private, multinational organisation committed to strengthening the capacity of the international community to anticipate, understand and act to prevent and contain conflict.

the Congo, Gabon, Kenya and also France and Belgium. The Tribunal has nine judges, three Trial Chambers, over 800 employees, and an annual budget of $90 million, 'but is bogged down by incompetence and bureaucratic infighting'. Five judges out of nine have spent more than a year and a half without hearing a substantial case: in March, one had not heard such a matter for 28 months. ICG Africa Programme Co-Director Fabienne Hara said: 'The Rwanda Tribunal is failing to meet its basic mandate – to deliver justice to the people of Rwanda and provide a record of events. We still don't know who committed the genocide. While the Tribunal claims a significant achievement in jailing the Prime Minister of Rwanda, the most important suspects have not been arrested'. The ICG report named a number of key suspects still at large, and the countries where they have found a home. In its Executive Summary, the report said that the judges' failure to fulfil their essential task, to render justice rapidly and establish the reality of facts, has prevented them from fulfilling one of the mandates given to them by the Security Council: national reconciliation between the Hutu and Tutsi communities. For the majority of the Rwandans, the Tribunal is a costly and ineffective institution, an expiatory mechanism of the international community to have its responsibility in the implementation of the genocide and its tolerance of the FPR crimes forgotten. The genocide survivors find the Tribunal distant and indifferent to their fate, while the victims of the FPR crimes denounce its use by the Kigali government and see the Tribunal as the symbol of victors' justice.

As a positive point, the report acknowledged the incontestable recognition of the Rwanda genocide and the international political neutralization of the eradication agenda of the Tutsi by the Hutu Power. The report recommended that the selection of judges should retain only judges having a real professional penal experience. Judges should be made accountable for their activity and performance. The independence of the Prosecutor's Office should be reinforced and incompetent members of the Registrar and Prosecution should be dismissed.

Adama Dieng, the Registrar, issued a statement on 11 June 2001 in response to the ICG report.[47] He recognised that the Tribunal had been criticised for a slow pace of trials in the past, 'with some justification'. 'However, its Rules of Procedure and Evidence have been progressively revamped by the judges to quicken the pace of trials without compromising the integrity and credibility of the judicial process. The Prosecutor's new strategy of joint trials of defendants accused of conspiracy and involvement in the same crimes is expected to expedite the judicial work of the court in the medium to longer term'. He affirmed that the Tribunal has provided the answer to the question as to 'who committed the genocide' to 'a very significant extent'. In his view, the Kambanda judgement – the first-ever conviction in history of a head of government for genocide – has set an important precedent for the judicial accountability of powerful political and military leaders for human rights crimes and the efficacy of international criminal justice in general. He added that Rwandans

47 Statement in ICTR/INFO/-9-3-01.EN, 11 June 2001.

'know that Kambanda and other accused ringleaders of the genocide who fled Rwanda after the genocide were effectively beyond their country's reach, and that without this International Tribunal that is bringing such individuals to trial, they would almost certainly have escaped justice'.

The reasons for the Tribunal's slow pace are well-known: its relative isolation in a small African country, the need to build a working international court from nothing, initial lack of support from African and European governments, lack of assistance from the UN headquarters, serious management problems, lack of interest by the international media, the hiring of incompetent or corrupt staff, the neglect by the successive Prosecutors, common to both Tribunals, who gave priority to the ICTY, until the appointment of Carla Del Ponte, the exacting, detailed procedural requirements of due process.

In the Akayesu case, the Tribunal interpreted and applied the Genocide Convention and delivered its first judgement for genocide by any international tribunal. The Tribunal defined rape in international law and held that rape, in this case, was an act of genocide. This was the first time in history that rape had been judged as a genocidal act by a court of justice. Previously, rape had been recognised in international law only as a crime against humanity and a war crime. Another 'first' is the detention of a woman, Pauline Nyiramasuhuko, former Minister of Family and Women Affairs on charges of genocide and crimes against humanity.

The Tribunal is now trying to catch up with its backlog and seems to be making progress. Most of the detainees are important political and military leaders and media propagandists who have played a key role in planning and implementing the genocide. Critics wonder why the 'real authors' of the genocide have not been prosecuted: the cases of individuals cited in the ICG report as 'key suspects' should be investigated and indicted if so justified. Their extradition should then be requested.

The Tribunal is still confronted with many problems, some of them well beyond its powers and competence. There is a statutory limitation which keeps the Tribunal from investigating crimes committed beyond 31 December 1994, even though these crimes may be connected with the genocide. The Tribunal will face major political obstacles in implementing the Prosecutor's intention to indict members of the RPF against whom evidence of atrocities is established. Such investigations are however required in order to show that the Tribunal is not only prosecuting Hutu leaders, although they planned and carried out the genocide. The charge of 'victors' justice' could be made against national Rwandan courts but cannot be retained for the Tribunal in view of the international origin of the judges and the Tribunal's detailed procedures which ensure due process for all the accused.

The Tribunal's mandate is the prosecution of persons responsible for serious violations of international humanitarian law committed in Rwanda and Rwandan citizens responsible for such violations committed in the territory of neighbouring States between 1 January 1994 and 31 December 1994, in accordance with its Statute. While the Security Council declared that it was 'convinced' that such prosecution 'would contribute to the process of national reconciliation and to the restoration and maintenance of peace', the Tribunal cannot be held responsible for the continuing fighting between Tutsi and Hutu within the regional context of political, military, ethnic and economic rivalries and anarchy.

Rwandan justice should, in principle, play a complementary role to that of the International Tribunal, by focusing on lesser actors of the genocide. However, its judicial processes are still faulty in view of the breakdown of its justice system: in spite of recent efforts, more judges and lawyers still need to be trained, better physical facilities (courtrooms, jails) need to be built, properly staffed and maintained. As noted above, it is hoped that the newly created gacaca courts will help in dealing more promptly with the mass of untried suspects in detention, thus preventing both impunity and abusively delayed justice: however, their impact and effectiveness remains to be tested. Organised justice at both international and national levels, in spite of their imperfections, should be seen as an indispensable alternative to impunity and/or widespread extrajudicial executions and private revenge killings.[48]

It is also noteworthy that a few countries, Switzerland and Belgium, have judged and sentenced Rwandan individuals for genocide and other crimes, thus enlarging the principle of universal jurisdiction.

More bluntly, besides all the possible legal and judiciary reservations concerning the creation and the functioning of both the ICTY and the ICTR, and the political limitations of their role, who could have anticipated, in the early 1990s, that such powerful leaders as Milosevic and Kambanda would be brought to international justice? Who would have believed that sentences of life or time imprisonment of indictees would have been pronounced by an international criminal tribunal, sentences which are then implemented?

Even if the two Tribunals have not contributed to national reconciliation and peace in their respective regions, an impossible task, they have contributed to the erosion of the impunity of top leaders and to the verification and recording of historical facts. Following the victors' justice of the Nuremberg and Tokyo tribunals, they have made international criminal justice a fair reality, albeit an imperfect and temporary reality. Their creation, functioning and jurisprudence have made an essential and significant contribution to the drafting of the Statute of the International Criminal Court. The experience slowly and, at times, painfully gained by the two Tribunals should also constitute an extended source of reference for the prosecutors and judges of the future Court.

---

48 Payam Akhavan, 'Beyond Impunity: Can International Criminal Justice Prevent Future Atrocities?', *American Journal of International Law*, Vol. 95, January 2001, p. 23.

CHAPTER 4

THE INTERNATIONAL CRIMINAL COURT

On 17 July 1998, the UN Diplomatic Conference held in Rome decided to establish a permanent International Criminal Court (ICC) by adopting its Statute by a vote of 120 in favour to seven against, with 21 abstentions. The USA, together with China, Israel, Libya, Iraq, Qatar and Yemen, voted against the establishment of the Court. The Russian Federation was among those states which abstained, although it signed the Statute on 13 September 2000. On 31 December 2000, the USA and Israel signed the Rome Treaty. The Statute will enter into force following the ratification, acceptance, approval or accession of 60 States. As of 19 January 2002, 140 countries had signed the Statute and 48 had ratified it. Out of the latter:

- 10 are African countries;
- five are from Asia and the Pacific;
- 12 are European Union members and 11 are other, non-EU, European countries;
- nine are from Latin America and the Caribbean;
- one (Canada) is from North America.

The list of countries having ratified the Statute by January 2002 is in Presentation 4.1.

The vote, after five weeks of difficult, at times acrimonious negotiations, was, in the words of Kofi Annan, the UN Secretary-General a 'giant step forward in the march towards universal human rights and the rule of law'. In a different assessment, Amnesty International (AI) asked whether the new Court was not 'crippled at birth'. AI recognised that the Court would be an historic step forward for international justice, but the organisation said that the Statute still requires radical surgery to ensure that the Court will be relevant and effective. Pierre Sane, AI's Secretary-General expressed his regret that a few powerful countries appeared willing to hold justice by threatening and bullying other states, and seemed sometimes to be more concerned to shield perpetrators from trial rather than producing a charter for victims.[1] Those states which voted against the Statute and others which abstained expressed openly or discreetly their firm opposition to creating an international criminal court, formally as a protection of their national sovereignty, in reality as a

[1] See AI News Service 138/98, AI INDEX: IOR 40/20/98, 17 July 1998. On the origin of the Court. See Beigbeder (1999), pp. 186–195.

Presentation 4.1. Ratification Status of the ICC Statute by Regions as of January 2002

Africa
(1) Senegal, 2 February 1999
(2) Ghana, 20 December 1999
(3) Mali, 16 August 2000
(4) Lesotho, 6 September 2000
(5) Botswana, 8 September 2000
(6) Sierra Leone, 15 September 2000
(7) Gabon, 21 September 2000
(8) South Africa, 27 November 2000
(9) Nigeria, 27 September 2001
(10) Central African Republic, 3 October 2001

Asia and Pacific
(1) Tajikistan, 5 May 2000
(2) New Zealand, 7 September 2000
(3) Fiji, 29 November 1999
(4) Marshall Islands, 7 December 2000
(5) Nauru, 12 November 2001

European Union
(1) Italy, 26 July 1999
(2) France, 9 June 2000
(3) Belgium, 28 June 2000
(4) Luxembourg, 8 September 2000
(5) Spain, 25 October 2000
(6) Germany, 11 December 2000
(7) Austria, 28 December 2000
(8) Finland, 29 December 2000
(9) Denmark, 21 June 2001
(10) Sweden, 28 June 2001
(11) The Netherlands, 17 July 2001
(12) United Kingdom, 4 October 2001

Europe (Non EU)
(1) San Marino, 13 May 1999
(2) Norway, 16 February 2000
(3) Iceland, 25 May 2000
(4) Andorra, 3 May 2001
(5) Croatia, 21 May 2001
(6) Yugoslavia (FRY), 6 September 2001
(7) Liechtenstein, 2 October 2001
(8) Switzerland, 12 October 2001
(9) Poland, 12 November 2001
(10) Hungary, 30 November 2001
(11) Slovenia, 31 December 2001

Latin America and the Caribbean
(1) Belize, 5 April 2000
(2) Trinidad and Tobago, 6 April 1999
(3) Venezuela, 7 June 2000
(4) Argentina, 8 February 2001
(5) Dominica, 12 February 2001
(6) Paraguay, 14 May 2001
(7) Costa Rica, 7 June 2001
(8) Antigua and Barbuda, 18 June 2001
(9) Peru, 10 November 2001

North America
(1) Canada

The Mediterranean and Middle East
None

Source: No Peace Without Justice Report: Ratification status: regional update. www.npwj.org/article.php?sid=123&mode=thread&order=0.www

shield against investigations and potential prosecution of their political and military leaders.

The Origins

Between the two World Wars, a few scholarly and professional organizations and NGOs initiated and promoted the concept and the creation of an international criminal court. In 1927, during the Paris Congress of the 'Fédération internationale des ligues des droits de l'homme', the Austrian League proposed to promote the creation of a 'Permanent International Court of Moral Justice', the action of which would ensure an effective and international protection of human rights within the framework of the League of Nations. This proposal was adopted by the Congress and has been included as one of the main demands of the Federation since then.

A first reference to an 'international penal tribunal' was made in Article VI of the 1948 Genocide Convention as an alternative to a competent national tribunal:

> Persons charged with genocide or any of the other acts enumerated in Article III shall be tried by a competent tribunal of the State in the territory of which the act was committed, or by such international penal tribunal as may have jurisdiction with respect to those Contracting Parties which shall have accepted its jurisdiction.

In part B of the same resolution adopted on 9 December 1948 (Res. 260 (III)), the UN General Assembly considered that there would be an increasing need of an international judicial organ for the trial of certain crimes under international law and invited the International Law Commission (ILC) to study the desirability and possibility of establishing such an organ for the trial of persons charged with genocide or other crimes. The ILC was requested to pay attention to the possibility of establishing a Criminal Chamber of the International Court of Justice.

Through the deliberate stalling of Member states, 50 years elapsed before the Court's Statute was adopted. As noted by Lee,[2] the explanations for the long delay are both political and legal. First, the prosecution and enforcement of the law are carefully guarded sovereign prerogatives: national jurisdiction prevails. Second, the subject matter relates to individual criminal responsibility for the most serious crimes, a matter in which important government departments, including defense, justice and the executive branches have a particular interest. These factors have made the subject matter extremely complex and sensitive. If an international court was to be established, a way had to be found to accommodate it without impairing national jurisdiction.

In 1950, the General Assembly set up a Special Committee to prepare a Draft Statute for an ICC, which produced a text in 1951, revised in 1953. The text was deferred over the next few years on the pretext that the crime of aggression had not been defined. Among the 'stalling' states, the USSR and other Socialist countries were ideologically hostile to 'bourgeois' international justice. The issue was only raised again in 1989, at the end of the Cold War, by Trinidad and Tobago in a Special Session of the General Assembly, proposing the creation of a specialized ICC for drug-related offences. As requested by the General Assembly in 1990, 1992 and 1993, the ILC prepared a Draft Statute in 1993, revised in 1994.

In December 1994, in another delaying move, the General Assembly rejected the ILC's recommendation to convene an international conference of plenipotentiaries to study the Draft Statute, but decided instead to establish an ad hoc committee open to all states Members of the UN or Members of specialized agencies or of the IAEA to review the issues arising from the Draft Statute (Res. 49/53). The Committee reported that the participating states differed so markedly on the major substantive and administrative issues that it would be more effective to combine further discussions with the actual drafting of a consolidated text of a Statute/Convention for the Court. In December 1995, the General Assembly established a preparatory committee, again open to all Member states of the UN and UN agencies (Res. 50/46). The Committee was not only to discuss issues but also to draft texts, with a view to preparing a widely acceptable consolidated text of a convention for an ICC as a next step towards consideration by a conference of plenipotentiaries.

The UN Diplomatic Conference was held in Rome from 15 June to 17 July 1998, when the Statute was finally adopted. 160 states participated in the Conference, with the assistance of more than 20 intergovernmental organisations, 14 specialized agencies of the UN, and a coalition of more than 200 NGOs. In addition, 474

---

[2] Roy S. Lee, 'Introduction, The Rome Conference and Its Contribution to International Law' in Roy S. Lee (ed.), *UNITAR, The International Criminal Court, The Making of the Rome Statute* (Kluwer Law International, The Hague, London, Boston, 1999), p. 5; See also pp. 14, 24–25.

journalists were accredited to cover the event. The Statute was the final result of battles and compromises between the determination of many 'like-minded countries' to set up an independent court, with the strong support of NGOs, and the opposition of states intent on limiting the autonomy of the future court. Among the reluctant states, the USA and France feared that their military personnel on peacekeeping missions might be indicted for war crimes by an overly independent court. The wishes of some countries were frustrated: among others, India, Turkey and Sri Lanka wanted to add the crime of terrorism among core crimes, other countries protested against the powers granted to the Prosecutor (China), or against the non-inclusion of the death penalty (Singapore). On the last day of the Conference, when the draft Statute was about to be adopted, India put forward two amendments. The first was to deprive the Security Council of the power to refer situations to the Court and to request the Court to defer investigation or prosecution. The second was to include the use of nuclear and other weapons of mass destruction in the list of war crimes. The US proposed an amendment sought to limit the Court's jurisdiction to those cases when only the state of the accused had accepted the jurisdiction of the Court. These amendments were rejected by a 'no action' motion proposed by Norway, thus allowing the adoption of the Statute on the same day.

In spite of the Statute's imperfections, in spite of these reservations and objections, its adoption was a considerable success for the promoters of international criminal justice and for those who believe that crimes committed, ordered or allowed by high-level leaders should not remain unpunished. The creation and functioning of the ICTY and ICTR had already proved that international criminal tribunals were a working proposition. However, the jurisdiction of both tribunals is limited and their creation by the Security Council has been criticised. Also, the Security Council appeared unwilling to create more ad hoc international criminal tribunals. Hence, the need for a permanent International Criminal Court with quasi-universal jurisdiction. Factors contributing to the success of the Rome Conference include the democratization of a number of former authoritarian or one-party states, the growing feeling among populations that leaders should be accountable for their crimes, the development of a human rights regime, the need to sanction effectively violations of the Hague and Geneva Conventions, the acknowledgement that national justice may be incompetent, that it is often unwilling to judge former or present leaders, and in many cases controlled by the executive, and the growing visibility and influence of human rights and humanitarian NGOs.

The Statute

The Statute has confirmed the Nuremberg principle of individual criminal responsibility without any distinction based on official capacity, and extended it over a comprehensive range of international crimes both in war and peace. For the first time in an international judiciary instrument, the gender issue and concern for children are explicitly referred to in several articles. The Statute incorporates both retributive (sanctions to the accused found guilty) and restorative (reparations to the victim) justice.

Its Preamble recalls that, during the 20th century 'millions of children, women and men have been victims of unimaginable atrocities that deeply shock the conscience of humanity'. It also recognises that these 'grave crimes threaten the peace, security and well-being of the world', referring in part to the language in Chapter VII of the UN Charter. It expresses the determination 'to put an end to impunity for the perpetrators of these crimes and thus to contribute to the prevention of such crimes'.

The main features of the Statute are summarised hereunder, together with comments.[3]

Status of the Court

The Court will be a permanent institution with the power to exercise jurisdiction over persons for the most serious crimes of international concern. It is to be complementary to national criminal jurisdictions (Art. 1). Unlike the Statutes of the ICTY and ICTY giving primacy to the international tribunals, national courts have primacy over the ICC in investigating and prosecuting crimes, unless the state is unwilling or unable genuinely to carry out the investigation or prosecution. The ICC will make such a determination, a significant and politically sensitive power, according to the following criteria: unwillingness may occur if national proceedings or decision are made for the purpose of shielding the person concerned from criminal responsibility for crimes within the jurisdiction of the ICC, and/or there has been an unjustified delay in the national proceedings, and/or the proceedings were not or are not being conducted independently or impartially. In order to determine inability in a particular case, the Court considers whether, due to a total or substantial collapse or unavailability of its national judicial system, the State is unable to obtain the accused or the necessary evidence and testimony or otherwise unable to carry out its proceedings (Art. 17).

The Court will not be part of the UN, unlike the International Court of Justice (ICJ) which is a principal organ of the UN. However, the new Court will be brought into relationship with the UN through an agreement (Art.2). There is a direct link between the ICC and the UN Security Council as shown below. Its seat will be in The Hague, which is already the seat of the ICJ and of the ICTY (Art. 3).

Established by treaty, and not by a decision of the Security Council as the ICTY and ICTR, its Statute will not be binding on non-ratifying states.

---

3 See Roy S. Lee (ed.), as per n. 2 above. Vesselin Popovski, 'The International Criminal Court: A Synthesis of Retributive and Restorative Justice', *International Relations*, vol. XV, no, 3, December 2000, pp. 1–10; *Fact sheets* of the International Justice Project on the ICC in <www.amnesty.org.>

Structure of the Court

The ICC will be composed of the following organs: the Presidency, an Appeals Division, a Trial Division and a Pre-Trial Division, the Office of the Prosecutor and the Registry (Art. 34).

Its 18 judges will be elected by secret ballot by the Assembly of States Parties for non-renewable terms of nine years. They should be persons of high moral character, impartiality and integrity who possess the qualifications required in their respective States for appointment to the highest judicial offices. Their selection should take into account the need for the representation of the principal legal systems of the world, equitable geographical representation and, as an innovation over the formulation of the Statutes of the ICJ, the ICTY and the ICTR, a fair representation of female and male judges. The NGO Coalition for an ICC has recently called for vigilance in respect of female representation, based on the experience of the ICTY and ICTR. For instance, in March 2001, a list of 25 candidates for 14 judicial posts at the ICTY included only one woman.[4]

Judges should have established competence in criminal law and procedure, and the necessary relevant experience, whether as judge, prosecutor, advocate or in any similar capacity, in criminal proceedings; or, have established competence in relevant areas of international law such as international law and the law of human rights and relevant experience. States Parties should also include judges with legal expertise on specific issues, including, but not limited to, violence against women or children. They should have an excellent knowledge of and be fluent in at least one of the working languages of the Court. No two judges may be nationals of the same State. The judges must be independent in the performance of their functions.

The Appeals Chamber is composed of all the judges of the Appeals Division, three judges sit in the Trial Chamber, while the functions of the Pre-Trial Chamber are carried out either by three judges or by a single judge (Art. 36, 39, 40).

The President and the First and Second Vice-Presidents, constituting the Presidency, are elected by an absolute majority of the judges for a term of three years. They are eligible for re-election once. The Presidency is responsible for the administration of the Court, with the exception of the Office of the Prosecutor (Art. 38).

The Office of the Prosecutor acts independently as a separate organ of the Court. It is responsible for receiving referrals and any substantiated information on crimes, for examining them and for conducting investigations and prosecutions before the Court. The Office is headed by the Prosecutor, assisted by one or more Deputy Prosecutors. The Prosecutors and Deputy Prosecutors should be persons of high moral character, highly competent in and have extensive practical experience in the prosecution or trial of criminal cases. They should have the same linguistic skills as

---

[4] Pam Spees, *The International Criminal Court Monitor, The Newspaper of the NGO Coalition for an International Criminal Court*, Issue 17, May 2001, p. 14.

the judges. The Prosecutor is elected by secret ballot by an absolute majority of the members of the Assembly of States Parties. The Deputy Prosecutors are elected in the same way from a list of candidates provided by the Prosecutor (Art. 42).

The Registry is responsible for the non-judicial aspects of the administration and servicing of the Court, without prejudice to the functions and powers of the Prosecutor. It is headed by the Registrar, as principal administrative officer of the Court. He exercises his/her functions under the authority of the President of the Court. He is assisted by a Deputy Registrar (Art. 43).

The Prosecutor and the Registry are required by Article 44(2) in the employment of staff to 'ensure the highest standards of efficiency, competency and integrity' and to respect the other criteria required for the selection of judges, mutatis mutandis.

Before taking up their respective duties, the judges, the Prosecutor, the Deputy Prosecutors, the Registrar and the Deputy Registrar make a solemn undertaking in open Court to exercise their functions impartially and conscientiously (Art. 45).

The Assembly of States Parties is the governing body of the Court. Each State Party has one representative to the Assembly who may be accompanied by alternates and advisers. Other States which have signed the Statute may be observers. The Assembly will consider and adopt, as appropriate, recommendations of the Preparatory Commission, provide management oversight to the Presidency, the Prosecutor and the Registrar regarding the administration of the Court, consider and decide the budget of the Court, and other functions (Art. 112).

The Crimes

The ICC's jurisdiction is limited to four crimes: genocide, crimes against humanity, war crimes, and the crime of aggression (Art. 5, 6, 7, 8).

However, 'The Court shall exercise jurisdiction over the **crime of aggression** once a provision is adopted in accordance with Articles 121 and 123 defining the crime and setting out the conditions under which the Court shall exercise jurisdiction with respect to this crime. Such a provision shall be consistent with the relevant provisions of the Charter of the United Nations'. This daunting task is entrusted to the Preparatory Commission and subject to the review and approval of the Assembly of States Parties (see below).

Article 6 of the Statute gives jurisdiction to the ICC over **genocide** as defined in the 1948 Convention on the Prevention and Punishment of the Crime of Genocide. In accordance with Article II of the Convention,

> Genocide means any of the following acts committed with intent to destroy, in whole or in part, a national, ethnical, racial or religious group, as such:
>
> (a) Killing members of the group;
> (b) Causing serious bodily or mental harm to members of the group;
> (c) Deliberately inflicting on the group conditions of life calculated to bring about its physical destruction in whole or in part;

(d) Imposing measures intended to prevent births within the group;
(e) Forcibly transferring children of the group to another group.

Crimes against humanity have been listed and defined in Articles 7.1 and 7.2 in detail for the first time in an international treaty.[5] They include murder, extermination, enslavement, deportation or forcible transfer of population, imprisonment or other severe deprivation of physical liberty in violation of the fundamental rules of international law, torture, rape, sexual slavery, enforced prostitution, forced pregnancy, enforced sterilization, or any other form of sexual violence of comparable gravity, persecution against any identifiable group or collectivity on political, national, ethnic, cultural, religious, gender, or other grounds that are universally recognised as impermissible under international law, in connection with any crime under the Statute, enforced disappearances of persons, the crime of apartheid, other inhumane acts of similar character intentionally causing great suffering, or serious injury to body or to mental or physical health. The definition of enslavement in Article 7(2)(c) recognises that women and children are particularly at risk of being subject to the course of trafficking in persons, which is defined as the exercise of the power attached to the right of ownership over a person.

Unlike the Charters of the Nuremberg and Tokyo Tribunals, no link to armed conflict is required: crimes against humanity can be committed and prosecuted in either times of peace or armed conflict. In order to constitute crimes against humanity, the acts must have been part of a widespread or systematic attack directed against any civilian population, with knowledge of the attack. They must have been committed pursuant to or in furtherance of a State or organisational policy to commit such an attack (Art. 7.2(a)).

Article 8 of the Statute gives the ICC jurisdiction over **war crimes** in particular when committed as part of a plan or policy or as part of a large-scale commission of such crimes. They include crimes committed both during an international armed conflict or in armed conflicts not of an international character. War crimes during an international armed conflict are defined as grave breaches of the four Geneva Conventions of 1949 and other violations of international humanitarian law, including violations recognised in The Hague Conventions and Protocol I to the Geneva Conventions. War crimes during internal conflicts include violations of the common Article 3 of the Geneva Conventions against civilians and violations of humanitarian law generally recognised in Protocol II of the Geneva Conventions.

On war crimes, Article 124 includes a controversial optional provision, introduced at the demand of the French delegation, under pressure by its military. A State, on becoming a party to the Statute, may declare that, for a period of seven years after the entry into force of the Statute for the State concerned, it does not accept the jurisdiction of the Court with respect to war crimes when a crime is alleged to have

---

5 See M. Cherif Bassiouni, *Crimes Against Humanity in International Criminal Law* (Kluwer Law International (The Hague/London/Boston/New York, 1999).

been committed by its nationals or on its territory: a self-incriminating clause which may not be availed of without considering the implication of such a declaration: does it mean that the concerned State will enjoy impunity for its war crimes for seven years, and then be subjected to the Court's jurisdiction?

A significant achievement of the Statute is to include in the war crimes the conscripting or enlisting of children under the age of 15 years into armed forces or groups or using them to participate actively in hostilities during international or non-international armed conflict (Art. 8(2)(b)(xxvi) and (e)(vii)).

Prosecution

The Court has jurisdiction to prosecute individuals when:

* Crimes have been committed in the territory of a State which has ratified the Statute;
  - Crimes have been committed by a citizen of a state which has ratified the Statute;
  - A state which has not ratified the Statute has made a declaration accepting the Court's jurisdiction over the crime (Art.12.3);
  - Crimes have been committed in a situation which threatens or breaches international peace and security and the Security Council has referred the situation to the Court pursuant to Chapter VII of the UN Charter (Art. 13)

The Court's jurisdiction will have no retroactive effect. It will have jurisdiction only over crimes committed after the Statute enters into force – after the 60th ratification – and only with regard to a state's ratification, if it occurred later than the entry into force of the Statute, unless that state has made a declaration under Article 12.3 (Art.11).

Initiating Prosecution

The Court may initiate prosecution in the following cases, under the conditions stated above:

(1) The Prosecutor may initiate investigations proprio motu on the basis of information on crimes within the jurisdiction of the Court (Art. 15);
(2) States which have ratified the Statute may ask the Prosecutor to investigate a situation where one or more of the crimes have been committed within the jurisdiction of the Court, for the purpose of determining whether one or more specific persons should be charged with the commission of such crimes (Art. 14);
(3) The UN Security Council, acting under Chapter VII of the UN Charter, can ask the Prosecutor to investigate a situation where one or more crimes appear to have been committed (Art. 13(b)). In such a case, the Court will have

jurisdiction even if the crimes occurred in the territory of a state which has not ratified the Statute or was committed by the national of such a state.

In all cases, only the Prosecutor, not states or the Security Council, assesses and decides whether to initiate an investigation and, based on its findings, whether to prosecute, subject to a decision by the Pre-Trial Chamber (Art. 15).

Limitations of the Court's Powers

Although the Preamble of the Statute refers to an 'independent' Court, a number of qualifications limits the powers of the Court and in particular those of its Prosecutor, in contrast with the broad autonomy of the Prosecutor of the ICTY and ICTR:

(1) The Court will determine whether the case is or is not admissible on the grounds of the primacy of national courts and its limitations (Art. 17).
(2) The Court may exercise its jurisdiction only for crimes committed on the territory of a State Party to the Statute, or of a State which has accepted the jurisdiction of the Court, or for crimes committed by a person who is a national of such a State (Art. 12).
(3) The Prosecutor's investigation has to be authorized by a Pre-Trial Chamber of the Court. The issue of a warrant of arrest of a person, based on the application of the Prosecutor, is also subject to approval by the Pre-Trial Chamber (Art. 57, 58).
(4) As another limitation of the Prosecutor's powers, no investigation or prosecution may be commenced or proceeded with for a period of 12 months after the Security Council, in a resolution adopted under Chapter VII of the UN Charter, has requested the Court to that effect – that request may be renewed by the Council under the same conditions (Art. 16). In this respect, such a resolution will require a majority of nine votes, including the five permanent members of the Council: a single veto would annul such a request.

Rights of the Accused

The general principles of criminal law are confirmed: nullum crimen sine lege, nulla poena sine lege, non-retroactivity ratione personae: 'no person shall be criminally responsible under this Statute for conduct prior to the entry into force of the Statute', individual criminal personality: the Court's jurisdiction applies [only] to natural persons, not to groups, organisations or other collective entities (Art. 22, 23, 24, 25). Under Article 25(3)(b) and (c) of the Statute, anyone who orders, solicits or induces the commission of a crime within the jurisdiction of the Court, crime which in fact occurs or is attempted, or aids, abets or otherwise assists in its commission will be individually responsible and liable for punishment in accordance with the Statute.

The Statute incorporates fundamental guarantees of the right to a fair trial recognised in the International Covenant on Civil and Political Rights of 1966 and by the Statutes of the ICTY and ICTR, e.g. the right 'to a fair and public hearing by a competent, independent and impartial tribunal established by law' and 'the right to be presumed innocent until proved guilty according to law' (Art. 14.1 and 14.2 of the Covenant). Everyone is presumed innocent until proved guilty before the Court. For the first time in an international instrument, Article 66(3) of the Statute expressly provides that in order to convict the accused, the ICC must be convinced of the guilt of the accused beyond reasonable doubt. The prosecution bears the burden of proof throughout the trial (Art. 66, 67). The accused must be informed of his right to a lawyer, to have one assigned in any case where the interests of justice so require and, if the accused cannot afford a lawyer, to have free legal assistance (Art. 67(1)(d)). He may obtain witnesses and have them examined on an equal footing with the Prosecutor. Finally, persons convicted by the ICC have the right to appeal to the Appeals Chamber on any of the following grounds: procedural error, error of fact, error of law or any other ground that affects the fairness or reliability of the proceedings or decision. The Prosecutor may also make an appeal on the grounds of procedural error, error of fact, or error of law (Art. 81.1).

The Court has no jurisdiction over any person who was under the age of 18 at the time of the alleged commission of a crime (Art. 26). The Statute applies to all persons without any distinction based on official capacity. Official capacity as a Head of State or Government, a member of a Government or Parliament, an elected representative or a government official do not exempt a person from criminal responsibility nor does it constitute a ground for reduction of sentence (Art. 27).

The accused 'shall be present during the trial', thus confirming the Statutes of the ICTY and of the ICTR. No trial in absentia is allowed except when the accused 'continues to disrupt the trial' (Art. 63).

Rights of Victims and Witnesses

Under Article 54(1)(b), the Prosecutor is required, during the course of an investigation and prosecution to respect the interests and personal circumstances of victims and witnesses, including age, gender and health, and take into account the nature of the crime, in particular where it involves sexual violence, gender violence or violence against children. Both the Pre-Trial Chamber and the Trial Chamber must take appropriate measures to protect the safety, physical and psychological well-being, dignity and privacy of victims and witnesses (Art. 57(3) and 68(1)). Article 68(3) requires the ICC to permit the views and concerns of victims to be presented and considered at appropriate stages in the proceedings in a manner which is not prejudicial to or inconsistent with the rights of the accused and a fair and impartial trial. Appropriate stages of proceedings encompass the trial, sentencing, award of reparations and post-trial proceedings including the appeal, sentence reduction hearings, review and release hearings. Article 15 authorizes the Prosecutor to initiate investigations based on information from any source. Victims may make representations to the Pre-Trial Chamber.

Women victims are implicitly or explicitly considered in several Articles of the Statute – some crimes may be committed against both men and women although most sexual crimes are likely to involve primarily women, some are gender-specific to women. Article 7(1) recognises rape, sexual slavery, enforced prostitution, forced pregnancy, enforced sterilization and any other form of sexual violence of comparable gravity as crimes against humanity. It also expressly recognises that the crime of enslavement includes, in particular, the trafficking in women and children(Art. 7.2(c)) Article 7(1)(h) states that persecution against any identifiable group or collectivity, on gender grounds, or other grounds that are universally recognised as impermissible under international law, if committed in connection with any other crime within the jurisdiction of the ICC, is a crime against humanity. Article 8.2(b)(xxii) provides that individual acts of the same crimes of sexual violence constituting a grave breach or violation of common Article 3 of the Geneva Conventions of 1949 can be prosecuted as war crimes.

Article 43(6) provides for the establishment of a Victims and Witnesses Unit in the Registry. It will provide protection measures, security arrangements and other appropriate assistance to victims, witnesses who appear before the Court and others, such as family members, who are at risk because of such testimony.

Reparations

As an improvement over the Statutes of the ICTY and ICTR, the Court will establish principles relating to reparations to, or in respect of, victims, including restitution, compensation, rehabilitation, satisfaction, guaranteed non-repetition, and any other type of reparations to victims it deems appropriate. The Court may issue an order directly against a convicted person specifying appropriate reparations to, or in respect of, victims either directly or through a Trust Fund (Art. 75).

Penalties

Applicable penalties include imprisonment not to exceed a maximum of 30 years, or life imprisonment when justified by the extreme gravity of the crime and the individual circumstances of the convicted person and, in addition, as applicable, a fine, a forfeiture of proceeds, property and assets derived directly or indirectly from the crime, without prejudice to the rights of bona fide third parties (Art. 77). Sentences are subject to appeal by the Prosecutor or the convicted person – either party may apply to the Appeals Chamber to revise a final judgement of conviction or sentence on established grounds (Art. 81, 84).

Cooperation with States

The ICC, like the ICTY and ICTR, will have no enforcement powers. Its arrest warrants can only be enforced by national authorities. It cannot seize evidentiary material, compel witnesses to give testimony, nor investigate the scene where crimes have been allegedly committed. The ICC will not have its own jails: sentences will have to be served in the facilities of State Parties which have volunteered to offer these. For all these purposes, the Court will have to turn to national authorities and request them to take action. States Parties have a general obligation to cooperate fully with the Court in its investigation and prosecution of crimes within the jurisdiction of the Court (Art. 86). However, Article 72 provides for an important exception: a state may refuse the disclosure of information or documents when such disclosure would, in the opinion of that state, prejudice its national security interests. States should then take steps to resolve such a matter by cooperative means, acting in conjunction with the Prosecutor, the Defence or the Pre-Trial or Trial Chamber.

Financing the Court

The expenses of the Court and of the Assembly of States Parties will be provided by assessed contributions made by States Parties – based on the UN scale of assessment for its regular budget. Additional funds will be provided by the UN in particular in relation to the expenses incurred due to referrals by the Security Council, and by voluntary funds (Art. 115, 116, 117).

Signatures and Ratifications

The Statute remained open for signature at the UN headquarters in New York until 31 December 2000. It is subject to ratification, acceptance or approval by signatory States, their instruments are to be deposited with the UN Secretary-General. The Statute is open to accession by all States. The Statute itself does not permit reservations (Art. 125 and 120).

The Statute will enter into force on the first day of the month after the 60th day following the date of the deposit of the 60th instrument of ratification, acceptance, approval or accession with the Secretary-General of the UN (Art. 126).

Amendments and Review of the Statute

After the expiry of seven years from the entry into force of the Statute, any State Party may propose amendments thereto. The Assembly of States Parties will decide whether to take up such proposals or convene a Review Conference if the issue involved so warrants.

Seven years after the entry into force of the Statute, the Secretary-General of the UN will convene a Review Conference to consider any amendments to the Statute.

The Conference will be open to those participating in the Assembly of States Parties and on the same conditions (Art. 121, 123).

THE PREPARATORY COMMISSION FOR THE ICC

The Commission (PrepComm) was established by the Rome Conference and its creation endorsed by the UN General Assembly.[6] All states invited to attend the Rome Conference can participate in the Commission, regardless of whether the state voted in favour of the Statute. As a result, the US initially participated actively and constructively in the discussions. However, following the installation of the Bush Administration, the former large US delegations were reduced to a bare-minimum two person delegation. Observers to the Commission include representatives of organisations and other entities that have received a standing invitation from the General Assembly, representatives of interested regional intergovernmental organisations and other interested international bodies, including the ICTY and the ICTR. NGOs may also participate in the work of the Commission by attending its plenary and its other open meetings, receiving copies of the official documents and making available their materials to delegates. The UN Secretary-General was requested by the General Assembly to make available to the Commission secretariat services, not including the preparation of working documents. The Director of the Codification Division of the Office of Legal Affairs of the UN acts as Secretary of the Commission.

The Commission first met at the UN headquarters on 16 and 22 February 1999.[7] At its fifth session on 30 June 2000, the Commission adopted the finalized draft texts of the Rules of Procedure and Evidence and the Elements of Crime, as requested by the General Assembly.

At its eighth session held from 24 September to 5 October 2001, the Commission finalized the Draft Relationship Agreement between the Court and the United Nations, the Draft Financial Regulations, the Draft Agreement on the Privileges and Immunities of the Court, the Draft Rules of Procedure of the Assembly of States Parties. It also reviewed the budget for the first year of the Court's operation, the Host State Agreement and the Crime of Aggression.[8]

One of the more difficult issues is the definition of the Crime of Aggression and the conditions for the exercise of the Court's jurisdiction over this crime, a highly-charged political issue long-debated by the UN. Among the critical questions under discussion: whether the definition of the crime of aggression should include an illustrative or exclusive list of acts constituting aggression or should be more general;

---

6 Final Act, Resolution F and General Assembly res. 53/105 of 8 December 1998 and res. 55/155.

7 The Commission's sessions were held on 16 and 22 February 1999, 26 July to 13 August 1999, 29 November to 17 December 1999, 13 to 31 March 2000 following an intersessional meeting in Siracusa 31 January to 6 February 2000. See <www.un.org/law/icc/prepcomm>.

8 See www.un.org/law/icc/prepcomm/eighth.htm., 22 January 2002.

how to differentiate between individual criminal acts versus acts of the State as a whole; and whether the Security Council holds the primary or the exclusive authority to determine that a State has committed an aggression; whether there is a role for the International Court of Justice in such determination.[9]

Once the Statute comes into force, draft texts adopted by the Commission will be submitted to the Assembly of States Parties for review and approval.

The US Position

President Clinton's announcement on 31 December 2000, the deadline established by the Rome Treaty, that the USA was signing the Treaty was unexpected in view of continuous US opposition to the Court's Statute. However, he said that 'we are not abandoning our concerns about significant flaws in the Treaty'. In particular, the US considers that the Court's jurisdiction over US personnel should come only with the US ratification of the Treaty. He did not recommend that his successor submit the Treaty to the Senate for advice and consent 'until our fundamental concerns are satisfied'. Although Clinton's decision looked like a coup against the incoming Republican Administration, he justified it by allowing US negotiators to promote US interests in productive discussions with other governments.

While Clinton's move won praise in press comments in Europe and Australia, the then Chairman of the US Senate Foreign Relations Committee, Senator Jesse Helms declared on 3 January 2001 that Clinton's decision in his final days in office is 'as outrageous as it is inexplicable'. He recalled the statement made two years before to Congress by the US chief negotiator, David Scheffer:

> The [Rome] treaty purports to establish an arrangement whereby United States armed forces operating overseas could be conceivably prosecuted by the International Criminal Court even if the United States has not agreed to be bound by the Treaty. Not only is this contrary to the most fundamental principles of treaty law, it could inhibit the ability of the United States to use its military to meet alliance obligations and participate in multinational operations.

As nothing had changed since then, Helms would make reversing this decision, and 'protecting America's fighting men and women from the jurisdiction of this international kangaroo court' one of his highest priorities.[10]

In May 2001, the US Senate Armed Services Committee Chairman John Warner and Helms introduced the 'American Service Members' Protection Act' strongly opposing the proposed International Criminal Court. Among its key provisions:[11]

---

9 Jennifer Schense, *The International Criminal Court Monitor*, May 2001, pp. 3 and 15.

10 *Public Diplomacy Query*, Doc. 25, 2 January 2001; Doc. 53, 2 January 2001; Doc. 13, 3 January 2001.

11 See <www.wfa,org/issues/issues/icc/aspasum.html>

- No governmental entity in the US, including State and local governments or any court, may cooperate with the ICC in matters such as arrest and extradition of suspects, execution of searches and seizures, taking of evidence, and similar matters;
- No agent of the ICC may conduct in the US any investigative activity;
- The President should use the US voice and vote at the Security Council to ensure that each resolution authorizing any UN peacekeeping operation permanently exempts members of the US armed forces from prosecution by the ICC;
- No country that has ratified the treaty establishing the Court can receive US military assistance (Exemption from NATO member countries and 'major non-NATO allies', cited in the bill as Australia, Egypt, Israel, Japan, the Republic of Korea and New Zealand, and Taiwan);
- The President is authorized to use all means necessary and appropriate to bring about the release from captivity of US and Allied personnel detained or imprisoned against their will by or on behalf of the Court. In other words, the President is authorized to 'invade the Hague' ...

Among the US opponents to the Court, Gary T. Dempsey[12] summarizes his objections as follows: the Court threatens to diminish America's sovereignty, produce arbitrary and highly politicized 'justice' and grow into a jurisdictional leviathan. It appears to him that many of the legal safeguards American citizens enjoy under the US Constitution would be suspended if they were brought before the Court. Endangered constitutional protections include the prohibition against double jeopardy, the right to trial by an impartial jury, and the right of the accused to confront the winesses against him. Alfred P. Rubin[13] has long opposed the establishment of an international court as unnecessary and even unwise. In 1996, he expressed his concern about the authority such a court would have and about how it would safeguard the rights of defendants. He believes that there are other options to preserve international order, such as the creation of truth commissions as in South Africa and Latin American countries, where issues are resolved in the moral rather than in the legal sphere. He argued in 1993 that attempts to successfully establish and enforce the authenticity of an international criminal court have failed because of complications in the structure of the state system on which existing legal order depends, rather than weak political commitment.

> Since the current international legal order rests on a notion of sovereign equality of states under the law, and the states that set it up are unwilling to submit themselves to its authority, the arrangement is inherently hypocritical;

[12] Gary T. Dempsey is a foreign policy analyst at the Cato Institute: see Cato Policy Analysis No. 311, 16 July 1998 in <www.cato.org/pubs/pas/pa-311es.htm>

[13] Alfred P. Rubin is professor of international law at the Fletcher School of Law and Diplomacy at Tufts University. See 'Global justice?' *Christian Science Monitor*, <icc-info@igc.apc.org>, 31 December 1996; 'International crime and punishment' in *The National Interest*, Fall 1993 n. 33 p. 73(3).

> another 'victor's tribunal' being set up belatedly by the winners of the Second World War. ... In sum, the world would do better grappling with the tragedies of former Yugoslavia and the Middle East, acknowledging that violations of international morality and rules of law are not analogous to violations of national criminal law ...

While some of these arguments have been overtaken by the approval of the Rome Statute in July 1998, US opponents still raise several objections to the present text of the Statute, considered as misunderstandings or misrepresentations by the Court's promoters. Objections and their rebuttal follow:

First objection: The ICC is 'significantly flawed' and the US should seek a full exemption from ICC jurisdiction.

The key flaw is generally construed as the jurisdiction of the future ICC over US citizens, even though the US has not ratified the Statute. At present, US citizens and soldiers who commit crimes abroad are subject to the jurisdiction of the territorial state in which the crime was committed. The ICC will have jurisdiction over the personnel of non-Party States only when these individuals commit crimes under the jurisdiction of the ICC in the territory of a State Party, or in the territory of a state that has chosen to accept the jurisdiction of the ICC. Any crime committed by an American would have to constitute a core crime under the ICC – genocide, crimes against humanity, war crimes – and would be subject to a rigorous threshold for investigation and prosecution, including review and decision by the Pre-Trial Chamber.

A major safeguard preventing the investigation and prosecution of US citizens is the principle of complementarity to national legal systems, e.g. that the ICC must defer to national courts' jurisdiction (Art. 17, 18, 19 of the Statute). The Court may not proceed with any case that is genuinely being investigated or prosecuted by a state which has jurisdiction, or already has been investigated by such a state and the state has decided not to prosecute the person concerned, or the person has already been tried for the same offence.

According to Judge Robinson O. Everett of the US Court of Military Appeals,[14]

> ... the existing provisions of the Uniform Code of Military Justice and the War Crimes Act [of 1996] have already created jurisdiction over war crimes on the part of US court-martial ... Therefore the principle of complementarity set out in the ICC statute would provide the United States with a basis for maintaining that American servicemembers accused of crimes prohibited by the Statute should be tried by a US court-martial, rather than by the ICC.

[14] Quoted by the Washington Working Group on the ICC. See <www.wfa.org/issues/wicc/safeguards.html>, and <www.wfa.org/issues/wicc/nationalsecurity.html>, 30 July 2001.

Furthermore, under Article 92.2 – inserted upon the insistence of US negotiators – the ICC may not proceed with a request for surrender which would require the requested State to act inconsistently with its obligations under international agreements, such as US Status of Forces Agreements. The US almost invariably requires such an Agreement before engaging in peacekeeping or humanitarian operations.

The ICC has no independent enforcement powers: the task of apprehending suspects will fall to States, which already have the authority to apprehend suspects within their territory.

Finally, according to Article 16, the UN Security Council may pass a resolution to prevent or stop the ICC from investigating and prosecuting crimes for twelve months, renewable.

Second objection: US military and civilian personnel may be subject to frivolous or politically-motivated charges by the ICC.

States that have not ratified the Statute may accept the jurisdiction of the Court by a 'declaration' under Article 12. Besides all the protection measures cited above, US negotiators have obtained the adoption of Rule 44(2) of the Rules of Procedure and Evidence. This Rule requires that any non-party state invoking an Article 12 procedure would expose its own conduct to the full scrutiny of the ICC, thus discouraging politically-motivated charges and efforts to hold only one state accountable for alleged crimes within a situation.

Third objection: The ICC seems unconstitutional, it does not provide for a jury trial.

The US Department of Justice has ruled that there are no constitutional barriers to joining the ICC. A few countries (such as France) have made amendments to their Constitution to ensure the applicability of the ICC Statute.

According to a 25 July 2000 statement to the House Committee on International Relations on behalf of the American Bar Association, former Assistant General Counsel for International Affairs in the Office of Secretary of Defence and Legal Adviser to the Department of State Monroe Leigh stated that the 'Treaty of Rome contains the most comprehensive list of due process protections which has so far been promulgated'. The right to jury trial in the Bill of Rights applies only to cases heard in the US. Americans have been extradited for trial abroad for many years, even to judiciary systems not providing jury trials.

Fourth objection: There is no oversight built into the current structure of the ICC.

The Assembly of States Parties provides management oversight to the Presidency, the Prosecutor and the Registrar regarding the administration of the Court and ... performs 'any other function consistent with this Statute or the Rules of Procedure and Evidence'. US ratification of the Statute and the presence of US representatives in the Assembly would reinforce the latter's oversight functions. Another safeguard consequent to US ratification would be the presence of a US judge and other legal personnel in the Court.

US efforts in the Preparatory Commission to restrict the power of the Court to request the surrender of suspects have, so far, failed. US seats in the plenary and all of the working group sessions (except that on the crime of aggression) stood empty during the seventh session of the Commission in March 2001.

By the end of 2001, the Bush Administration had not yet issued its policy regarding the ICC. According to international law experts, a signature cannot be 'withdrawn'. Although the Statute has withdrawing provisions (Article 127), the US cannot withdraw from a treaty which it has not ratified. It seems that the only option for the Bush Administration would be to send a letter to the UN Secretary-General notifying him that the US has no intention to ratify the Statute.

On 7 December 2001, the US Senate passed Helms' 'American Service Members' Protection Act' as an amendment to the Defense Appropriations Act. On 20 December, as a welcome but limited reversal, both the House of Representatives and the Senate dropped the amendment from the final version of the Act when it adopted the Defense Department appropriations bill for Fiscal Year 2002. However, this bill contains a provision adopted by the House to prohibit the use of the Year 2002 Department's funds to cooperate with the Court. A similar amendment applying to the 2002 budgets for the State, Commerce and Justice Departments was approved by Congress in November 2001 and then signed by President Bush.[15]

The opposition of the US Congress and government to the ICC remains solid.

Promoting the ICC

For those who support the ICC, the creation of a permanent independent international criminal court is a significant progress in international relations and justice, which will provide an international judiciary mechanism to judge and sanction those responsible for the 'most serious crimes of concern to the international community as a whole' as a complement to national criminal jurisdictions, when national courts are either unwilling or unable to carry out investigations and prosecution. It will also, hopefully, have a preventive role. Even if the Statute is not perfect, it was the product of difficult negotiations, and should not be compromised by exemptions which might lead to more challenges and damage the promising ratification process. A permanent court would also obviate the need to create more ad hoc international criminal tribunals, and ensure consistency of international criminal jurisprudence. Finally, a global court would tend to be more independent than temporary ad hoc tribunals with limited jurisdiction.

[15] No Peace Without Justice, Essays, 'Anti-ICC American Servicemembers Protection Act dropped by House', Don Kraus, www.npwj.org/article.php?sid=115&mode=thead&order=0&thold=o.www.

European Countries

Before the adoption of the Statute, at a meeting of the Sixth Committee (Legal) of the UN General Assembly, Germany, on behalf of the EU, Australia and Austria spoke in favour of the creation of a permanent court while the US expressed reservations. On 17 July 1997, the UK Secretary of State for Foreign and Commonwealth Affairs, Robin Cook, gave strong support to the proposed creation of the court.

On 21 October 1998, Austria, speaking on behalf of the European Union and its associated countries and Iceland, said that the EU was 'extremely satisfied with the outcome of the Diplomatic Conference ... A major gap in the international legal order had been closed ... Such an institution would make the world a safer place ... The purpose of the Court was not only to punish those who committed crimes but through its mere existence to deter individuals from committing crimes in the first place'.[16]

Unlike the US, most of the Western democracies have signed and ratified the Statute and issued declarations of support. They have also opposed any proposal for amendments (read 'US proposals') that would weaken the integrity of the future ICC.

During the November 2000 session of the Preparatory Commission, the German representative announced the German ratification of the Treaty with a unanimous vote in the Bundestag. He said that the representatives of all parties emphasized the necessity to fully safeguard the integrity of the Rome Statute. The German government was warned not to admit any changes of or exemptions from the Statute, in particular related to the jurisdiction of the Court and to cooperation with the Court.[17]

In congratulating the states that had ratified the Statute at the time, a resolution of the European Parliament adopted on 18 January 2001[18] urged, in part,

> the Member States of the European Union and the applicant countries that have not yet ratified the Rome Treaty to do so as soon as possible, without opting out on war crimes pursuant to Article 124 of the Treaty;
> Welcomes US President Bill Clinton's signing of the Treaty on 31 December 2000, as well as the relevant signing by the Yugoslav Federation on 19 December 2000, and calls on both Parliaments to ratify the Treaty;

---

16 UN Doc. A/C.6/53/SR.9, 21 October 1998. This and other statements are found in 'Views and Comments by Governments' in Lee R. S. (ed.), *UNITAR, The International Criminal Court, The Making of the Rome Statute* (Kluwer Law International, The Hague, London, Boston, 1999), pp. 573–639.

17 UN *Press Release* DH/1759, 26 October 1994; UK Mission to the UN *Press Release*, 4 August 1997; Washington Working Group on the ICC, <www.wfa.org/issues/wicc/nationalsecurity.html>, 30 July 2001.

18 *The International Criminal Court Monitor*, May 2001.

> Asks EU Member States to take action in all appropriate seats to maintain and protect the integrity of the ICC Rome Statute, rejecting any proposal for amendment that would weaken the fairness, effectiveness or impartiality of the future ICC; (...)

On 11 June 2001, the EU Council adopted a common position on the ICC[19] stating that:

> The establishment of the International Criminal Court, for the purpose of preventing and curbing the commission of the serious crimes falling within its jurisdiction, is an essential means of promoting respect for international humanitarian law and human rights, thus contributing to freedom, security, justice and the rule of law as well as contributing to the preservation of peace and the strengthening of international security (...)

By January 2002, 12 European Union countries and 11 non-EU countries had ratified the Statute. Within the EU, further ratifications are expected shortly by Greece, Ireland and Portugal. Among non-EU countries, further ratifications are expected shortly by Bulgaria, Estonia, Macedonia, Romania and Slovakia.

African Countries

On 20 October 1998, South Africa, speaking on behalf of the Southern African Development Community, welcomed the adoption of the Statute, 'which would serve notice to those responsible for acts of genocide and other serious crimes that the culture of impunity was at an end ...The Statute would also serve as a reminder that even during armed conflict the rule of law must be upheld'. On 22 October 1998, Nigeria expressed support for the proposal to convene a Review Conference to consider the possibility of including terrorism, drug crimes and the use of nuclear weapons and landmines in the list of crimes within the jurisdiction of the Court.[20]

Ministers and Heads of Delegations of West African countries met in Bamako on 1–2 December 2000 for the African Intergovernmental Conference on the signing and ratification of the Rome Statute. In the Bamako Declaration, they noted, in general, that national legal systems have failed to punish the perpetrators of serious violations of International Humanitarian Law and Human Rights such as genocide, crimes against humanity and war crimes. They were aware of the importance of the early entry into force of the Statute of the ICC for Africa and for the international community as a whole in order to end this impunity and act as a powerful deterrent, and of the fact that an effective Court can obviate the need to resort to ad-hoc tribunals when massacres and other massive acts of violence are committed. In a

[19] *Official Journal of the European Communities*, 12.6.2001 L. 155/19.

[20] UN Doc. A/C.6/53/SR.9, 20 October 1998, and A/C.6/53/SR.12, 22 October 1998.

message to the Conference, the government of South Africa appealed to all the African States to ratify the Statute as soon as possible.

Even though Kenya signed the Statute on 11 August 1999, Connie Ngondi, Executive Director of Kenya's branch of the International Commission of Jurists warned that the ICC could be used to harass nations of the South. She added that there was also apprehension in Africa that an international criminal court would have too much power to intrude in a country's internal affairs.[21]

By January 2002, 10 African countries had ratified the Statute. Further ratifications are expected shortly from Angola, Benin, Cameroon, Congo Brazzaville, the Democratic Republic of the Congo, Côte d'Ivoire, Gambia, Guinea, Madagascar, Malawi, Mauritius, Namibia, Sao Tome and Principe, Cape Verde and Seychelles.

Asia and the Pacific

By January 2002, 5 countries had ratified the Statute. Further ratifications were expected shortly from Australia, Bangladesh, Cambodia, the Republic of Korea, Mongolia, the Philippines and Thailand. Japan is not yet a signatory and is only starting to study the Statute. As China found the Statute finally adopted 'riddled with deficiencies', it did not sign it and it is unlikely that it will adopt it in the foreseeable future.[22]

North America

Canada ratified the Statute on 7 July 2000.

The Mediterranean and Middle East

On 17 July 1998, Sudan, on behalf of the Arab Group of States, declared that Arab States were not happy with the adopted document: 'It was regrettable that just reference to aggression was included, as aggression is "the mother of all crimes". Also nuclear weapons should also be have been included ... The Prosecutor must also be under reasonable and logical control and not be ex-officio only ... Reservations should have been allowed'. On the other hand, Egypt said on 22 October that 'The Arab world had need for such a Court'.[23] In spite of Sudan's criticisms, 11 Arab countries are signatories of the Statute and Egypt will shortly ratify it.

[21] B. Crossette, 'World Criminal Court Having Painful Birth', in *New York Times*, 13 August 1997.

[22] UN Doc. A/C.6/53/SR.9, 21 October 1998.

[23] Press Release, L/ROM/22, 17 July 1998, and UN Doc. A/C.6/53/SR.12, 22 October 1998.

UN Organisations

Besides the strong support given by the UN Secretary-General, Kofi Annan, the heads of two UN agencies have vigorously and courageously endorsed the creation of the Court.

Former UN High Commissioner for Refugees, Sadako Ogata (Japan), in an article published by *The Washington Post* on 4 May 1997, deplored that in the decades since the Holocaust, 'we have not been able to prevent or halt even the most brutal forms of violence against whole groups of people'. Providing protection against evil lies at the heart of refugee protection. She said:

> We need a strong United Nations human rights machinery to prevent but also expose violations of human rights. We also need an International Criminal Court. The potential Pol Pots of this world – yes, the planners and not just the perpetrators – must be deterred by the prospects of criminal justice. And is it fair and realistic to expect the survivors to forgive and to cooperate if there is no justice? In the absence of justice, private revenge may prevail.

Carol Bellamy (US), Executive Director of UNICEF, declared at the opening session of the Hague Appeal for Peace on 12 May 1999:

> (...) UNICEF is ... insistent on the need to fight atrocities against children including rape as a weapon of war, by deploying a permanent, fully empowered International Criminal Court. The purveyors of genocide and ethnic cleansing and other unspeakable crimes must be made to understand that as surely as the sun rises, they will be called to account – and that impunity will not stand.

In May 1997, Bellamy had already called for the establishment of an international criminal court and a permanent prosecutor's office so that atrocities committed against children in conflict cannot go unpunished. She said:

> We have to recognise that these incidents [in Algeria, Zaire, Rwanda, Uganda, Bosnia and Herzegovina, in Central America] represent a deliberate targeting of children as part of an orchestrated campaign to terrorize and subjugate entire communities (...). UNICEF believes that those responsible cannot and must not be allowed to act with impunity. A permanent international criminal court, and a permanent prosecutor's office would mean that, for the first time, the world will have the capacity to bring to justice those responsible for the torture, the rape and the murder of children.[24]

Her call for action endorsed the recommendation of a UN-sponsored report prepared by Graça Machel (Mozambique), Expert of the UN Secretary-General on the Impact of Armed Conflict on Children. The report, presented to the UN General

---

[24] Amnesty International, 'The International Criminal Court, Fact Sheet 8, Ensuring justice for children', 1 August 2000; <cicc@igc.apc.org>, 'UNICEF ED calls for ICC', 9 May 1997.

Assembly in November 1996, warned that if perpetrators of war crimes go unpunished, it will lead to contempt for the law and renewed cycles of violence. Ms Machel stated that, unless those at every level of political and military command fear that they will be accountable for crimes and subject to prosecution, there is little prospect of restraining their behaviour during armed conflicts. She said: 'A permanent court would only speed up the process. It would be a major step towards protecting children caught up in armed conflict'.

The International Committee of the Red Cross (ICRC)

While the Geneva Conventions of the Red Cross require that sanctions be applied by national authorities to those who violate their obligations, the ICRC has itself recognised that the existing system for the repression of war crimes (relying only on national justice) is still too often ignored. This is the reason why the ICRC has consistently and actively supported the establishment of a fair and effective International Criminal Court and welcomed the adoption of its Statute.

On 22 October 1998, the Observer for the ICRC said that a particularly welcome feature of the Statute was that the Court could try crimes committed during non-international armed conflicts: it had been recognised that rape, torture, wilful killing, hostage-taking and attacks against the civilian population were war crimes in internal armed conflicts as well as in wars between States. It was to be hoped that the use of weapons of mass destruction, anti-personnel mines and blinding weapons would be added to the list of war crimes at the Review Conference. 'An even greater disappointment arose from Article 124, which created a distinction between war crimes and other crimes'.[25]

As an Observer, the ICRC has contributed to the drafting of the Rules of Procedure and Evidence and to the definition of the Elements of Crimes adopted by the ICC Preparatory Commission.

In October 2000, the ICRC continued to call upon States which had not already done so to promptly sign and ratify the Statute, for three reasons: First, to send a strong message of deterrence to those who would continue to flout the most elementary laws of mankind. Second, to bring the ICC into force at the earliest possible moment, thereby losing no opportunity to bring to justice those who commit the most heinous crimes against their fellow humans. Third, to convey a message in support of the ICC to those States that have not yet become convinced of the Court's rightful place in the scheme of international justice – a place reflecting the recognition that certain crimes are so serious that they concern the international community as a whole. The ICRC invited States to avail themselves of the technical assistance of its Advisory Service on international humanitarian law in connection with ratification and national implementation of the Rome Statute. The ICRC expressed the hope that the continuing work of the Preparatory Commission would

[25] UN Doc. A/C.6/53/SR.12, 22 October 1998.

not result in a dilution of the integrity of the Rome Statute. The Committee also reaffirmed its wish to see States refrain from declaring, as they are entitled to under Article 124, that they do not accept the jurisdiction of the Court for a period of seven years with respect to war crimes alleged to have been committed by their nationals or on their territory.

In a direct rebuttal of some of the US objections (without referring by name to the US), with regard to the jurisdiction of the Court, the ICRC has usefully recalled that a state on whose territory a crime is committed has the authority to prosecute a national of another state, without regard to the consent of that other state. There is no doubt about the right of a state to delegate this authority to an international tribunal. Secondly, war crimes, crimes against humanity and genocide are already subject to universal jurisdiction under customary international law. Thus, any State may prosecute anyone for such crimes, regardless where they are committed. The Geneva Conventions go even further, imposing an obligation on States to either try or extradite those who may have committed war crimes qualified as grave breaches.[26]

The Influence of NGOs

The NGO Coalition for an ICC, created in 1995, has had a determining influence over governments in obtaining a successful outcome to the Rome Conference. In 1996, the Coalition had 78 participating organisations, including law associations (comprising the International Commission of Jurists and the International Bar Association), human rights groups (among them, Amnesty International, Fédération internationale des Ligues des droits de l'homme, Human Rights Watch), parliamentarian associations, Church or religious groups (Coordinating Board of Jewish Organisations, Evangelical Lutheran Church in America, Quaker UN Office), universities and institutes concerned with international humanitarian and criminal law, from the USA, Canada, Denmark, India, Italy, the Netherlands, France. As reported by Pace and Thieroff,[27] from its inception, the Coalition brought together a broad-based network of NGOs and international law experts to develop strategies on substantive legal and political issues relating to the proposed Statute. The key goal of the Coalition was to foster awareness and support for the Court among a wide range of civil society organisations, including those focusing on human rights, international law, humanitarian issues, peace, the rights of women and children, religion and other issues. The Coalition served as both a facilitator for civil society involvement in the negotiating process as well as the world's principal source of information on the ICC. By the beginning of the Conference, the Coalition had

[26] UN General Assembly, 55th session, Sixth Committee, agenda item 162, *Statement by the ICRC*, New York, 19 October 2000; agenda item 158, *Statement by the ICRC*', New York, 22 October 1999.

[27] William R. Pace and Mark Thieroff, 'Participation of Non-Governmental Organisations' in Lee R. S. (ed.), *UNITAR, The International Criminal Court, The Making of the Rome Statute* (Kluwer Law International, The Hague, London, Boston, 1999), p. 392.

grown into a movement involving more than 800 organisations. Of the 236 NGOs accredited to the Conference, most were members of the Coalition. These organisations were represented by an estimated 450 individuals.Many governments, the UN Secretary-General, other UN officials and media experts have commented on the decisive role of NGOs at the Conference.

Following the Rome Conference of 1998, the Coalition has continued and expanded its work, bringing together a network of over 1000 NGOs, international law experts and other civil society groups. The multi-track approach of the Coalition involves promoting education and awareness of the ICC and the Rome Statute at the national, regional and global level; supporting the successful completion of the mandate of the Preparatory Commission and facilitating NGO involvement in this process; strengthening its global network. Its main current objective is to promote the universal ratification of the Rome Statute, including the adoption of comprehensive national implementing legislation following ratification.

Some of its activities include:

- Convening sectoral caucuses (Women's, Children's, Faith, Peace, and Victims), national and regional networks, and working groups on specific issues;
- Maintaining a World Wide Web site and e-mail lists to facilitate the exchange of NGO and expert documentation and information concerning the ICC negotiations and the ad hoc Tribunals and to foster discussion and debate about substantive issues;
- Facilitating meetings between the Coalition and government representatives, UN officials and others involved in ICC negotiations;
- Promoting education and awareness of the ICC negotiations at relevant public and professional conferences – including UN conferences, committees, commissions and preparatory meetings;
- Producing newsletters, bulletins, media advisories, reviews and papers on all aspects of efforts to establish the ICC.[28]

'No Peace Without Justice' (NPWJ), one member of the Coalition, has a broader mandate than that of the Coalition, like many other NGOs participating in the Coalition. It has its own membership and activities. NPWJ is an international committee of parliamentarians, mayors and citizens, whose objective is the establishment of an effective system of international justice. In particular, its goals are to contribute to the development and reform of existing international institutions, to support the mandate of the ICTY and ICTR, to ensure that human rights are enforced in member States of the UN and to campaign for the establishment of the ICC.

NPWJ was created in 1993 with the support of the Transnational Radical Party, following the outbreak of the war in the Former Yugoslavia and shocked by the atrocities committed there. Since then, NPWJ has played a prominent role, together

[28] See <www.igc.org/icc/html/coalition.htm>.

with other NGOs, in the campaign for creation of the ICTY, and more recently for the creation of the ICC. In 1996, NPWJ launched its first International Appeal promoted by Emma Bonino (Italy), European Commissioner and signed by more than 30 world leaders and over 600 parliamentarians of various countries. The Appeal demanded that a Diplomatic Conference for the establishment of the ICC be held in 1998. In 1997–1998, a NPWJ Campaign for the establishment of the ICC was launched at the Conference held in Paris on 19 and 20 June 1997. The meeting was convened by Emma Bonino and Senator Robert Badinter, former President of the French Constitutional Council. A number of conferences were organised by NPWJ during and after the Rome Conference.

On 26 January 2001, a solemn appeal was launched by Emma Bonino, Professor Giovanni Conso, Ambassador Philippe Kirsch, Professor Cherif Bassiouni and Senator Robert Badinter, signed by more than 50 global leaders and fully endorsing the proposal by the NGO Coalition for the ICC to secure the 60 ratifications as soon as possible and, in any case, by the target date of 17 July 2002. At a meeting on 30 March to 1 April 2001, the participants at the NPWJ Strategy Meeting held in Ischia, adopted a Plan of Action to obtain the effective implementation and entry into force of the Rome Statute through the organisation and facilitation of a series of coordinated activities at country and regional levels, including awareness raising, judicial assistance and technical cooperation.[29]

The Potential Immunity of North States

One potential problem for the future ICC is whether its investigations and prosecutions will be limited to 'situations' and alleged perpetrators in South countries, while the leaders in rich, powerful or important North States, including the permanent members of the Security Council, will enjoy a de facto immunity.

Among the five permanent members of the Security Council, the Russian political and military leaders would be well-identified targets for crimes allegedly committed by the Russian army in the 'Chechnya war situation', with the blessing if not the encouragement of the highest authorities in Moscow (see Chapter 1).

If Russia continues its violations of human rights and humanitarian law in Chechnya after the entry into force of the ICC Statute, investigations and prosecutions by the Court would be subject to the basic condition that Russia becomes a Party to the Statute (Russia has signed the Statute on 13 September 2000), or lodges a declaration with the Registrar accepting the exercise of jurisdiction by the Court with respect to these crimes, as Chechnya is part of the Russian Federation. Investigations could then be initiated by the Prosecutor proprio motu, or at the request of a State Party (Art. 12, 15 and 14 of the Statute). The Security Council, acting under Chapter VII of the UN Charter, may ask the Prosecutor to investigate the Chechnya situation (Art. 13(b)): however, Russia could veto such a request.

[29] See <www.npwj.org/who.html>, <www.npwj,org/campaigns/ischia/index.htm>.

Finally, the Security Council could request the Court not to commence or proceed with an investigation or prosecution for a renewable period of 12 months, in a resolution adopted under Chapter VII of the UN Charter (Art. 16): this would require a majority of nine votes, including the five permanent members of the Council.

Other 'powerful' or important countries, including democracies, may also become targets for prosecution by the Court, unless they show that alleged violations of international criminal law are being investigated by their own national courts.

CONCLUSION

The adoption of the Statute by 120 states on 17 July 1998 was an unexpected achievement and it is now probable that the Statute of the ICC will be ratified by 60 states in 2002 or in 2003, giving birth to the new Court. In itself, this process is a significant and innovative advance in international law, as it will create for the first time in history a permanent, global international judiciary mechanism to identify, investigate, judge and sanction those individuals found responsible for the "most serious crimes of concern to the international community as a whole'. The new institution will judge, not the indifferent and unaccountable states, but those criminal leaders responsible directly or indirectly for genocide, crimes against humanity, war crimes and, when these are defined, crimes of aggression. Through the expected implementation of the Statute on the basis of a reconstructed international criminal law, the Court should be an effective tool to erode progressively the long-standing impunity of untouchable leaders protected by the sovereignty of their state and their own status. It should also give a measure of relief to the millions of innocent victims and their families who have suffered violence, torture and death. It may, hopefully, act as a deterrent against the potential crimes of present or future leaders.

The negotiation and adoption of the Statute required compromises between the universal human demand for justice and governments' fears of loss of sovereignty. The final 'product', with its limitations, necessarily reflects most of the current political forces in the international community, without fully satisfying all governmental and non-governmental actors.

There are important caveats before one adopts a complacent and perhaps illusory belief that the Court will solve all the world's problems, or more specifically, that justice will now prevail over politics, and that advances in international law and justice will be effective in the short- or mid-term. Obstacles and problems are many.

The first hurdle is to obtain the ratification of 60 states, a process which is strongly supported and actively promoted by 'like-minded' states, all Western countries except the USA, influential national and international personalities and groups, a few intergovernmental organisations, many vocal human rights and humanitarians NGOs. It is noteworthy that the International Committee of the Red Cross has actively and constructively supported the creation of the ICC in spite of its long-standing doctrine of neutrality. Most ICC supporters have called against any dilution of the integrity of the adopted Statute, and several have asked State Parties not to have recourse to Article 124.

With the entry into force of the Statute, the major problem to be faced by the Court will be to obtain the cooperation of State Parties and/or of the Security Council in identifying situations in which one or more crimes within its jurisdiction have allegedly been committed. Will State Parties and/or the Security Council then allow the Prosecutor to initiate investigations and the Judges to exercise their jurisdiction? The new Court, like Gulliver, will be tied by many visible and invisible bonds, which may paralyze or at least delay its action. Its lack of enforcement powers, as shown by the experience of the ICTY and ICTR, may prevent or delay the arrest and transfer of accused to the Court, hamper the production of evidence and the testimony of witnesses.

It is likely that the action of the Court will soon be faced by sensitive political obstacles. Its Prosecutor and Judges will need to demonstrate publicly and repeatedly their competence, independence and impartiality in order to overcome these obstacles and establish and maintain the integrity of the Court. The issue faced by the ICTY regarding allegations of NATO crimes, and that faced by the ICTR concerning alleged crimes committed by Tutsi forces illustrate the type of problems to be resolved by the future Court.

The negative vote of China, the possible refusal of Russia to ratify the Statute, and, even more, the refusal of the USA to become a State Party without major amendments to the Statute will constitute serious handicaps for the installation, financing and functioning of the Court. US support has been a determining factor in the creation and relative achievements of the Nuremberg and Tokyo Tribunals, and of the ICTY and ICTR. It is unfortunate that the position of the US Administration and Congress is that international law, international human rights and international justice are meant for foreign countries and their citizens, not for the USA and Americans. One can only hope that the present or a future US Administration will understand that the US has a major role to play in the creation of permanent international justice in line with its strong support for the rule of law at the national level. More concretely, the new Court would benefit from American legal expertise and experience, and from the presence of US legal specialists among its staff. Once a State Party, the US could exercise its influence from within, rather than playing the part of the odd state out.

The Court's value will have to be established and weighed on the basis of the performance of its members, e.g. their competence, integrity, independence and courage. ICC supporters will have to watch carefully over the selection and appointment process of the Prosecutor and Judges.

In the words of Amnesty International,[30]

---

30 Pace and Thieroff, p. 396.

The true significance of the adoption of the Statute may well lie, not in the actual institution itself in its early years, which will face enormous obstacles, but in the revolution in legal and moral attitudes towards the worst crimes in the world. No longer will these crimes be simply political events to be addressed by diplomacy at the international level, but crimes which all states have a duty to punish themselves or, if they fail to fulfil this duty, by the international community in accordance with the rule of law.

CHAPTER 5

THE PINOCHET EFFECT

On 16 October 1998, General Augusto Pinochet, former President of Chile, was arrested in London by the London police at the request of a Spanish warrant charging the former dictator with human crimes committed in Chile during his 17-year rule.

This arrest and its subsequent legal and political developments, a few weeks after the adoption of the Statute of the International Criminal Court, uncovered and triggered a number of initiatives based on the concept of universal jurisdiction, in parallel to the slow process towards international criminal justice.

PINOCHET'S CHILE

In 1970, Dr Salvador Allende, a Marxist and member of Chile's Socialist Party, who headed the 'Popular Unity' (UP) coalition of Socialists, Communists, Radicals, and dissident Christian Democrats, was elected with 36% of the vote and by a plurality of 36 000 votes.[1] His programme included nationalization of private industries and banks, including nationalization of US interests in major copper mines, land expropriation and collectivization. Under the influence of the Chilean extreme right and part of the army, with US covert support, a strategy of destabilization, kidnapping and assassination was designed in order to provoke the fall of the Allende government. The economy deteriorated following shortages of consumer goods and industrial products, strikes and violence. By 1973, Chile had split into two hostile camps. A US-supported military coup overthrew Allende on 11 September 1973. As the armed forces bombarded the presidential palace, Allende reportedly

[1] Facts in this section are based, in part, from <www.worldrover.com/history/chile_history.html>, 29 March 2001, and <www.lcweb2.loc.gov/cgi-bin/query/r?frd/cstdy@field(DOCID+c10042-43,44,45>, 29 March 2001. The involvement of the Nixon Administration and of the CIA is documented in Christopher Hitchens, 'The Case Against Henry Kissinger – Part I: The making of a war criminal – Part II: Crimes Against Humanity', *Harper's Magazine*, February 2001, pp. 33–58; March 2001, pp. 49–74. On 30 June 1999, the US released approximately 5800 documents (approximately 20 000 pages) containing detailed reports – some of which were prepared by the CIA – of widespread human rights abuses by the Chilean military after the 1973 coup: see S. D. Murphy (Ed.), 'US Assistance Regarding Information on Former Chilean President Pinochet', *American Journal of International Law*, Vol. 94, April 2000, pp. 368–369.

committed suicide. General Augusto Pinochet soon emerged as the dominant figure and became president. The government evolved into a one-man dictatorship, with the rest of the junta acting as a sort of a legislature. Pinochet made himself not only the chief executive of the state but also the commander in chief of the military.

The armed forces justified the coup as necessary to stamp out Marxism, avert class warfare, restore order, and salvage the economy. The first phase of the dictatorship (1973–1975) was mainly destructive, aimed at the physical elimination of the political opponents. The armed forces treated the members of the UP as an enemy to be obliterated. The worst human rights abuses occurred in the first four years of the junta, when thousands of civilians were murdered, jailed, tortured or exiled, especially those connected with the UP parties. In the first 19 days of Pinochet's rule summary executions totaled 320. The secret police, reporting to Pinochet through the National Intelligence Directorate (Direccion Nacional de Inteligencia – DINA), replaced in 1977 by the National Information Centre (Centro Nacional de Informacion – CNI), kept political opponents in fear of arrest, torture, murder or 'disappearance'. Throughout the second half of the 1970s, leftist political parties in Europe and other democratic groups outside of Chile, human rights NGOs, the Roman Catholic Church and other Christian denominations denounced the widespread violations of human rights in Chile. Former members of UP went underground or into exile.

The US gave strong military, logistic and financial support to Pinochet's Chile during the presidencies of Richard Nixon and Gerald R. Ford. Relations soured after Jimmy Carter was elected President in 1976 on a platform promising vigorous pursuit of human rights as a major component of his foreign policy. During Carter's administration, a source of contention was the assassination in Washington, D.C., of the former Chilean ambassador to the US, Orlando Letelier and his aide, Ronni Moffitt, in September 1976, by agents of Pinochet's secret police.

According to a new Constitution approved in a controlled plebiscite in 1980, Pinochet would remain President through 1989 and would retain his control of the Army as its commander. A plebiscite in 1988 would determine if he would have an additional eight years in office. From 1982 to 1990, Chile went through a prolonged journey back to democracy. Revived political parties took charge during the 1988 plebiscite that effectively ended the Pinochet regime and the 1989 elections for president and Congress. After being surroundered by other dictators in Latin America, Pinochet became isolated as democratization was progressing in the region, and the US and Europe applied pressure for Chile to join the trend.

The Christian-Democrat Patricio Aylwin won the presidential elections in December 1989 with 55% of the votes. He was president from 1990 to 1993, and was then succeeded by Eduardo Frei, of the same party. The socialist Ricardo Lagos, a faithful ally of Allende and a minister in both previous presidencies, won the elections in January 2000. His six-year term of office started in March 2000.[2]

[2] *Le Monde*, 16 January 2000.

In April 1990, President Aylwin created the National Commission for Truth and Reconciliation (the Rettig Commission, by the name of its chairman). The Commission's report, released on 4 March 1991, implicated the military and secret police at the highest levels in the deaths or disappearances of 2279 persons between September 1973 and March 1990. By the end of 1994, the total number of people who had been killed or had disappeared under the military dictatorship was officially acknowledged to be more than 3000. However, as a result of the protection provided by an amnesty law for all political crimes issued by the Pinochet government in 1978, only a few perpetrators were judged and sentenced by civilian courts for human rights violations.[3]

THE PROSECUTION OF PINOCHET

In 1996, lawyers acting on behalf of victims of military repression in Argentina and Chile who were unable to pursue their claims in those countries filed criminal complaints in Spain against the former military leaders, including General Pinochet, using the principle of 'universal jurisdiction' over human rights violations.[4]

In October 1998, Pinochet travelled to England. On 16 October, he was arrested by the London police on the basis of an arrest warrant of Baltasar Garzon, a Spanish judge, that he be held in London prior to extradition to Madrid, on charges of genocide, torture and kidnapping in connection with the death or disappearance of 3197 people in the period 1973–1990, and more specifically the murder of Spanish citizens in Chile. These alleged crimes were in breach of Spanish law relating to genocide, torture and terrorism. At the time of his arrest, Pinochet was in a London clinic, recuperating from back surgery and planning to return to Chile a week later. Extradition was also sought by Belgium, France, Italy, Luxembourg, Sweden and Switzerland for alleged crimes committed against their own nationals in Chile.

On 17 October, the Chilean government protested his arrest on the ground that, as a former head of state, he had sovereign immunity. This view was upheld in a unanimous verdict by a three-judge panel of England's High Court on 28 October, but reversed in a three-to-two decision of five Law Lords on 25 November. In this judgement, the Law Lords ruled that although a former head of state enjoys immunity for acts committed in his functions as head of state, crimes such as torture and crimes against humanity were not 'functions' of a head of state. On the same date, Mary Robinson, the UN High Commissioner for Human Rights, welcomed the Lords' decision, raising hope that Augusto Pinochet would finally be brought before a court to face allegations of violations of human rights. On 1 December, the US Administration declared publicly that it was in favour of Pinochet's return to Chile while firmly condemning abuses committed by his regime. On 17 December, the

3 See Beigbeder (1999), pp. 107–108.

4 See 'The Pinochet Precedent, How Victims can pursue Human Rights Criminals Abroad', Human Rights Watch <www.hrw.org/campaigns/chile98/precedent.htm>, 13 March 2000.

Appeals Committee of the House of Lords quashed the Law Lords' decision of 25 November in view of the links with Amnesty International of one of the three judges who had voted with the majority. On 19 February 1999, the Vatican made a diplomatic intervention to the British government in favour of the liberation of Pinochet. On 24 March, the Law Lords, in a six-to-one decision, ruled that Pinochet must remain in England and face possible extradition to Spain but they significantly narrowed the charges. Immunity as a former head of state was still rejected, but only for the period 1988–1990: the UK had signed the UN Convention against Torture in 1988. The accused could therefore not be extradited on allegations of crimes committed before 1988: all but three of the 32 charges issued by the Spanish judge were thus dismissed. On 15 April, Home Secretary Jack Straw authorized the start of extradition proceedings. The remaining charges were sufficient and the Spanish extradition request well-founded. He concluded that Mr Pinochet 'does not enjoy immunity in relation to the extradition crimes of conspiracy to torture and torture'.[5]

On 2 March 2000, Jack Straw refused Pinochet's extradition to Spain and allowed him to return to Chile, on the basis of a medical examination by four British specialists concluding that he no longer had the mental capacity to stand trial. According to the *Daily Telegraph* of 3 March 2000, the Foreign Office Secretary, Robin Cook and his Spanish counterpart, Abel Matutes, had agreed, during a meeting in June 1999 in Rio de Janeiro, to avoid the death of the former dictator, sick and 84 years-old, in the UK or in Spain.[6]

The next day, a smiling General Pinochet walked unaided to the helicopter on his arrival in Santiago, with a hero's welcome staged by the armed forces, a welcome deplored by the Chilean government.

Also in March 2000, judiciary proceedings started in Chile against the former dictator. On 6 March, Chilean Judge Juan Guzman, investigating 61 civil cases of rights abuses, formally asked a Santiago court of appeals to consider whether Pinochet should lose his immunity from prosecution as a 'senator for life', and would be tried for a 'Death Caravan' that killed at least 74 political opponents after the coup of 1973. As the corpses of 19 of the victims had not been found, Judge Guzman had claimed these were 'permanent' crimes which could not be protected by the amnesty imposed by Pinochet in 1978. This law covers homicides committed between 1973 and 1978. Pinochet then appealed against the court's decision to lift his parliamentary immunity as a 'senator for life', a function he held since 1998, when he was no longer commander in chief of the armed forces. On 8 August 2000, Chile's Supreme Court rejected his appeal by a clear majority of 14 against 6, a non-appealable decision. The judgement was based on Pinochet's responsibility in the crimes of the Death Caravan. The Court considered that there were founded

5 The Opinions of the five Law Lords read on 25 November 1988 are in www.reports.guardian.co.uk/sp_reports/pinochet/judgements/pino01.htm. See also *IHT*, 25 March and 14 April 1999; *Le Monde*, 16 April 1999. Mary Robinson's statement is in www.un.or./News/dh/latest.htm//11, 25 November 1998.

6 As reported in *Le Monde*, 4 March 2000. See also *IHT*, 13 January 2000.

suspicions on the fact that Pinochet had directly ordered these summary executions. The ruling gave further impetus to the legal doctrine followed by Guzman that 'disappearances' are not covered by the amnesty law. On 11 December, the Santiago Appeals Court dismissed criminal charges filed on 1 December by Judge Guzman against General Pinochet, on a procedural point. By a 3-to-0 vote, the Court ruled that Judge Guzman should have first interrogated General Pinochet before putting him under arrest and charging him. On 20 December, the Supreme Court first upheld the Appeals Court ruling that revoked the indictment of General Pinochet: in a 4-to-1 vote, it agreed that Judge Guzman's indictment was invalid because the judge failed to question the accused. The Court then ordered Judge Guzman to interview General Pinochet within 20 days about his responsibility for homicides and kidnappings committed after the 1973 coup. The Court stated that the interview must be carried out regardless of whether medical tests have been done to establish whether the 85-year-old former dictator was mentally fit to stand trial. Pinochet underwent medical tests from 10 to 12 January 2001, which reportedly found that he suffered from a degree of mental impairment. On 23 January, Judge Guzman finally questioned Pinochet at his Santiago home. On 29 January, the Judge again indicted General Pinochet for kidnapping and murder. Also in January, the armed forces admitted that the bodies of 130 of the 1 200 people who disappeared during Pinochet's 1973–1990 dictatorship had been thrown into the sea or into Chile's lakes. This admission formally confirmed previously-known information.[7]

On 9 July 2001, the Santiago Appeals Court suspended the proceedings against Pinochet on health grounds, thus ending the belated, unexpected and suspenseful judiciary prosecution of the former dictator at the international and national levels.[8]

THE PINOCHET PRECEDENT

General Pinochet was neither extradited to and judged in Spain, nor judged in Chile. However, these apparent defeats were at the same time a significant advance in the legal and judiciary fight against the impunity of criminal leaders at both the international and national levels.

This advance has been the result of tenacious, competent and courageous judges, Baltasar Garzon in Spain and Juan Guzman in Chile, and other judges and lawyers in other countries, with the strong motivation given by victims or their families and

[7] See *Le Monde*, 10 August 2000; *IHT*, 7 March, 2–3 December and 12 December 2000; – 'Chile Supreme Court Rejects Pinochet Immunity', Human Rights Watch, hrwatchnyc@igc.org, 8 August 2000, 'Chilean Appellate Court Ruling on Pinochet Criticised, Mounting Pressure On Chilean Judiciary', HRW hrwatchnyc@igc.org, 11 December 2000, HRW 'Chile: Pinochet to Undergo Questioning, Supreme Court leaves dor open for Pinochet prosecution', hrwatchnyc@igc.org, 20 December 2000, HRW 'Re-Instatement of Pinochet Charges Hailed', hrwatchnyc@igc.org, 29 January 2001; *The Economist*, 3 February 2001.

[8] Human Rights Watch World Report 2001, Chile, 'Pinochet Decision Lamented, but rights group says case a Landmark', www.hrw.org/press/2001/07/pino0709.htm, 9 July 2001.

their representatives and, in general, the concern for justice for all, with the determined and persistent support of human rights organisations such as Human Rights Watch, Amnesty International, the International Federation of Human Rights Leagues and others.

At the international level, for the first time, a former head of state has been arrested and indicted in a country other than his own for crimes allegedly committed during his tenure in his own country against Chilean and other nationals. His immunity was lifted by the Law Lords in a first judgement, later annulled, on the grounds that, although a former head of state enjoys immunity for acts committed in his functions as head of state, international crimes such as torture and crimes against humanity were not 'functions' of a head of state. In the second, more limited judgement, the Lords held that once the UK and Chile had ratified the 1984 UN Convention against Torture and Other Cruel Inhuman or Degrading Treatment or Punishment, Pinochet could not claim immunity for torture. A British magistrate then determined that Pinochet could be extradited to Spain (which had also ratified the Convention) on charges of torture and conspiracy to commit torture. As Lord Browne-Wilkinson, the senior Judge in the Pinochet Case, said: 'The purpose of the Convention was to introduce the principle aut dedere aut punire – either you extradite or you punish'.[9]

At the national level, the second victory was that, after his return to Chile, Pinochet was indicted and prosecuted in his own country in spite of the angry resistance of the military, a considerable achievement due to the progress of Chilean democracy and the evolution of public opinion when Pinochet was arrested in London and the object of judiciary proceedings. Thanks again to the persistence and ingenuity of the judges, the amnesty law of 1978 intended to shield the military was circumvented. The courts have reinterpreted that law, ruling that because relatives of the 'disappeared' live in constant torment, not knowing the fate of their loved ones, the disappearances are a continuing crime, extending beyond the years covered by the amnesty. Pinochet's subordinates will face human rights trials. It is ironical that the junte's strategy of having their victims 'disappeared', thus suppressing potential witnesses, was turned against the military, who had to confess to some of their crimes.

Universal Jurisdiction

For centuries, jurisdiction over a crime has depended on a link, usually territorial, between the prosecuting state and the crime.

Universal jurisdiction was first initiated by the Geneva Conventions which defined war crimes, then developed on the basis of the new legal concept of 'crimes against

[9] Quoted in HRW 'The Pinochet Precedent', www.hrw.org/campaigns/chile98/precedent/htm, 13 March 2000. Credits are also given to the same HRW document for the definition of 'universal jurisdiction' and its application.

humanity', inscribed in the Nuremberg Charter, the Statutes of the ICTY and ICTR, and the Statute of the ICC, then on the basis of the Convention against Genocide and the Convention against Torture. Such grave crimes are of concern to all mankind and their perpetrators, whatever their rank or status, must be brought to justice, no matter where the crime was committed, and regardless of the nationality of the perpetrators or their victims. Universal jurisdiction should ensure that there is no safe haven for those responsible for the most serious crimes.

A first area where universal jurisdiction may be claimed is that of war crimes. Traditionally, war crimes refer to crimes in international armed conflicts, and more precisely to 'grave breaches' of the four Geneva Conventions of 1949 and their first Additional Protocol of 1977. Each of the widely ratified four Geneva Conventions prescribe that 'each High Contracting Party shall be under the obligation to search for persons alleged to have committed, or to have ordered to be committed, such grave breaches, and shall bring such persons, regardless of their nationality, before its own courts. It may also, if it prefers, and in accordance with the provisions of its own legislation, hand such persons over for trial to another High Contracting Party concerned, provided such High Contracting Party has made out a prima facie case'. Article 88 of Protocol I prescribes that ' (...) when circumstances permit, the High Contracting Parties shall cooperate in the matter of extradition. They shall give due consideration to the request of the State in whose territory the alleged offence has occurred'.[10] More recently, the concept of war crimes has extended to internal conflicts, in accordance with Article 3 common to all the Geneva Conventions, thus giving third party states the right to exercise universal jurisdiction.

Under customary international law, universal jurisdiction may be the basis for prosecution for genocide. The Genocide Convention of 1948 provides for the trial and penalties by national tribunals, and by 'such international penal tribunal as may have jurisdiction with respect to those Contracting Parties which shall have accepted its jurisdiction'. The Contracting Parties also 'pledge themselves to grant extradition in accordance with their laws and treaties in force' (Art. VI and VII).

The second judgement of the British Lords was based on the Convention against Torture adopted by the UN General Assembly on 10 December 1984. Article 4 of the Convention prescribes that 'Each State Party shall ensure that all acts of torture are offences under its criminal law (...)'. Under Article 5

> 1. Each State Party shall take such measures as may be necessary to establish its jurisdiction over the offences referred to in Article 4 in the following cases:
>
> (a) When the offences are committed in any territory under its jurisdiction or on board a ship or aircraft registered in that State;
> (b) When the alleged offender is a national of that State;

[10] First Geneva Convention, Art. 49, Second Geneva Convention, Art. 50, Third Geneva Convention, Art. 129, Fourth Geneva Convention, Art. 146, Protocol I, Art. 85–88, Protocol II, Art. 6.

(c) When the victim is a national of that State if that State considers it appropriate (. . .)

Article 8 provides for extradition: '(. . .) States Parties undertake to include such offences as extraditable offences in every extradition treaty to be concluded between then'.

However, in each case, whether a prosecution may be brought based on universal jurisdiction will depend on the laws of the particular state in which the case is brought (the prosecuting state).

In many civil law countries, ratified treaties (and even customary international law in some cases) are automatically part of national legislation, without need for specific legislation to implement the instrument. In many other countries, treaties must be specifically incorporated into domestic law before they can be relied on.

Kissinger's Case Against Universal Jurisdiction

In a recent article,[11] Henry A. Kissinger has underlined 'The Pitfalls of Universal Jurisdiction'. For the author,

> The doctrine of universal jurisdiction asserts that some crimes are so heinous that their perpetrators should not escape justice by invoking doctrines of sovereign immunity or the sacrosanct nature of national frontiers. Two specific approaches to achieve this goal have emerged recently. The first seeks to apply the procedures of domestic criminal justice to violations of universal standards, some of which are embodied in United Nations conventions, by authorizing national prosecutors to bring offenders into their jurisdictions through extradition from third countries. The second approach is the International Criminal Court (. . .)

He adds that the notion that heads of state and senior public officials should have the same standing as pirates, hijackers and similar outlaws whose crimes were typically committed outside the territory of any state 'is quite new'. For Kissinger,

> The danger lies in pushing the effort to extremes that risk substituting the tyranny of judges for that of governments; historically, the dictatorship of the virtuous has often led to inquisitions and even witch-hunts.

Calling the Pinochet case 'a dangerous precedent', he considers that the

> Unprecedented and sweeping interpretation of international law in Ex parte Pinochet would arm any magistrate anywhere in the world with the power to demand extradition, substituting the magistrate's own judgement for the

[11] Henry A. Kissinger, 'The Pitfalls of Universal Jurisdiction', *Foreign Affairs*, Vol. 80, No. 4, July/August 2001, pp. 86–96. This essay is adapted from his book *Does America need a Foreign Policy? Toward a Diplomacy for the 21st Century.*

> reconciliation procedures of even incontestably democratic societies where alleged violations of human rights may have occurred.

Kissinger allies himself with the US opposition to the ICC Statute, which, in the views of the US, should be renegotiated. He rejects any formal system which would not contain the following three provisions:

> First, the UN Security Council should create a Human Rights Commission or a special subcommittee to report whenever systematic human rights violations seem to warrant judicial action. Second, when the government under which the alleged crime occurred is not authentically representative, or where the domestic judicial system is incapable of sitting in judgement on the crime, the Security Council would set up an ad hoc international tribunal on the model of those of the former Yugoslavia or Rwanda. And third, the procedures for these international tribunals as well as the scope of prosecution should be precisely defined by the Security Council, and the accused should be entitled to the due process safeguards accorded in common jurisdictions.

Kissinger's opposition both to universal jurisdiction and to the ICC is understandable for a former US Secretary of State and National Security Adviser with a record as a realpolitic practitioner and promoter of US interests through overt and covert means. His rejection of international justice however ignores the pleas of past and new victims for making their tormentors accountable for their crimes, and for some measure of reparation. For an American, his reference to a 'tyranny of the judges' sounds shallow, as the US Supreme Court has often ruled on political and social issues. In many countries, national justice has long been subjected to the 'tyranny' of governments, and their relative independence from government pressures or fiats has only appeared recently in a few democratic countries through democratic progress and the courage of a few judges, determined that the law should apply to all. However, their work is to apply national and international laws, not to take illegal initiatives. International criminal prosecutors and judges are not free of control: their work is constrained by the Statutes of their Tribunal, and they depend on the cooperation of governments to accomplish many of their procedures.

Henry Kissinger has recently been the object of judiciary requests by French and Latin American judges asking for his testimony. On 28 May 2001, he was asked by French Judge Roger Le Loire to appear as a witness in an investigation into the disappearance of French citizens during the Chilean dictatorship. The US Embassy told the court that Mr Kissinger had other obligations and was unable to appear. On 30 July 2001, the Chilean Supreme Court authorized the questioning, in the US, of Mr Kissinger in the murder of the US journalist Charles Horman during the Pinochet regime. A questionnaire had been prepared by judge Guzman. The Argentine federal judge Rodolfo Canicoba Corral formally requested the US Department of Justice, on 10 August 2001, to question Mr Kissinger in order to determine whether he knew about the Condor Plan when he was the head of US diplomacy. The Condor Plan was an operation of repression organised in the 1970s and 1980s by the dictatorships in Argentina, Bolivia, Brazil, Chile, Paraguay and Uruguay to assist each other in eliminating their respective political opponents.[12]

The Difficult Expansion of Universal Jurisdiction

Called the 'Pinochet effect', the concept of universal jurisdiction has been availed of more frequently in recent years, with more or less success. As noted in Chapter 3, a few Rwandans have been judged and sentenced in Switzerland (May 1999) and in Belgium (June 2001). Before the Pinochet episode, in Germany, the Bavarian High Court sentenced a Bosnian Serb, Novislav Djajic, to five years' imprisonment in 1997 under the Geneva Conventions for aiding and abetting the killing of 14 Muslim men in Bosnia in 1992. In September 1997, a former leader of a paramilitary Serb group, Nikola Jorgic, was convicted on 11 counts of genocide and 30 counts of murder, and sentenced to life imprisonment on 18 December 1999 by the Düsseldorf High Court. In Denmark, Bosnian Muslim Refik Saric is serving an eight-year sentence for war crimes, charged under the Geneva Conventions with torturing detainees in a Croat-run prison in Bosnia in 1993.[13]

In Latin American cases, on 10 October 1997, the former Navy Captain Adolfo Scilingo was indicted in Madrid of genocide and imprisoned in preventive custody.[14] In October 1998, French Prosecutors initiated a criminal investigation for 'illegal confinement followed by torture' on the basis of the complaints of several families of French citizens 'disappeared' in Argentina. In May 2000, French Judge Le Loire issued an international rogatory commission to hear, in Argentine, approximately 150 persons. In September 2000, Judge Garzon asked the Spanish government to request the extradition from Mexico of the former Argentine officer, Ricardo Miguel Cavallo, detained in that country since 24 August 2000. Known under the nickname of 'Serpico' or 'Ricardo', Cavallo is alleged to have committed personally 21 summary executions, 227 disappearances, 110 cases of torture and 17 kidnappings of new-born babies delivered by their mothers in jail. Spanish judges had already started in March 1996 a criminal investigation into the torture, disappearance and murder of 600 Spanish citizens in Argentina. The investigators in Spain charged 110 former and active Argentine military and police officers, including army officers, intelligence chiefs and even medical doctors, who are said to have supervised torture sessions during the dictatorship (1976–1983). Argentine contended that Spain had no jurisdiction over events in Argentine and that the leaders of its security forces were tried in 1985 and 1986, imprisoned and finally pardoned in 1989 by President Carlos Saul Menem. The Spanish judge still ruled that he had jurisdiction, as crimes against humanity enjoy universal jurisdiction and have no statute of limitations. On 6

[12] *IHT*, 30 May 2001; *Le Monde*, 18 August 2001.

[13] See www.hrw.org/campaigns/chile98/precedent.htm, 13 March 2000.

[14] Beigbeder (1999), p. 133.

August 2000, a former Argentine lieutenant-colonel, Jorge Olivera, was arrested in Italy. He is alleged to be one of the leaders of the commandos who abducted a 24-year-old French woman, Anne-Marie Erize Tisseau, in San Juan, in the north-west of Argentine. Judge Le Loire was to request Olivera's extradition to France. Again, Argentine rejected, on 14 August 2001, requests submitted by Italy and France to extradite the former Navy Captain Alfredo Astiz: he was immediately released from preventive jail in his country. He is alleged to be responsible for the disappearance, between 1976 and 1977, of three Italian women, Angela Maria Aleta, Giovanni Pegoraro and his daughter Susana. Susana's daughter, born in jail was illegally adopted by another navy officer. In Paris, Astiz had been condemned in absentia, in December 1990, to life imprisonment for the abduction and disappearance, in 1977, in Buenos Ayres of two French nuns, Alice Domon and Léonie Duquet. Argentine rejects the principle of universal jurisdiction, in favour of the principle of territoriality of justice and the exclusive competence of Argentine judges. In spite of the amnesty laws ordered by President Alfonsin in the 1980s, former heads of the dictatorship, including the former General Jorge Videla and the former Admiral Emilio Massera were in jail in 2001, for the abduction of new-born babies, a crime not subject to these laws nor to statutory limitations.[15]

The Failed Prosecution of Hissène Habré

Encouraged by the Pinochet precedent, in 1999, the Chadian Association for the Promotion and Defense of Human Rights requested Human Rights Watch's assistance in bringing Habré to justice in Senegal.[16]

Habré ruled Chad from 1982 with the military and financial support of the US and France, which sought his help in opposing Colonel Moammar Ghadafi of Libya. He was deposed in 1990 by current President (General) Idriss Deby and fled to Senegal. A 1992 Truth Commission report documented 4000 political killings which it said amounted to less than a tenth of the crimes committed, and accused the regime of systematic torture on 200 000 Chadians. The report described a 'veritable genocide against the Chadian people'.

On 25 January 2000, the Chadian Association of Victims of Political Repression and Crime (AVCRP) and seven individual Chadian plaintiffs, with the support of a coalition of national and international NGOs,[17] filed a criminal complaint in the Dakar Criminal Court, accusing Habré of torture and crimes against humanity. The

[15] *Le Monde*, 16 August 2001, *IHT*, 21 August 2001.

[16] The main facts in this section are based on Human Rights Watch's 'The Case Against Hissène Habré', www.hrw.org/justice/habre/intro_web2.htm, 29 August 2001, and other HRW releases. See also *IHT*, 29 November 2000; *Le Monde*, 27 January, 5 February, 7 July 2000, 22 March and 10 April 2001.

[17] Including the Dakar-based African Assembly for the Defense of Human Rights, the Paris-based International Federation of Human Rights Leagues, two Chadian and one Senegal human rights groups, the London-based Interights and the French association 'Agir ensemble pour les Droits de l'Homme.

torture charges were based on the Senegalese statute on torture and on the 1984 Convention against Torture, which Senegal ratified in 1987. The plaintiffs also cited Senegal's obligations under customary international law to prosecute those accused of crimes against humanity. It was the first time that the principle of universal jurisdiction was called upon in Africa to initiate a prosecution against a former dictator. Within two days, the Prosecutor gave his favourable advice. Judge Demba Kandji then called in Habré on 3 February 2000 and indicted him on charges of 'complicité d'actes de torture' and placed him under house arrest. He also opened an investigation against persons to be named for crimes against humanity, disappearances and barbarous acts, which could be used as later indictments of Habré and others.

In March 2000, Abdoulaye Wade was elected President of Senegal, the first democratically elected president. When Habré filed a motion to dismiss the case, the state prosecutor, reversing his previous position, supported the motion. On 4 July 2000, the indicting Chamber dismissed the charges against Habré, ruling that Senegal had not enacted legislation to implement the Convention against Torture and therefore had no jurisdiction to pursue the charges because the alleged crimes had not been committed in Senegal. On 20 March 2001, Senegal's highest court (Cour de Cassation) affirmed this decision. On 7 April, president Wade declared to the BBC and a private Senegalese radio station that he had asked Habré to leave Senegal. On 23 April, the UN Committee against Torture asked Senegal 'not to expel Mr Hissène Habré and to take all necessary measures to prevent Mr Hissène Habré from leaving Senegalese territory except pursuant to an extradition'.

Senegal was the first country in the world to ratify the Statute of the International Criminal Court.

Although the prosecution against Habré had been stopped in Senegal, on 26 October 2000, 17 victims lodged criminal complaints in Chad for torture, murder and 'disappearance' against named members of the Documentation and Security Directorate (DDS). The case was initially rejected, but was reinstated by a decision of the Constitutional Court. In May 2001, an investigating judge began to hear witnesses. President Déby had met earlier with the Chadian Association of Victims' leadership to tell them that 'the time for justice has come' and that he would support their cases. He also promised to clean up the administration of all former DDS agents and to grant full access to the files of the Truth Commission.

The Complaint Against Ariel Sharon

On 18 June 2001, 23 survivors of the Sabra and Shatilla massacre lodged a complaint in Brussels against Ariel Sharon, Israel's Prime Minister, for war crimes, crimes against humanity and genocide. The complaint was based on the Belgian law of 16 June 1993 (modified by the law of 10 February 1999) regarding the repression of grave violations of the international humanitarian law: acts of genocide, crimes against humanity, crimes committed against persons or property protected by the

Geneva Conventions of 12 August 1949. It was also based on customary international law and jus cogens concerning these crimes.[18]

The massacre had been committed in the Palestinian refugee camps of Sabra and Chatila in September 1982 following the occupation of Beirut by the Israeli army. After the murder of the Lebanese president Béchir Gemayel, a friend of Israel, Sharon, then minister of defense, decided that the camps should be 'cleaned' of the 2000 fighters of the Palestine Liberation Organisation (PLO) which had remained there in spite of the expulsion of the Organisation from Beirut. Sharon authorized the Lebanese Christian Phalangist militias, Israel's allies, to enter the camps. The militiamen found few guerillas, but during more than three days, they killed at least 700 Palestinian refugees – some estimates run to 2000 or more. Among the victims were women, children and the elderly, some of whom were tortured, disfigured or raped before they were mowed down with machine guns.

During a BBC programme aired on 17 June 2001, Morris Draper, the US Special Envoy to the Middle East at the time, said that, after the killings began, he cabled Sharon 'You must stop the slaughter. The situation is absolutely appalling. They are killing children. You have the field completely under your control and are therefore responsible for that area'.

A resolution of the UN General Assembly adopted on 16 December 1982[19]

(1) Condemns in the strongest terms the large-scale massacre of Palestinian civilians in the Sabra and Shatila refugee camps;
(2) Resolves that the massacre was an act of genocide.

An Israeli investigation conducted in 1982 by the President of the Supreme Court, Itzhak Kahan, ackowledged that the massacre had been committed by the militias, led by the Lebanese military leader Elie Hobeika. The report of the Commission underlined that 'Minister of Defense bears personal responsibility' and should 'draw the appropriate personal conclusions arising out of the defects revealed with regard to the manner in which he discharged the duties of his office'. The Commission recommended that Prime Minister Menachem Begin remove Sharon from office if he did not resign. Sharon did resign as minister of defense, but later assumed other cabinet positions. Another investigation carried out by the Lebanese army exonerated the militias of all charges.

On 23 June 2001, Human Rights Watch urged that a criminal investigation into Sharon's role in the massacre should be launched. For HRW, the Kahan Commission's findings and conclusions, however authoritative in terms of investigation and documentation of the facts surrounding the massacre, could not be a substitute for proceedings in a criminal court in Israel or elsewhere that would bring to justice those responsible for the killing of hundreds of innocent civilians. HRW recognised that Sharon, in his capacity as Prime Minister, enjoys temporary

[18] *IHT*, 25 June 2001; *Le Monde*. 3 and 28 July 2001.

[19] Res. 37/123 D.

immunity: 'however, that should not preclude an active criminal investigation into his conduct whether in Israel, Belgium or elsewhere'.[20] The International Federation of Human Rights Leagues (FIDH) agreed that there were extremely serious elements to consider that war crimes and crimes against humanity were involved in this episode. The Federation was however concerned about the need to target judiciary cases as solid as possible.

On 1 July, the Brussels Public Prosecutor's Office took the position that the complaint was receivable, subject to a decision by the court.

In an interview published by *Le Monde* on 9 August 2001, the Belgian lawyer Michèle Hirsch appointed by the State of Israel to defend the case, explained her intention to demonstrate that the Belgian court was not competent to hear the complaint. She considered that the Kahan Commission had worked like a judge and had referred only to an indirect, political or 'ethical' responsibility of the former minister of defense. As the Israeli State decided not to prosecute, the Belgian government cannot pass judgement on the manner in which Jerusalem assessed facts examined more than 20 years before. More importantly, she stressed the need for a territorial basis, a 'lien de rattachement'. The Belgian criminal law prescribes that the accused or suspect must be in the territory of the country. She also questioned whether the Belgian law could apply to facts prior to 1993. Finally, she recalled that, in international law, a head of state or of government enjoys an absolute immunity of jurisdiction and execution. International practice confirms this absolute immunity in relation to national courts. While she recognised that the Belgian law was a good law, corresponding to the obligation of states to fight against impunity, she considered that universal jurisdiction is not a permit to do anything under any conditions: 'The Belgian judges cannot judge the whole world'.[21]

In the meantime, another complaint has been introduced, under the 1993 law, against Saddam Hussein, the head of the Iraqi state by five Iraqi nationals of Kurdish origin, refugees in Belgium and in the Netherlands.[22]

CONCLUSION

Universal jurisdiction is far from being achieved, but it is now a growing trend which is being used more often than in the past by judges and courts, effectively prodded by human rights organisations, both at international and national level. It is finally offering a judiciary recourse, emotional relief and possible reparation to long-forgotten victims and/or their kins, it allows the truth to be restored and publicized, it helps to identify and make accountable those responsible for grave crimes under international humanitarian law. While the International Criminal Court (ICC), when created, will have no retroactive jurisdiction, national courts are able to judge

[20] Human Rights Watch hrwatchnyc@igc.org, 25 June 2001 and other HRW releases.

[21] *Le Monde*, 9 August 2001.

[22] *Le Monde*, 5 July 2001.

war crimes, genocide and crimes against humanity without statutes of limitation under relevant international instruments and under customary international law: the Geneva Conventions and Protocols, the Convention against Genocide, the Convention against Torture.

The Law Lords judgements have established that there is no immunity for former heads of state or of governments, although they enjoy legal and judiciary immunity during their tenure. Only the ICC will be entitled to indict dictators in office. The Lords also made clear that torture, crimes against humanity, genocide are not 'functions' of those dignitaries whose criminal actions make them subject to criminal proceedings.

In the cases of Pinochet, the judiciary proceedings initiated by Spain and other countries and carried out by the English courts, even though they ended with a rejection of extradition, had a deep effect in Chile itself. Public opinion, ashamed to see that 'their' dictator might have been judged abroad, finally supported the Chilean judges' efforts to prosecute Pinochet in his own country, a move which helped the people to face their past and force political and military officials to face their own responsibilities. The aborted trial of Habré in Sénégal gave courage to victims' and human rights groups in Chad to initiate criminal proceedings against the perpetrators of crimes during Habré's dictatorship.

However, universal juridiction is still facing formidable obstacles. The principal one is the protection provided by the principle of national sovereignty, the rejection of interventions or interference in matters within the domestic jurisdiction of states. Other obstacles include the lack of national legislation to implement international instruments, the rejection of extradition through the assertion of the principle of territoriality of justice (Argentine), the domination exercised by government authorities over justice in many countries. Another major difficulty arises from political, economic and diplomatic links binding states: the British government was not inclined to upset its relations with Chile by extraditing Pinochet to be judged in Spain, nor was the Spanish government eager to judge Pinochet on its soil, for similar reasons. The solidarity of current and former chiefs of state was demonstrated by the pressures exercised by president Wade to stop judiciary proceedings against Habré in Senegal. As another example, Ethiopia's requests to Zimbabwe and to South Africa for the extradition of former dictator Mengistu Haile Mariam have been ignored. He is charged in his own country with genocide, crimes against humanity, summary or arbitrary executions, detentions, disappearances and forcible resettlement as head of the junta which ruled Ethiopia from 1974 to 1991. Briefly hospitalized in South Africa, he returned to his safe political asylum in Zimbabwe.[23]

Finally, countries like Belgium which have adopted legislation authorizing proceedings under the principle of universal jurisdiction find that they may have opened Pandora's box. A number of Belgian judges now feel that the law of 1993,

[23] Beigbeder (1999), pp. 129–132; *Le Monde*, 10 December 1999.

Chapter 5

Presentation 5.1. The Princeton Principles on Universal Jurisdiction (2001) (Excerpts)

The participants in the Princeton Project on Universal Jurisdiction propose the following principles for the purposes of advancing the continued evolution of international law and the application of international law in national legal systems:

Principle 1 – Fundamentals of Universal Jurisdiction

(1) For purposes of these Principles, universal jurisdiction is criminal jurisdiction based solely on the nature of the crime, without regard to where the crime was committed, the nationality of the alleged or convicted perpetrator, the nationality of the victim, or any other connection to the state exercising such jurisdiction.

(2) Universal jurisdiction may be exercised by a competent and ordinary judicial body of any state in order to try a person duly accused of committing serious crimes under international law as specified in Principle 2(1), provided the person is present before such judicial body.

(3) A state may rely on universal jurisdiction as a basis for seeking the extradition of a person accused of or convicted of committing a serious crime under international law as specified in Principle 2(1) provided that it has established a prima facie case of the person's guilt and that the person sought to be extradited will be tried or the punishment carried out in accordance with international norms and standards on the protection of human rights in the context of criminal proceedings.

(4) In exercising universal jurisdiction or in relying upon universal jurisdiction as a basis for seeking extradition, a state and its judicial organs shall observe international due process norms including but not limited to those involving the rights of the accused and victims, the fairness of the proceedings, and the independence and impartiality of the judiciary (hereinafter referred to as 'international due process norms').

(5) A state shall exercise universal jurisdiction in good faith and in accordance with its rights and obligations under international law.

Principle 2 – Serious Crimes Under International Law

(1) For purposes of these Principles, serious crimes under international law include: (1) piracy; (2) slavery; (3) war crimes; (4) crimes against peace; (5) crimes against humanity; (6) genocide; and (7) torture.

(2) The application of universal jurisdiction to the crimes listed in paragraph 1 is without prejudice to the application of universal jurisdiction to other crimes under international law.

Principle 3 – Reliance on Universal Jurisdiction in the Absence of National Legislation

With respect to serious crimes under international law as specified in Principle 2(1), national judicial organs may rely on universal jurisdiction even if their national legislation does not specifically provide for it.

Principle 4 – Obligation to Support Accountability

(...)

Principle 5 – Immunities

With respect to serious crimes under international law as specified in Principle 2(1), the official position of any accused person, whether as head of state or government or as a responsible government official, shall not relieve such person of criminal responsibility nor mitigate punishment.

Principle 6 – Statutes of Limitations

Statutes of limitations or other forms of prescription shall not apply to serious crimes under international law as specified in Principle 2(1).

Principle 7 – Amnesties

(1) Amnesties are generally inconsistent with the obligation of states to provide accountability for serious crimes under international law as specified in Principle 2(1).

(2) The exercise of universal jurisdiction with respect to serious crimes under international law as specified in Principle 2(1) shall not be precluded by amnesties which are incompatible with the international legal obligations of the granting state.

Principle 8 – Resolution of Competing National Jurisdictions

(. . .)

Principle 9 – Non Bis In Idem/Double Jeopardy

(. . .)

Principle 10 – Grounds for Refusal of Extradition

(1) A state or its judicial organs shall refuse to entertain a request for extradition based on universal jurisdiction if the person sought is likely to face a death penalty sentence or to be subjected to torture or any other cruel, degrading, or inhuman punishment or treatment, or if it is likely that the person sought will be subjected to sham proceedings in which international due process norms will be violated and no satisfactory assurances to the contrary are provided.

(2) A state which refuses to extradite on the basis of this Principle shall, when permitted by international law, prosecute the individual accused of a serious crime under international law as specified in Principle 2(1) or extradite such person to another state where this can be done without exposing him or her to the risks referred to in paragraph 1.

Principle 11 – Adoption of National Legislation

A state shall, where necessary, enact national legislation to enable the exercise of universal jurisdiction and the enforcement of these Principles.

Principle 12 – Inclusion of Universal Jurisdiction in Future Treaties

In all future treaties, and in protocols to existing treaties, concerned with serious crimes under international law as specified in Principle 2(1), states shall include provisions for universal jurisdiction

Principle 13 – Strengthening Accountability and Universal Jurisdiction

(. . .)

Principle 14 – Settlement of Disputes

(. . .)

Source: Princeton University Programme in Law and Public Affairs, University of Minnesota, Human Rights Library, www1.umn.edu/humanrts/instree/princeton.html, 13 November 2001.

revised in 1999, cannot be implemented and should be modified in a more restrictive way. Their argument is that Belgium cannot judge the whole world. Belgian courts do not have the capacity to deal with numerous complaints attracted by the liberal Belgian law: the ICTY employs more than 1000 persons to prosecute and judge only those crimes committed in the Former Yugoslavia, while the Belgian Prosecution Section in charge of such complaints has less that 100 persons to deal with them.[24]

In spite of all obstacles and reservations, universal jurisdiction is expanding: more countries will feel compelled to either punish (or rather judge) or extradite.

A group of leading international legal scholars and jurists has proposed, in 2001, 'The Princeton Principles on Universal Jurisdiction'. Convinced that more public figures are likely in coming years to face trials for war crimes and other serious crimes under international law when there are no traditional jurisdictional links to the victims or perpetrators, the group believes that, if adopted by governments around the world, the Principles would go far to bring war criminals to justice.[25] Excerpts from these Principles are shown in Presentation 5.1.

It is hoped that these Principles will be widely publicized and that many governments will integrate them in their legislation, under the pressure of national and international public opinion, prodded by human rights NGOs.

[24] *Le Monde*, 28 July 2001.

[25] The Princeton Project was sponsored by the Programme in Law and Public Affairs and the Woodrow Wilson School of Public and International Affairs, Princeton University; the International Commission of Jurists; the American Association for the International Commission of Jurists; the Netherlands Institute of Human Rights and the Urban Morgan Institute for Human Rights. In two conference sessions, in November 2000 and January 2001, judges and scholars from the UK, Canada, China, Japan, India, the Netherlands, Turkey and the US met with experts from the European Court of Human Rights and the UN.

CHAPTER 6

MIXED NATIONAL/INTERNATIONAL TRIBUNALS

Under the protection of national sovereignty, national courts have long had exclusive jurisdiction over crimes committed in their territory. National courts have requested the extradition of their own nationals from other countries for crimes committed in their home country, or of foreign nationals alleged to have committed crimes in the national courts' country. Under the concept of universal jurisdiction, national courts in a few countries have judged foreign nationals alleged to have committed crimes in their own or other countries: German courts have judged Serb criminals for war crimes or crimes against humanity. A Belgian court has judged four Rwandans for genocide committed in Rwanda.

The Security Council has created temporary, ad hoc international criminal tribunals to judge alleged perpetrators of war crimes, crimes against humanity committed in the Former Yugoslavia since 1991, and alleged perpetrators of war crimes, crimes against humanity and genocide committed in connection with the Rwanda Genocide in 1994.

Finally, the probable creation of the International Criminal Court will expand the scope of international criminal justice in accordance with its Statute. However, the new Court will have no retroactive jurisdiction: the authors of many past massacres will not be subject to prosecution, judgement and sentences by the Court.

In the meantime, it is unlikely that the Security Council will create any new international criminal tribunals, for political and/or financial reasons. One or more of its permanent members may have been involved in supporting a criminal government and would fear public revelations unearthed by independent prosecutors – the costs of running the present ICTY and ICTR are more than $176 million per year.

In the cases described below, there is doubt that the judicial system of the countries referred to would be either willing or capable to carry out prosecutions and hearings in accordance with set international standards. Hence the recent attempts to create mixed national/international courts in Cambodia and in Sierra Leone, by negotiation between the governments concerned and the United Nations.

Proposals to set up an international tribunal or a mixed national/international tribunal for crimes committed in East Timor have failed except for the creation of a Serious Crimes Panel at the Dili District Court in East Timor which includes national and international judges. However, Indonesia has consistently rejected the creation of an international human rights tribunal, claiming abusively that Indonesian justice is both willing and capable to prosecute and judge the initiators and perpetrators of the violence and atrocities committed in East Timor.

Finally, the Trial of the alleged perpetrators of the Lockerbie crash, combining Scottish judges in The Netherlands to judge Libyan accused persons is sui generis: even though justice was rendered by a national court, the Trial is mentioned in this Chapter because of its international background and innovative arrangements.

JUDGING THE KHMER ROUGE LEADERS?

The genocide, initiated and carried out by the Khmer Rouge regime between 1975 and January 1979, caused the death of at least 1.7 million Cambodians, widespread suffering and economic disruption. There are strong doubts that the principal Khmer Rouge leaders will ever be judged and sentenced by an independent tribunal.

Historical Background

Cambodia gained independence from France in 1953 under the leadership of Prince Norodom Sihanouk and the 1954 Geneva Conference on Indochina recognised its neutrality.[1] Massive US air bombing carried out in Cambodia from February to August 1973 caused deaths, suffering and a strong hate of the Americans, which gave popular support to the communist Khmer Rouge forces, led by Pol Pot. The Khmer Rouge took over the country in April 1975 from the Lon Nol government, supported by the US.

The new leaders ordered the evacuation of the cities, causing a gigantic exodus of more than 2 million people, with thousands of deaths. Hospitals, schools, factories and monasteries were closed and all individual rights and freedoms abolished. The 'old society', the bourgeoisie, the 'corrupt city dwellers' and educated people had to be eliminated to leave only a young fanatic class of revolutionaries. Chiefs of cooperatives and soldiers had full powers to punish and kill. Identified members of the condemned groups were subject to deportation, torture, massacres, starvation and uncared-for diseases, leading to more deaths. Deaths caused by deliberate killings, exhaustion, disease or starvation are estimated at 1.7 million out of a population of 7.3–7.9 million in 1975. They were the consequences of a governmental policy that imposed massive migration, forced labour and inhumane living conditions on the people and attacked perceived enemies of the revolution.

The well-hidden genocide committed by the Khmer Rouge leaders and their indoctrinated followers was a product of ill-conceived Marxism and Maoism, mixed with feelings of national pride, economic self-sufficiency, rejection of foreign imperialism, hate of the Vietnamese, and a spirit of revolutionary violence.

---

1 For a more detailed historical description, see Beigbeder (1999), pp. 95–101 and related references.

In December 1978, the Vietnamese army intervened, meeting no resistance except from the retreating Khmer Rouge forces, which took refuge in forest sanctuaries along the Thai border. A pro-Vietnamese government was installed in Phnom Penh as the People's Republic of Kampuchea, and was soon recognised by Vietnam, Laos, and the USSR and her allies.

The USA, China and Thailand, all enemies of Vietnam continued to support and send arms to the Khmer Rouge. The USA was still grieving from its defeat in the Vietnam war, China was opposed to the Soviet-supported Vietnam, both China, Thailand and other countries in Asia feared the political and military expansion of Vietnam. The Khmer Rouge continued to represent Kampuchea in the United Nations, the Vietnamese intervention being condemned as 'aggression'. In 1991, the Paris Conference on Cambodia adopted the 'Agreements on a Comprehensive Political Settlement of the Cambodia Conflict', which created the UN Transitional Authority in Cambodia (UNTAC). UNTAC was to deal with the four competing factions of Cambodia, including the genocidal Khmer Rouge Party of Democratic Kampuchea. In spite of Khmer Rouge harassment, refusal to disarm and refusal to participate in the UN-organised elections, these were held in May 1993 with a high voter participation. This was the beginning of the final loss of power and influence of the Khmer Rouge, which accelerated with defections from the Pol Pot core group, and the death of Pol Pot himself in April 1998.

The First Political Trials

Following the Vietnamese intervention, the Revolutionary People's Tribunal, sitting in Phnom Penh in August 1979, ruled that Pol Pot, alias Saloth Sar, and Ieng Sary were guilty of the crime of genocide, condemned them both to death in absentia and ordered that all their properties be confiscated.[2] The judgement was final. Pol Pot was the Secretary of the Angkar (Party Organisation) and held the highest office in leading the entire State apparatus. Ieng Sary, as Standing Political Bureau member of the Angkar and Deputy Prime Minister in charge of foreign affairs, shared leadership with Pol Pot. They were found guilty of genocide on the following counts as defined in Decree-law No. 1 of 15 July 1979:

- (a) Planned massacre of innocent people;
- (b) Forced evacuation of people from towns and villages;
- (c) Concentrating people and forcing them to do hard labour in physically and morally exhausting conditions;
- (d) Abolition of religion and destruction of economic and cultural structures and family and social relations.

According to the judgement, their crimes were 'much more serious than the definition of genocide in the 9 December 1948 Convention'. It linked the 'Pol Pot

[2] UN Doc. A/34/491, ANNEX, August 1979.

clique' with the 'Peking reactionaries'. The Khmer Rouge 'People's Commune', that huge concentration camp was copied from the Chinese model. The instigation of the youth and their use for killing Kampucheans were lessons learned from the Chinese cultural revolution.

Witnesses for the prosecution who made on-the-spot investigations were lawyers from Cuba, Japan and from the USA. The accused were 'defended' by two Cambodian lawyers and one American lawyer. However, the defence admitted that the criminal acts of genocide of which the defendants were accused had been fully proved.

The court exercised revolutionary 'victors' justice' at the national level. The international standards for 'a fair and public hearing by a competent, independent and impartial tribunal established by law'[3] were not respected. The openly political trial was not monitored by independent international observers. The participation of a few lawyers from Cuba, Japan and the USA was no guarantee of a fair trial. Rights of the defense were not observed: the competence and independence of the defense lawyers is doubted in view of their admission of the guilt of the accused.

In a letter dated 21 June 1997 addressed to the UN Secretary-General, Prince Norodom Ranariddh, Cambodia's First Prime Minister (later removed from this position by Hun Sen) and Hun Sen, Second Prime Minister, asked for the assistance of the UN and the international community in bringing to justice those persons responsible for the genocide and crimes against humanity during the rule of the Khmer Rouge from 1975 to 1979:[4]

> Cambodia does not have the resources or expertise to conduct this very important procedure. Thus, we believe it is necessary to ask for the assistance of the United Nations. We are aware of similar efforts to respond to the genocide and crimes against humanity in Rwanda and the former Yugoslavia, and ask that similar assistance be given to Cambodia.

In transmitting this letter to the Security Council, Kofi Annan stated that

> The facts which gave rise to the request remain unclear. The Office of my Representative in Cambodia is presently seeking to clarify the situation, while the Secretariat is examining the legal and institutional issues involved. The letter is brought to your attention for any action which may be deemed appropriate.

It appears that neither the Secretariat nor the Security Council was prepared to act promptly in this matter: no proposal was then made for creating an International Criminal Tribunal for Cambodia.

---

3 Article 14.1 of the International Covenant on Civil and Political Rights, which entered into force on 23 March 1976.

4 UN Doc. A/51/930, S/1997/488, 24 June 1997.

On 23 July 1997, the 'surreal trial' of Pol Pot, in the words of the *New York Times* was held in Anlong Veng in the north of Cambodia. It was witnessed by Nate Thayer, the correspondent for the Far Eastern Economic Review. The aged and sickly Pol Pot was publicly humiliated by a small, disciplined Khmer Rouge group and condemned to life imprisonment. The spectators periodically lifted their fists in unison and shouted 'Crush, crush, crush Pol Pot and his clique'. Pol Pot was tried for political reasons internal to the Khmer Rouge, not because he had directed genocide. His trial had no pretense of fair justice or due process. In an interview with Thayer held on 15 October 1997, Pol Pot said that he had no regrets, his conscience was clear.

The Khmer Rouge announced on 16 April 1998 that Pol Pot, age 73, had died the day before of a heart failure.[5]

The Stalled International Justice

On 30 April 1998, a US representative told the Security Council that the US was working to establish a tribunal to bring to justice senior Cambodian Khmer Rouge leaders during the period 1975–1979.[6]

Hun Sen's policy was to give priority to national reconciliation and peace rather than to justice. Hun Sen was a former Khmer Rouge leader who defected and helped Vietnamese forces to overthrow the Pol Pot regime. He encouraged Khmer Rouge troops to defect, telling them 'We were not at fault at all in creating the war and the genocidal regime' ... 'During the 1970s there was a small group of people who created the war, and we were all just victims'.

In September 1996, King Norodom Sihanouk conferred pardon on Ieng Sary, at the request of the two Prime Ministers. Ieng Sary asserted that he was not involved in the genocide. He said: 'I have no regrets, because this was not my responsibility'. In January 1997, more than 200 former Khmer Rouge were appointed as senior officers in the Cambodian army. Eighteen thousand former Khmer Rouge would form eight new army divisions and two regiments. On 25 December 1998, two senior Khmer Rouge leaders, Khieu Samphan, former head of state of the Khmer Rouge, and Nuon Chea, main ideologist and responsible for the security, surrendered to the Hun Sen government. They said they were 'very sorry' not only for the human lives, but also for the loss of animal lives lost during the war. They rejected any personal responsibility. Hun Sen said that they should be welcomed 'with bouquets of flowers, not with prisons and handcuffs'. A trial would only open old wounds and lead to possible instability: 'We should dig a hole and bury the past and look ahead to the 21st century with a clean slate'.

On 12 December 1997, the UN General Assembly endorsed the comments of the UN Special Representative for human rights in Cambodia that the most serious

---

5 *New York Times*, 30 July 1997; *Le Monde*, 2 August, 25 October 1997 and 17 April 1998.

6 UN *Press Release* SC/6510, 30 April 1998.

human rights violations in Cambodia in recent history have been committed by the Khmer Rouge and that their crimes, including the taking and killing of hostages, have continued to the present.[7] It noted with concern that no Khmer Rouge leader had been brought to account for his crimes. It requested the Secretary-General to examine the request by the Cambodian authorities for assistance in responding to past serious violations of Cambodian and international law, including the possibility of the appointment, by the Secretary-General, of a group of experts to evaluate the existing evidence and propose further measures, as a means of bringing about national reconciliation, strengthening democracy and addressing the issue of individual accountability. The Special Representative had expressed his concerns about the problem of impunity in Cambodia.

Only two Khmer Rouge leaders were arrested, as they had failed to negotiate surrender deals:[8] Kang Kek Ieu, head of the Khmer Rouge secret police and commandant of the infamous Tuol Slen prison, arrested in March 1999, and Ta Mok, a notorious military commander known as 'The Butcher', arrested in May 1999.

As suggested by the General Assembly, in the Spring of 1998, the UN Secretary-General appointed an expert group with the following mandate: (1) to evaluate the existing evidence with a view to determining the nature of the crimes committed by Khmer Rouge leaders in the years 1975–1979; (2) to assess the feasibility of their apprehension; and (3) to explore legal options for bringing them to justice before an international or national jurisdiction.[9] The group carried out its work from July 1998 until February 1999. It submitted its 60-page report to the Secretary-General on 22 February 1999.

On the basis of the material and documents made available to it, the group concluded that the evidence gathered to date testified to the commission of serious crimes under international and Cambodian law, and that sufficient physical and witness evidence existed to justify legal proceedings against the Khmer Rouge leaders for these crimes. It considered that the crimes committed by Khmer Rouge leaders during the 1975–1979 period included crimes against humanity, genocide, war crimes, forced labour, torture and crimes against internationally protected persons, as well as crimes under Cambodian law. It recommended that trials be confined to 'those persons most responsible for the most serious violations of human rights in

7 Res. 52/135, adopted without a vote on 12 December 1997, paras. 3, 15, 16. The Special Representative was Thomas Hammarberg, a Swedish diplomat.

8 *IHT*, 16 and 19 September, 13 December 1996, 29 December 1998, 8 March 1999; *Le Monde*, 12–13 January 1997, 17 April, 31 December 1998.

9 The group consisted of Sir Ninian Stephen, a former Governor-General of Australia and former judge of the ICTY, as chair; judge Rajsoomer Lallah, member of the Human Rights Committee and Steven R. Ratner, who had participated in the Cambodia settlement talks and served as a consultant to the US Department of State on bringing the Khmer Rouge to justice. See the article by Steven R. Ratner, 'The United Nations Group of Experts for Cambodia', *The American Journal of International Law*, Vol. 93, 1999, pp. 948–953. The Expert Group Report is in UN Doc. A/53/850, ANNEX, 16 March 1999.

Cambodia ... includ[ing] senior leaders with responsibility over the abuses as well as those at lower levels who are directly implicated in the most serious atrocities'.

In the view of the group, the question of the feasibility of apprehending Khmer Rouge leaders turned on the ability and willingness of the government to effectuate their arrest or extradition. Both Hun Sen and the government of Thailand expressed their willingness and readiness to apprehend any person indicted by the independent prosecutor of an international tribunal, should one be established.

The group examined the following legal options for bringing Khmer Rouge leaders to justice: a tribunal established under Cambodian law; a tribunal established by the Security Council or the General Assembly as an ad hoc international tribunal; a mixed option of a Cambodian tribunal under UN administration; an international tribunal established by multilateral treaty and trials in third states. It recommended that the UN should establish an ad hoc international tribunal to try Khmer Rouge officials for crimes against humanity and genocide committed from 17 April 1975 to 7 January 1979, that the Security Council establish this tribunal, or, should it not do so, that the General Assembly establish it. The group favoured the Council as facilitating swifter action.

In rejecting trials in both a Cambodian criminal court and a UN-supervised Cambodian court, the group reasoned that such options were too prone to manipulation by the government of Cambodia and other political forces.[10] The level of corruption of Cambodia's courts was so high that the population had justifiably lost confidence in them. In the group's view, even extensive involvement of foreign personnel – perhaps through a mixed tribunal – would not solve the problem, as the government could exert undue influence during prosecutions. As for a UN-supervised Cambodian court, it would still place too much initiative on the Cambodian government, which would find ways to stall the process.

The group recommended that the trials be held outside Cambodia, as an international court sitting in Cambodia could be manipulated in terms of interference with the work of the prosecutors, investigators and judges. The report proposed trials in 'a State situated somewhere in the Asia-Pacific region', meaning Australia, Singapore or the Philippines.

The UN Secretary-General transmitted the expert group's report under cover of his identical letters dated 15 March 1999 to the President of the General Assembly and the President of the Security Council.[11] He mentioned that the government of Cambodia, having considered the report, in a letter addressed to him dated 3 March 1999, cautioned that any decision to bring Khmer Rouge leaders to justice must take account of Cambodia's need for peace and national reconciliation, and that, 'if improperly and heedlessly conducted, the trials of Khmer Rouge leaders would panic other former Khmer Rouge officers and rank and file, who have already surrendered,

---

[10] See Ratner's article.

[11] UN Doc. A/53/850, S/1999/231, 16 March 1999.

into turning back to the jungle and renewing the guerrilla war in Cambodia'.[12] In January 1999, Hun Sen had finally agreed to the principle that a tribunal should judge the Khmer Rouge. However, he believed that the period to consider should not be restricted to 1975 to 1979 but that it should extend to the period 1970–1975, during which nearly 1 million Cambodians died as a result of the US bombing, and the period 1979–1998. He did not specify the type of tribunal and its competence. In a letter to the Secretary-General dated 24 March 1999, Hun Sen stated that an existing national tribunal of Cambodia should take up the case to charge and convict Ta Mok and other Khmer Rouge leaders if found guilty of crimes of genocide in Cambodia, under Article 33 of the Cambodian Constitution and Article VI of the Genocide Convention. Assistance of legal experts from foreign countries would be welcome, in order to ensure that the Cambodian tribunal meets international standards. It will be up to the tribunal to determine the number of these legal experts. The tribunal 'will enjoy complete independence from the executive and legislative powers'.[13] The Secretary-General then reminded the Cambodian Foreign Minister that the group of experts had carefully considered the feasibility of a national tribunal, but concluded that the Cambodia judiciary in its current state was unlikely to meet minimal international standards of justice, even with external assistance. Kofi Annan added that, in his view, the trial of a single Khmer Rouge military leader which would leave the entire political leadership unpunished would not serve the cause of justice and accountability: 'Impunity is unacceptable in the face of genocide and other crimes against humanity'. His firm view was that the tribunal in question must be international in character. However, the success of any international tribunal of whatever character presupposes the full cooperation of the government of Cambodia. On 18 April 1999, Hun Sen affirmed to US Senator John Kerry that, to meet international standards, the trial of Ta Mok would be conducted by the existing national court with the assistance of foreign countries, in which foreign judges and prosecutors would be allowed to take part. The indictment and prosecution of other Khmer Rouge leaders were to be within the sole competence of the court.[14]

According to a UN plan issued in August 1999, a joint tribunal would have either five judges, two of them Cambodians, or seven judges, three of them Cambodians. The UN Secretary-General would select an independent prosecutor and the international judges. The UN had thus abandoned the earlier proposal of an international tribunal. In October, Hun Sen endorsed a US initiative reversing the proportions of Cambodian and international judges: three Cambodian judges and two UN-appointed judges. At least, one of the international judges would have to agree with any verdict passed by the tribunal. Following long and fruitless negotiations between the UN and the Cambodian government, the deadlock was resolved by US Senator John Kerry. Under the agreement, indictments against

[12] UN Doc. A/53/851, S/1999/230, 3 March 1999.
[13] UN Doc. A/53/875, S/1999/324, 24 March 1999.
[14] UN Doc. A/53/916, S/1999/443, 19 April 1999.

suspects would be drawn by two prosecutors – one appointed by the UN, the other by the Cambodian government. In the event of a disagreement between the two prosecutors, the three Cambodian and two international judges could prevent an indictment from being issued, but only if four of these five judges vote to do so.[15]

In January 2001, the Cambodian General Assembly approved the creation of the tribunal. In a concession to Hun Sen, the Assembly specified that only 'those persons who are most responsible' could face the tribunal. On 10 August 2001, King Norodom Sihanouk promulgated the law creating the special joint court, a Cambodian court with an international character. The Cambodian government and the UN would still have to agree to the terms of a memorandum of understanding.[16]

The long delays were caused initially by the reluctance of many countries, including permanent members of the Security Council, to uncover Khmer Rouge atrocities while they had supported the regime. Delays were later caused by the conflict between the UN insistence on an independent international court, based on the fact that Cambodian courts were neither competent nor independent from government authorities, and Cambodian concerns for national sovereignty, Hun Sen's insistence on peace and reconciliation at the cost of impunity of the senior Khmer Rouge leaders and the fear that former senior members of the Khmer Rouge now serving in the government could be prosecuted by an independent tribunal. Hun Sen's resistance and stalling tactics have successfully overcome international pressures and human rights concerns: no international tribunal will be created and the Cambodian tribunal, yet to be created, will not be independent: it will be subject to pressures and interference by the Cambodian government.

Sierra Leone's Special Court

'Nothing had quite prepared me', said Secretary-General Kofi Annan of his visit to Freetown, Sierra Leone, in July 1999, remarking on the sight of thousands of limbless children and adults, their arms and legs hacked off by rebel forces during the nine-year civil war. From March 1991 to July 1999, the civil war created from 1 to 2 million refugees, 50 000 deaths, 5000–10 000 amputated persons, 5000–10 000 women and girls raped, 10 000 children forcibly recruited as soldiers.[17]

---

15 *Le Monde*, 16 and 22 January, 19 March 1999; *IHT*, 26 March, 13 August, 20 October 1999. See also Mark A. Drumbl, 'Legal Issues' in John Tessitore and Susan Woolfson (eds), *A Global Agenda, Issues Before the 55th General Assembly of the United Nations, An annual publication of the UN Association of the USA* (Rowman & Littlefield Publishers, Inc., Lanham, New York, Boulder, Oxford, 2000), p. 251.

16 *IHT*, 3 January 2001; *Le Monde*, 12–13 August 2001.

17 UN *News Wire*, 2 August 1999; *Le Monde*, 30 November 1999.

Historical Background

The conflict in Sierra Leone dates from March 1991 when fighters of the Revolutionary United Front (RUF), led by Foday Sankoh, launched a war from the east of the country near the border with Liberia to overthrow the government.[18] With the support of the Military Observer Group (ECOMOG) of the Economic Community of West African States (ECOWAS) Sierra Leone's army tried at first to defend the government but, the following year, the army itself overthrew the government. Despite the change of power, RUF continued its attacks. Parliamentary and presidential elections were held in February 1996, and the army relinquished power to the winner, Alhaji Dr. Ahmed Tejan Kabbah However, the RUF did not participate in the elections and did not recognise the results. The conflict continued.

UN Special Envoy Berhanu Dinka (Ethiopia) assisted in negotiating a peace agreement, in November 1996, between the government and RUF, the Abidjan Accord. The agreement was derailed by another military coup d'état in May 1997. This time, the army joined forces with the RUF and formed a ruling junta. President Kabbah and his government went into exile in neighbouring Guinea. In February 1998, ECOMOG launched a military attack that led to the collapse of the junta and its expulsion from Freetown. On 10 March, President Kabbah was returned to office.

In June 1998, the Security Council established the UN Observer Mission in Sierra Leone (UNOMSIL). Unarmed UNOMSIL teams, under the protection of ECOMOG, documented reports of on-going atrocities and human rights abuses committed against civilians. Fighting continued with the rebels gaining control of more than half the country. In January 1999, the RUF overran most of Freetown. Over 6000 Sierra Leoneans were killed in the four days of an orgy of destruction that followed: among them police officers, judges, human rights activists, journalists, civil servants, government officials and ordinary citizens. During the first few days of occupation, the rebels were reported to have amputated the limbs of 1500 adults and children. Over the years, rebel forces abducted thousands of children for use as labourers, fighters, and, in the case of girls, cooks and sexual partners. Between early January and mid-February 1999, childcare agencies in Freetown reported that 2000 children had disappeared from the city alone. A UN human rights assessment team found that 'the ultimate responsibility for the fighting, for most of the civilian casualties and for the related humanitarian emergency in Freetown rested with the rebel forces'.[19] Later the same month, ECOMOG troops retook the capital and again installed the civilian government, although thousands of rebels were still hiding out in the surrounding countryside. By then, over a fifth of the population

18 See 'Sierra Leone – UNAMSIL Background', <www.un.org/Depts/dpko/unamsil/UnamsimB.htm>, 21 November 2000.

19 Nick Birnback, 'Sierra Leone', in John Tessitore and Susan Woolfson (eds), *A Global Agenda, Issues Before the 54th General Assembly of the United Nations, An Annual Publication of the UN Association of the USA* (Rowman & Littlefield Publishers, Inc., Lanham/New York/Boulder/ Oxford, 1999), pp. 16–18.

had been uprooted: 450 000 Sierra Leonans had fled the country and 700 000 were internally displaced. By the spring of 1999, the rebels controlled roughly two-thirds of the country.

Negotiations between the government and the rebels began in May 1999 and on 7 July the parties to the conflict signed an agreement in Lomé to end hostilities and form a government of national unity. In addition to providing for a cease-fire between the parties and for disarmament of the RUF, the agreement granted an 'absolute and free pardon and reprieve to all combatants and collaborators and respect of anything done by them in pursuit of their objectives ...' Moreover, the agreement granted the RUF several cabinet seats in the transition government and provided that the RUF may participate in planned national elections. Foday Sankoh was offered the Chairmanship of the Board of the Commission for the Management of Strategic Resources, National Reconstruction and Development, with the status of Vice President. Rather than providing for the prosecution of war crimes, the agreement established a Truth and Reconciliation Commission 'to address impunity, break the cycle of violence, provide a forum for both the victims and perpetrators of human rights violations to tell their story, [and] get a picture of the past in order to facilitate genuine healing and reconciliations'.[20] The Special Representative of the UN Secretary-General entered a reservation to the Lomé agreement, that the 'United Nations holds the understanding that the amnesty provisions of the Peace Agreement shall not apply to international crimes of genocide, crimes against humanity, war crimes and other serious violations of international humanitarian law'. The UN Secretary-General recommended the creation of an Inquiry Commission on the atrocities committed during the civil war.[21] On 20 August 1999, the Security Council welcomed the signing of the agreement, commended the Government of Sierra Leone for its courageous efforts to achieve peace and also the leadership of the RUF for taking this decisive step towards peace. Human Rights Watch and Amnesty International denounced the amnesty provision in the agreement. HRW wrote to the Secretary-General: 'Time and time again, the United Nations' experience has shown that peace accords built on impunity are shaky and do not hold'.

In October 1999, the Security Council authorized the establishment of the UN Mission in Sierra Leone (UNAMSIL), a larger mission with a maximum of 6000 military personnel including 260 observers to assist the government and the parties in carrying out the provisions of the Lomé peace agreement. The strength of UNAMSIL was increased by the Security Council in February 2000 to a maximum of 11 100 military personnel, and, in May 2000, to 13 000.[22]

---

20 Peace Agreement between the Government of Sierra Leone and the Revolutionary United Front of Sierra Leone, July, 1999, UN Doc. S/1999/777, 12 July 1999, Art. IX(2), XXVI(1).

21 Security Council resolution 1260(1999) adopted on 20 August 1999; *IHT*, 27 July 1999; *Le Monde*, 4 August 1999. See also HRW Letter of 19 May 2000, www.hrw.org/press/2000/05/sl-ltr0519.htm.

22 Security Council res. 1289 and 1299.

Foday Sankoh was captured by the Sierra Leone government on 17 May 2000, raising hopes for a progress towards peace. However, fighting and atrocities continued in 2000 and 2001.

In July 2000, the UN Security Council expressed its concern at the role played by the illicit trade in diamonds in fuelling the conflict in Sierra Leone and at reports that such diamonds transit neighbouring countries, including Liberia. The Council asked all States to take the necessary measures to prohibit the direct or indirect import of rough diamonds from Sierra Leone to their territory. The resolution established a UN Panel of Experts. In its report, the Panel found that diamonds represent a major and primary source of income for the RUF, that the bulk of RUF diamonds leave Sierra Leone through Liberia, and that such illicit trade cannot be conducted without the permission and involvement of Liberian Government officials at the highest levels. In March 2001, the Council expressed its deep concern at the unequivocal and overwhelming evidence presented by the Panel's report that the Government of Liberia is actively supporting the RUF at all levels. The Council determined that the active support provided by the Government of Liberia for armed rebel groups in neighbouring countries, and in particular its support for the RUF in Sierra Leone, constituted a threat to international peace and security in the region. Acting under Chapter VII of the UN Charter, the Council demanded that the Government of Liberia immediately ceased its support for the RUF in Sierra Leone and for other armed rebel groups in the region, expel all RUF members from Liberia, cease all financial and military support to the RUF, cease all direct or indirect import of Sierra Leone diamonds not controlled through the Certificate of Origin regime and other measures.[23]

On 20 April 2001, the UN Commission on Human Rights adopted resolution 2001/20 which, in part, expressed its grave concern

> 2 (a) At abuses of human rights and international humanitarian law that have been committed in Sierra Leone, generally with impunity, in particular atrocities against civilians, including women and children, perpetrated by the Revolutionary United Front and others, including other armed groups, including summary and extrajudicial executions, mutilations, abductions, arbitrary detention, hostage-taking, forced recruitment, forced labour, forced displacement, harassment, looting, destruction of property, attacks on and killings of journalists and the continued detention of abductees;
>
> (b) At the targeting and abuse of women and girls that have been committed in Sierra Leone by the Revolutionary United Front and others, including other armed groups, in particular murder, sexual violence, rape, including systematic rape, sexual slavery and forced marriages ...

[23] Security Council res. 1306 (2000), 5 July 2000; res. 1343 (2001), 7 March 2001.

The Commission also expressed concern at the recruitment and continuing victimization and use of child combatants by the RUF and others. According to HRW reports, 'others' include pro-government militias.[24]

The Creation of an Independent Special Court

In 2000, several proposals were made for the creation of an international tribunal to try the perpetrators of atrocities in Sierra Leone. On 19 May, Human Rights Watch called on the Security Council to authorize and establish as soon as possible an International Criminal Tribunal for Sierra Leone with jurisdiction over all crimes of genocide, crimes against humanity, war crimes and other serious violations of human rights and international humanitarian law committed at least since March 1991, when the RUF launched a rebellion to overthrow the Sierra Leone government. Because of the inevitable time required to establish such a tribunal, the Council should send investigators to Sierra Leone to collect evidence of war crimes and crimes against humanity committed both before and after the Lomé agreement, in anticipation of its use by the future tribunal. In another letter to the Security Council dated 20 June, HRW urged that the process of justice for the crimes in Sierra Leone should be broad-based and inclusive, going beyond rebel leader Foday Sankoh, and look at the conduct of all parties involved in the brutal conflict. The trials will have to meet international standards of due process and fairness. On 12 June, the government of Sierra Leone asked the Security Council to set up an international tribunal on crimes against humanity to try Foday Sankoh and others, under a combination of domestic and international law. At the end of July, the US submitted a draft resolution asking the Security Council to establish a special court which would try senior Sierra Leone nationals who bear the greatest responsibility for the most systematic and egregious criminal violations. The court would combine elements of Sierra Leonean and international law.[25]

On 14 August 2000, the Security Council adopted resolution 1315 (2000), expressing its deep concern at the very serious crimes committed within Sierra Leone against the people of Sierra Leone and UN personnel and at the prevailing situation of impunity. The Council reinterated that the situation in Sierra Leone continued to be a threat to international peace and security in the region. The Council requested the Secretary-General to negotiate an agreement with the government of Sierra Leone to create an independent special court, recommended that its jurisdiction should include notably crimes against humanity, war crimes and other violations of international humanitarian law, as well as crimes under Sierra Leonean law

[24] See for instance HRW 'Sierra Leone: Most Serious Attacks in Months, UN Peacekeepers Needed to Protect Civilians', hrw-news@igc.topica.com, 24 July 2001.

[25] See HRW's 'Expedited UN Criminal Tribunal Urged, Letter to UN Security Council on Sierra Leone', www.hrw.org/press/2000/05/sl-ltr0519.htm, 19 May 2000; 'Decisive UN action on Sierra Leone urged', hrw-news@igc.topica.com, 20 June 2000; *IHT*, 21 June and 29–30 July 2000.

committed within the territory of Sierra Leone. It recommended further that the court should have jurisdiction over persons who bear the greatest responsibility for these crimes, including those leaders who have committed these crimes, have threatened the establishment and implementation of the peace process in Sierra Leone, emphasized the importance of ensuring the impartiality and credibility of the process, in particular with regard to the judges and the prosecutors. The Secretary-General was requested to submit a report on the implementation of this resolution not later than 30 days following the adoption of the resolution.

On 4 October 2000, the Secretary-General submitted his Report on the establishment of a Special Court for Sierra Leone.[26] Unlike the ICTY and the ICTR, which were established by resolutions of the Security Council and constituted as subsidiary organs of the United Nations, and unlike national courts established by law, the proposed Special Court would be established by an Agreement between the United Nations and the Government of Sierra Leone: it would therefore be a treaty-based sui generis court of mixed jurisdiction and composition. Its implementation at the national level will require that the Agreement be incorporated in the national law of Sierra Leone. Its applicable law will include both international and Sierra Leonean law. As a treaty-based organ, the Special Court will not be anchored to any existing system, such as the UN internal administrative law or national law of the seat of the Court. Rules will need to be developed for such purposes as recruitment, staff administration, procurement etc. In the view of the Secretary-General, the support and technical assistance of UNAMSIL in providing security, logistics, administrative support and temporary accommodation would be necessary in the first operational phase of the Special Court. Regarding the financing of the Court, the Secretary-General's view was that the only realistic solution was financing through assessed contributions. The proposed Agreement between the UN and the Government of Sierra Leone followed as an Annex to the Report. The Court will have its seat in Sierra Leone. It will function in accordance with its Statute, annexed to the Agreement as an Enclosure, forming an integral part of the Agreement.

The Proposed Statute of the Special Court

The main elements of the Statute, as proposed by the Secretary-General, are summarised hereunder. Some of these were later amended by the Security Council.

- *Competence of the Court*: the Court will have the power to prosecute persons most responsible for serious violations of international humanitarian law and Sierra Leonean law committed in the territory of Sierra Leone since 30 November 1996 (Art. 1);

[26] UN Doc. S/2000 915 dated 4 October 2000, Annex 'Agreement between the United Nations and the Government of Sierra Leone on the Establishment of a Special Court for Sierra Leone', Enclosure 'Statute of the Special Court for Sierra Leone'.

- The Court will have the power to prosecute persons who committed crimes against humanity as part of a widespread or systematic attack against civilian population (Art. 2). It will have the power to prosecute persons who committed or ordered the commission of serious violations of Article 3 common to the Geneva Conventions of 12 August 1949 for the Protection of War Victims, and of Additional Protocol II thereto of 8 June 1977 (Art. 3). The Court's power will extend to other serious violations of international humanitarian law, including abduction and forced recruitment of children under the age of 15 years into armed forces or groups for the purpose of using them to participate actively in hostilities (Art. 4). It will also include crimes against specified Sierra Leonean Law (Art. 5);
- The provisions concerning individual criminal responsibility are the same as in the Statutes of the ICTY and ICTR, except that individual criminal responsibility for the crimes against Sierra Leonean Law will be determined in accordance with the respective laws of Sierra Leone (Art. 6);
- The Court will have jurisdiction over persons who were 15 years of age or over at the time of the alleged commission of the crime. In the trial of a juvenile offender, the Court will consider as a priority the release of the juvenile under certain conditions. The Court will constitute a 'Juvenile Chamber' composed of at least one sitting judge and one alternate judge possessing the required qualifications and experience in juvenile justice (Art. 7);
- The Special Court and the national courts of Sierra Leone will have concurrent jurisdiction. The Special Court will have primacy over the national courts. At any stage of the procedure, the Special Court may formally request a national court to defer to its competence (Art. 8);
- Under the principle of non bis in idem, no person shall be tried before a national court of Sierra Leone for acts for which he or she has already been tried by the Special Court. A person who has been tried by a national court may be subsequently tried by the Special Court under specific conditions (Art. 9);
- An amnesty granted to any person falling within the jurisdiction of the Special Court in respect of the crimes referred to in Article 2 to 4 of the Statute will not be a bar to prosecution (Art. 10);

- *Organisation of the Special Court*:
  The Special Court will consist of the following organs:
  The Chambers, comprising two Trial Chambers and one Appeals Chamber;
  The Prosecutor, and
  The Registry (Art. 11),

The Chambers will be composed of 11 independent judges, serving as follows:

- three judges serve in each of the Trial Chambers, of whom one will be a judge appointed by the government of Sierra Leone, and two judges appointed by the UN Secretary-General;

- five judges serve in the Appeals Chamber, of whom two judges appointed by the government of Sierra Leone and three judges appointed by the Secretary-General;
- In addition to these judges, the presiding judge of a Trial Chamber or the Appeals Chamber will designate an alternate judge appointed by either the Government of Sierra Leone or the Secretary-General, to be present at each stage of the trial, and to replace a judge, if that judge is unable to continue sitting (Art. 12);
- Judges should have the same qualifications as those of the ICTY and ICTR. They are independent in the performance of their functions. They are appointed for a four-year period, renewable (Art. 13);
- **The Rules of Procedures and Evidence** of the ICTR obtaining at the time of the establishment of the Special Court will be applicable mutatis mutandis to the conduct of legal proceedings before this Court (Art. 14);
- **The Prosecutor** will be responsible for the investigation and prosecution of the persons most responsible for serious violations of international humanitarian law and crimes under Sierra Leonean law committed in the territory of Sierra Leone since 30 November 1996. The Prosecutor acts independently as a separate organ of the Special Court. The Prosecutor is appointed by the Secretary-General for a four-year term and is eligible for reappointment. He is assisted by a Sierra Leonean Deputy Prosecutor (Art. 15);
- **The Registry** is responsible for the administration and servicing of the Special Court. The Registrar is appointed by the Secretary-General after consultation with the President of the Special Court. He or she is a UN staff member. He or she serves for a four-year term, renewable (Art. 16);
- **Rights of the accused**: The accused are entitled to a fair and public hearing, they are presumed innocent until proved guilty according to the provisions of the Statute (Art. 17);
- **Judgements** are rendered by a majority of the judges of the Trial Chamber or Appeals Chamber, they are delivered in public. They are accompanied by a reasoned opinion in writing, to which separate or dissenting opinions may be appended (Art. 18);
- The Trial Chamber imposes upon a convicted person, other than a juvenile offender, imprisonment for a specified number of years. In determining the terms of imprisonment, the Court will, as appropriate, have recourse to the practice regarding prison sentences in the ICTR and the national courts of Sierra Leone. In addition to imprisonment, the Trial Chamber may order the forfeiture of the property, proceeds and any assets acquired unlawfully or by criminal conduct, and their return to their rightful owner or to the State of Sierra Leone (Art. 19);
- The Appeals Chamber hears appeals from persons convicted by a Trial Chamber or from the Prosecutor on the grounds of a procedural error, an error on a question of law invalidating the decision, an error of fact which has occasioned a miscarriage of justice. The Appeals Chamber may affirm, reverse, or revise the decision of a Trial Chamber (Art. 19);

- An application for review of a judgement is submitted to the Appeals Chamber (Art. 20);
- Imprisonment is served in Sierra Leone. If circumstances so require, imprisonment may also be served in any of the States which have concluded with the ICTR or the ICTY an agreement for the enforcement of sentences and which have indicated to the Registrar of the Court their willingness to accept convicted persons (Art. 22).

In a letter dated 1 November 2000 to the Security Council, the Executive Director of Human Rights Watch (HRW) recommended a few amendments to the proposed Statute. He urged that the Court should be vested with Chapter VII powers of enforcing international cooperation at every stage. It deplored the restrictive scope of temporal jurisdiction, i.e. that the Court would only try crimes committed since 30 November 1996, rather than from the war's inception in March 1991. HRW recommended that the Court does not try persons who were under the age of 18 at the time when they allegedly committed a crime within the Court's jurisdiction. The Court's 'limited resources would be far better used in pursuit of justice for adult offenders, rather than children'.[27]

The Security Council's Amendments

In a letter of 22 December 2000 from the President of the Security Council to the Secretary-General,[28] the members of the Council maintained their view that the Court should have personal jurisdiction only 'over persons who bear the greatest responsibility' for the listed crimes. They believed that, 'by thus limiting the focus of the Court to those who played a leadership role, the simpler and more general formulations suggested in the appended draft will be appropriate'. In the view of the Council's members, the Truth and Reconciliation Commission would have a major role to play in the case of juvenile offenders. To this end, the Council members encouraged the government of Sierra Leone and the UN to develop suitable institutions, including specific provisions related to children.

The Council rejected the Secretary-General's recommendation that the new Court be financed through mandatory fees levied on all UN Member States, as is the case for the ICTR and ICTY. They recommended instead that the Court be funded through voluntary contributions. However, Council members understood that the Secretary-General could not be expected to create any institution for which he did not have adequate funds in hand for at least 12 months and pledges to cover anticipated expenses for a second year of the Court's operations. The Council also disagreed with the Secretary-General's proposal of setting up two Trial Chambers and the use of alternate judges, at least from the very outset. The Council members

---

[27] HRW *Press Release*, 'Justice and the Special Court for Sierra Leone, Letter to the United Nations Security Council', 1 November 2000.

[28] UN Doc. S/2000/1234, 22 December 2000 and Annex.

recommended a single Trial Chamber, 'with the possibility of adding a second Chamber should the developing caseload warrant its creation'.

In the Annex to the same document, the Council's President suggested amendments to both the Agreement between the UN and the Government of Sierra Leone and the Statute of the Special Court. The main changes in the Statute were:

Competence of the Special Court (revised article 1):

(a) The Special Court shall, except as provided in subparagraph (b), have the power to prosecute persons who bear the greatest responsibility for serious violations of international humanitarian law and Sierra Leonean law committed in the territory of Sierra Leone since 30 November 1996, including those leaders who, in committing such crimes, have threatened the establishment of and implementation of the peace process in Sierra Leone.

(b) Any transgressions by peacekeepers and related personnel present in Sierra Leone pursuant to the Status of Mission Agreement in force between the United Nations and the Government of Sierra Leone or agreements between Sierra Leone and other Governments or regional organisations, or, in the absence of such agreement, provided that the peacekeeping operations were undertaken with the consent of the Government of Sierra Leone, shall be within the primary jurisdiction of the sending State.

(c) In the event the sending State is unwilling or unable genuinely to carry out an investigation or prosecution, the Court may, if authorized by the Security Council on the proposal of any State, exercise jurisdiction over such persons.

Article 11 (a) was to be modified, showing that the Chamber would comprise '... one or more Trial Chambers ... ' instead of 'two trial Chambers'. Article 12 would prescribe that the Chamber would be composed of '...not less than eight (8) or more than eleven (11) independent judges, ... ', instead of 11 judges plus alternate judges.

In his letter of 12 January 2001 addressed to the President of the Security Council,[29] the Secretary-General first stressed that the determination of the meaning of the term 'persons who bear the greatest responsibility' in any given case falls initially to the prosecutor and ultimately to the Special Court itself, thus recalling implicitly the independence of the Court. He proposed the following part revision of Article 7,

Jurisdiction over persons of 15 years of age:

7.1 The Special Court shall have no jurisdiction over any person who was under the age of 15 at the time of the alleged commission of the crime. Should any person who was, at the time of the alleged commission of the crime, between 15 and 18 years of age come before the Court, he or she shall be treated with dignity and a sense of worth, taking into account his

[29] UN Doc. S/2001/40, 12 January 2001.

or her young age and the desirability of promoting his or her rehabilitation, reintegration into and assumption of a constructive role in society, and in accordance with international human rights standards, in particular, the rights of the child.

7.2 In the disposition of his or her case, [the Special Court] order any of the following: care guidance and supervision orders, community service orders, counselling, foster care, correctional, educational and vocational training programmes, approved schools and, as appropriate, any programmes of disarmament, demobilization and reintegration or programmes of child protection agencies [former Article 7.3(f)].

The Secretary-General cautioned against the establishment of the Court on the basis of availability of funds for one year and pledges for the following year, as unlikely to ensure a regular flow of funds in the subsequent years. He proposed that the process of establishing the Court should not commence until the UN Secretariat had obtained sufficient contributions in hand to finance the establishment of the Court and 12 months of its operations, as well as pledges equal to the anticipated expenses of the following 24 months.

The President of the Security Council, in his letter of 31 January 2001,[30] conveyed the agreement of the Council's members to most of the Secretary-General's proposals,[31] but expressed their belief that it was extremely unlikely that juvenile offenders would in fact come before the Special Court and that other institutions, such as the Truth and Reconciliation Commission, were better suited to address cases involving juveniles. Council members agreed with the Secretary-General's proposal to seek concurrent information from States with respect to their preparedness to contribute funds, services and personnel before the entry into force of the agreement with the Government of Sierra Leone.

On 9 February 2001, the Government of Sierra Leone expressed its willingness to accept the revised texts of the draft Agreement and the draft Statute of the Court. In his letter of 13 July 2001[32] to the President of the Security Council, the Secretary-General recalled that the UN Secretariat had presented to the group of interested States revised (reduced) budget estimates amounting to approximately to $57 million for the first three years of operation of the Court, with $16.8 million for the first year. These estimates reflected a scaled-down operation of the Court, while maintaining its nature and sui generis character, international standards of justice and the applicable law. Although renewed appeals to States had produced a shortfall of contributions in relation to the reduced budget, the Secretary-General considered that the amount of

[30] UN Doc. S/2001/95, 31 January 2001.

[31] Except for the Secretary-General's proposal to empower the President of the Special Court to notify the Security Council and seek its intervention with an 'unwilling or unable' sending State in order to induce it to conduct an investigation and prosecution in its own courts, or to surrender the accused to the jurisdiction of the Special Court (see new Article 1(c)).

[32] UN Doc. S/2001/693, 13 July 2001.

these contributions was sufficient to commence the establishment and operation of the Court. States' contributions were to be deposited into a Trust Fund, following which the Legal Counsel would conclude on behalf of the UN the Agreement on the Establishment of the Special Court with the Sierra Leone Government. On 23 July, the members of the Security Council welcomed these developments, 'as a positive step forward in bringing justice to the people of Sierra Leone'.[33]

On 16 January 2002, in Freetown, the Government of Sierra Leone and the United Nations signed the Agreement formally establishing the Special Court for Sierra Leone. The Government expressed its gratitude to the international community, as represented by the UN, for its continuing determination to ensure that those who bear the greatest responsibility for the crimes committed during the conflict will be held to account and the rule of law re-established within Sierra Leone.[34]

The Truth and Reconciliation Commission

The Peace Agreement signed in Lomé on 7 July 1999 between the Government of Sierra Leone and the RUF provided for, inter alia, the establishment of a Truth and Reconciliation Commission.[35] The Report of the Secretary-General on the Establishment of a Special Court for Sierra Leone of 4 October 2000 did not address in detail specifics of the relationship between the Court and the National Truth and Reconciliation Commission. It however recognised that relationship and cooperation arrangements would be required between the Prosecutor and the Commission, including the use of the Commission as an alternative to prosecution, and the prosecution of juveniles in particular.[36]

In February 2000, the Sierra Leone Parliament adopted the Truth and Reconciliation Commission Act 2000. The Office of the UN High Commissioner on Human Rights (OHCHR) had assisted the Government in the drafting process of the Act. A seminar on the operational and managerial aspects of the Commission was held in Freetown from 29 May to 1 June 2001. It was attended by representatives of the government and the local diplomatic community, and the leadership of the UN Mission in Sierra Leone (UNAMSIL). NGOs directly involved in truth and reconciliation, disarmament, demobilization and reintegration processes also attended. As recommended by the national seminar on the Commission organised in November 2000 by OHCHR, in cooperation with UNAMSIL and the National Forum for Human Rights, a technical meeting of experts was hosted by

---

33 UN Doc. S/2001/722, 23 July 2001. As of mid-July, Canada, the Czech Republic, Denmark, Germany, Mauritius, the Netherlands, Norway, Sweden, the UK and the US had pledged contributions: see HRW 'Funds Urged for Sierra Leone Court', www.hrw.org/press/2001/07/un_courts0724.htm, 24 July 2001.

34 See www.specialcourt.org/SLMission/PlanningMission/PressReleases/16JAN02.html.

35 See Security Council res. 1260 (1999), para. 10, 20 August 1999.

36 UN Doc. S/2000/915, para. 8.

UNICEF in Freetown from 4 to 6 June 2001. The aim was to define the framework for participation and protection of children in the Commission's process. National and international experts explored the extent to which children had been affected by the armed conflict in Sierra Leone and the role of the Commission for children. A target date of October 2001 was established for the appointment of commissioners and the Commission was expected to commence operations in January 2002. The interim secretariat, to be made up of international and national staff will eventually succeed the UNAMSIL Human Rights Section and assume full responsibility for organizing and managing the preparatory phase of the Commission. The Commission will be composed of four national commissioners and three international commissioners.

The Commission will require approximately $8 million for one year. Efforts are made to ensure Sierra Leonean ownership of the Commission process and to include it in its traditional structures and methods. On 24 July 2001, the UNAMSIL Human Rights Section met with the RUF leadership in Makeni. The Front indicated support for the Commission and acknowledged that it is a party to it by virtue of the Lomé Peace Agreement.[37]

Assessment

The Special Court was created at the initiative of the Sierra Leone government, in part because the government did not have the legal capacity nor the financial resources, after a decade of civil war, to set up a national court to try those responsible for serious violations of international humanitarian law. But the most important reason, as reported by Michelle Sieff,[38] was to establish the credibility of the Court. In the words of John Leigh, Sierra Leone Ambassador to the US: 'We don't want the Court to be seen as victor's justice, and international involvement will prevent this perception'. The creation of the Court had strong support from the UK and the US governments. None of the Security Council members supported the creation of another international criminal tribunal on the lines of the ICTY or ICTR, in part because of the heavy costs incurred by these tribunals, and, perhaps, on the expectation that the adoption of the Statute of the International Criminal Court in July 1998 was leading towards a universal criminal justice system, thus preempting the need for more ad hoc international criminal tribunals.

The Special Court will be located in Sierra Leone, while the ICTY is located in The Hague, not in the former Yugoslavia, and the ICTR is located in Tanzania, not in Rwanda. The geographical distance of the ICTY and ICTR from the scenes of the crimes may have prevented the populations concerned from a sense of participation in the trials and from benefiting from an educational process, while legal and

[37] UN Doc. A/56/281, 9 August 2001, 'Situation of human rights in Sierra Leone'.

[38] M. Sieff, 'A "Special Court" for Sierra Leone's War Crimes', in www.globalpolicy.org/security/issues/sierra/court/2001/analysis.htm, 11 October 2001.

linguistic problems of the trials themselves, political, nationalistic, historical, cultural, religious and ethnic factors have constituted other obstacles. The location of the Special Court in Sierra Leone may be a significant asset, provided the UN and the Sierra Leone government accompany the judicial process with an effective public education and sensitization programme.[39]

The Special Court for Sierra Leone differs from the ICTY and ICTR insofar as these are genuine international tribunals, while the Court is a mixed national/international tribunal. The ICTY and ICTR have been created by the Security Council under Chapter VII of the UN Charter as subsidiary bodies of the Council, while the Court will be a sui generis international treaty-based organ created by agreement between the UN and the Sierra Leone government, a new model for the prosecution and trial of those persons who have committed serious violations of international humanitarian law.

Both the ICTY and the ICTR have the power to prosecute 'persons' responsible for serious violations of international humanitarian law, while the Court will rightly focus on 'persons who bear the greatest responsibility for serious violations of international humanitarian law and Sierra Leonean law', 'including those leaders who, in committing such crimes, have threatened the establishment of and implementation of the peace process in Sierra Leone'.

In contrast with the ICTY and ICTR, the Court will not have competence over the crime of genocide, which is understandable as the killings in Sierra Leone were not perpetrated with the intent to destroy in whole or in part, a national, ethnical, racial or religious groups. The mixed nature of the Court is reflected by the inclusion, in Article 5 of its Statute, of 'Crimes under Sierra Leonean law', in addition to 'Crimes against humanity', 'Violations of Article 3 common to the Geneva Conventions and of Additional Protocol II' (found in the Statute of the ICTR), and 'Other serious violations of international humanitarian law'. The Statute of the Special Court integrates the same provisions of 'individual criminal responsibility' as the ICTY and ICTR, but adds that individual criminal responsibility for crimes committed under Sierra Leonean law will be determined in accordance with the respective laws of the country.

The Statute of the Special Court, unlike the Statutes of the ICTY and ICTR, includes a novel reference to potential transgressions by peacekeepers and related personnel present in Sierra Leone under the terms of agreements between the UN and the Sierra Leone government or between Sierra Leone and other governments or regional organisations, or in the absence of an agreement, provided that the peacekeeping operations were undertaken with the consent of the Sierra Leone government. The purpose of this reference is to establish that such transgressions should be within the primary jurisdiction of the sending state. The Court could

---

39 See Alison Smith, 'A Response to "A "Special Court" for Sierra Leone's War Crimes', in www.globalpolicy.org/security/issues/sierra/court/2001/critique.htm, *No Peace Without Justice*, 15 August 2001.

exercise jurisdiction over such persons only if the sending State is unwilling or unable genuinely to carry out an investigation or prosecution, and only if authorized by the Security Council on the proposal of any State. Even if such cases are likely to be few, the recognition of the possible criminal responsibility of peacekeepers is a useful warning to their commanders.

As an innovation over the Statutes of the ICTY and ICTR, Article 7 of the Statute of the Special Court provides detailed instructions and guidance to the Court concerning its jurisdiction over persons of 15 years of age, and those between 15 and 18 at the time of the alleged commission of crimes, their treatment, protection and reintegration. Another innovation is the constitution of a 'Juvenile Chamber' by the Court. These innovations were justified by the exposure of widespread practices of abduction, forced recruitment of children during the civil war, and the participation of children in crimes against humanity and other violations of international humanitarian law, practices not observed in Former Yugoslavia or in Rwanda. Considering that it is most unlikely that juvenile offenders would be identified as 'persons who bear the greatest responsibility for the commission of crimes', the members of the Security Council rightly believed that the Truth and Reconciliation Commission would have a major role to play in the case of juvenile offenders. The interconnection and relationship between the Court and a non-judiciary Commission should contribute to the ultimate aim of national civil peace through justice and reintegration of offenders. The experience of South Africa and Latin American countries will be useful to both national and international experts and actors in the judiciary and non-judiciary areas.[40]

The Special Court will have primacy over national courts in Sierra Leone, similarly to the ICTY's and ICTR's primacy over national courts. The Court's structure is similar to that of the ICTY and ICTR. The composition of the Chambers of the Sierra Leone Court reflects its mixed national/international nature, with a numerical majority given to those appointed by the Secretary-General of the UN. International preeminence is also shown by the appointment of the independent Prosecutor by the UN Secretary-General. These elements are in contrast with the status of the proposed tribunal for Cambodia, a national court with only an 'international character'.

The Court may impose a prison sentence, the death penalty is rightly excluded, as in the Statutes of the ICTY, the ICTR and the International Criminal Court.

The two operating international criminal tribunals have faced serious obstacles in their quest to obtain custody of indicted persons, even though they were created by the Security Council under Chapter VII of the UN Charter, and states were under obligation to cooperate with the Tribunals and to comply with the Tribunals' requests for assistance or orders.[41] The Special Court may face even more obstacles for the reasons given by the Secretary-General in his report of 4 October 2000. First,

[40] See Beigbeder (1999), Chapter 5, 'Truth and Reconciliation', pp. 104–124.

[41] Art. 29 of the Statute of the ICTY and Art. 28 of the Statute of the YCTR.

the Special Court lacks the power to assert its primacy over national courts in third countries, second, the Court lacks the power to request the surrender of an accused from any third state and to induce the compliance of its authorities with any such request. The Secretary-General's suggestion that the Security Council might wish to consider endowing the Court with Chapter VII powers for the specific purpose of requesting the surrender of an accused from outside the jurisdiction of the Court was rejected by the Security Council in its President's letter of 31 January 2001.[42] While a number of alleged perpetrators of crimes, including Foday Sankoh, are in custody in Sierra Leone, others have fled to Liberia and other West African countries, where they may enjoy undue impunity.

Finally, it is worth noting that the final terms of the Statute of the Special Court were negotiated between the UN Secretariat and the Sierra Leone government, concurrently with a dialogue between the UN Secretariat and the Security Council, subject to the latter's final authority over the UN Secretariat.

East Timor: Indonesian Impunity

The UN General Assembly placed East Timor on the international agenda in 1960, when it added the territory to its list of Non-Self-Governing Territories. East Timor was then administered by Portugal. In 1974, Portugal sought to establish a provisional government and a popular assembly which would determine the status of the territory. Civil war broke out between those who favoured independence and those who advocated integration with Indonesia. Unable to control the situation, Portugal withdrew. Indonesia then intervened militarily and later integrated East Timor as its 27th province. The UN never recognised this integration, and both the Security Council and the General Assembly called for Indonesia's withdrawal. Following periodical talks between the UN Secretary-General, Portugal and Indonesia, in June 1998, Indonesia proposed a limited autonomy for East Timor within Indonesia. In light of the proposal, further talks resulted in a set of agreements signed in New York on 5 May 1999 between Indonesia and Portugal to finally resolve the status of the East Timor. The two governments entrusted the UN Secretary-General with organizing and conducting a 'popular consultation' in order to ascertain whether the East Timorese people accepted or rejected a special autonomy for East Timor within the Republic of Indonesia. In June 1999, the Security Council established the UN Mission in East Timor (UNAMET) to carry out the consultation and oversee a transition period after the vote. In a climate of high tension, the voters decided on 30 August 1999 by a 78.5% majority to reject the proposed autonomy and begin a process of transition towards independence. Following the announcement of the result, pro-integration militias, supported by the Indonesian security forces, launched a systematic campaign of violence, looting and arson throughout the whole territory. An estimated 70% of homes and buildings

[42] UN Doc. S/2000/915, 4 October 2000, para. 10; S/2001/95, 31 January 2001.

across East Timor were destroyed, more than two thirds of the population was displaced, and more than 200 000 East Timorese fled or were forcibly taken, often at gunpoint, across the border into Indonesian West Timor. Hundreds of civilians were killed and thousands were injured. The 1999 violence was the most recent incident in 24 years of Indonesian occupation, over the course of which an estimated 200 000 East Timorese have been killed.[43] On 15 September 1999, the Security Council, inter alia, condemned all acts of violence in East Timor, called for their immediate end and demanded that those responsible for such acts be brought to justice. The Council also authorized a multinational force (INTERFET) under Australian command to restore peace and security in East Timor and to facilitate humanitarian assistance operations.

On 23 September, the UN High Commissioner for Human Rights declared, 'there was overwhelming evidence that there had been a deliberate, vicious, and systematic campaign of gross violations of human rights in East Timor, including mass killings, forcible expulsions, violence against women, and a breakdown of law and order. The extreme violence ... was initiated by different militia groups, in which elements of security forces were also involved'.[44]

On 19 October, the Indonesian People's Consultative Assembly formally recognised the result of the consultation. On 25 October, the Security Council established, by resolution 1272, the UN Transitional Administration in East Timor (UNTAET) as an integrated, multidimensional peacekeeping operation fully responsible for the administration of East Timor during its transition to independence.[45]

On 10 December, the UN Secretary-General transmitted to the General Assembly the report of a joint mission to East Timor undertaken by the Special Rapporteurs of the Commission on Human Rights on extrajudicial, summary or arbitrary executions, on the question of torture and on violence against women, its causes and consequences, in accordance with the Commission resolution 1999/S-4/1 of 27 September 1999.[46] The report concluded that

> it was too early, on the basis of a short visit and the absence of many witnesses, more than 200 000 of whom are, at the conclusion of the visit, still held in precarious conditions in West Timor or elsewhere in Indonesia, to assess the full extent of the human rights violations and crimes which were perpetrated before and after the 30 August consultation. What is clear is that they took

---

43 M. A. Drumbl, 'Legal Issues' in J. Tessitore and S. Woolfson (eds), *A Global Agenda, Issues Before the 55th General Assembly of the United Nations* (Rowman & Littlefield Publishers, Inc., Lanham/New York/Boulder/Oxford, 2000), p. 252.

44 UNCHR *Press Release* HR/CN/99/67, 23 September 1999.

45 See (UN) www.org/peace/etimor/UntaetB.htm, 31 May 2000. See also Human Rights Watch 'Justice for East Timor, Press Backgrounder', March 2000, www.hrw.org/backgrounder/asia/timor/etimor-back0330.htm, 8 June 2000.

46 UN Doc. A/54/660, 10 December 1999.

> place in the context of an attack against the East Timorese population that overwhelmingly supported independence from Indonesia. They include murder, torture, sexual violence, forcible transfer of population and other persecution and inhumane acts, including destruction of property. These have all been committed on a scale that is widespread or systematic or both.

The report said that the East Timorese judicial system, which still needed to be created and tested, could not hope to cope with a large and sustained investigative process. The record of impunity for human rights crimes committed by Indonesia's armed forces in East Timor over almost a quarter of a century could not instil confidence in their ability to ensure a proper accounting. The Rapporteurs suggested that, unless, in a matter of months, the steps taken by the Indonesian government to investigate the Indonesian armed forces' involvement in the past year's atrocities bear fruit, both in the way of credible clarification of the facts and the bringing to justice of the perpetrators – both directly and by virtue of command responsibility, however high the level of responsibility – the Security Council should consider the establishment of an international criminal tribunal for the purpose. This should preferably be done with the consent of the government, but such consent should not be a prerequisite. Such a tribunal should then have jurisdiction over all crimes under international law committed by any party in the territory since the departure of the colonial power.

On 31 January 2000, the UN Secretary-General wrote to the President of the General Assembly, the President of the Security Council and the Chairperson of the Commission on Human Rights to transmit the report of the International Commission of Inquiry on East Timor, established by him in accordance with resolutions of the Commission on Human Rights endorsed by the Economic and Social Council.[47] The Inquiry Commission found that

> There is no doubt that the evidence gathered clearly demonstrates a pattern of serious violations of fundamental human rights and humanitarian law in East Timor. The violations include, but are not limited to, violations of the rights to life and to freedom from torture, cruel, inhuman or degrading treatment or punishment, violence against women, and violations of rights relating to freedom of assembly, association, opinion and expression, freedom from arbitrary arrest and exile, and freedom of movement and residence, and the right to own property. In addition, and particularly after the proclamation of the results of the consultation, further human rights were violated through the large-scale destruction, including the right to work, the right to an adequate standard of living, including food, clothing, housing and medical care, and the right to education.

[47] UN Doc. S/2000/59, A/54/726, 31 January 2000. paras. 142, 152, 153 – UNCHR res. 1999/S-4/1 of 27 September 1999, ECOSOC decision 1999/293, 15 November 1999.

The Inquiry Commission recommended the establishment of an independent investigation and prosecution body. It also recommended the establishment of an international human rights tribunal consisting of judges appointed by the UN, preferably with the participation of members from East Timor and Indonesia. The tribunal would sit in Indonesia, East Timor and any other relevant territory to receive the complaints and to try and sentence those accused by the independent investigation body of serious violations of fundamental human rights and international humanitarian law which took place in East Timor since January 1999 regardless of the nationality of the individual and where that person was when the violations were committed.

The Indonesian government opposed the creation of an international tribunal. It had rejected the resolution adopted by the Commission on Human Rights on 27 September 1999 which established the Inquiry Commission, although it had approved the visit of the Commission to Indonesia from 5 to 8 December 1999. In a letter dated 26 January 2000,[48] the Indonesian Minister for Foreign Affairs denied the charges in the Commission report as 'sweeping, uncorroborated allegations, one-sided and selective in approach'. He argued that human rights violations had been committed by both sides and deplored that the Commission had not shown any interest in such facts as an intensified campaign of terror and intimidation and incidents of armed attacks and other violent acts perpetrated by the pro-independence groups and armed separatist groups in East Timor against civilian and military personnel. 'The accusation of the International Commission that the Indonesian Police and TNI [the Indonesian armed forces] were involved in the violation of human rights in East Timor is totally false and baseless'.

The Minister stated that it was the firm position of his government that the recommendation of the Commission to establish an international human rights tribunal was totally unacceptable for several reasons: Indonesian laws are the only laws applicable to the alleged violations of human rights, as these were committed when East Timor was still an integral part of Indonesia, and the Indonesian judicial mechanism is the exclusive mechanism for bringing the perpetrators of the violations to justice; the national judicial mechanism of Indonesia is functioning and capable of dispensing justice, in contrast with the case of the International Criminal Tribunals established for the former Yugoslavia and Rwanda; the principle of exhaustion of national remedies should be respected; the degree and extent of the alleged violations do not justify the establishment of an international human rights tribunal; its establishment would only create obstacles to the promotion of friendly relations between Indonesia and East Timor.

The Indonesian government had welcomed the establishment by the National Commission on Human Rights of the National Commission of Inquiry on Human Rights Violations in East Timor, which had sent a fact-finding mission to the

48 UN Doc. S/2000/65, A/54/727, 31 January 2000.

territory. Its report would be transmitted to the Attorney-General who will decide what legal action to take through the existing national judicial mechanism.

On 19 August 2000, the Indonesian People's Consultative Assembly adopted Amendment 28(1) to the Constitution which invokes the right not to be prosecuted on the basis of a retroactive law. Since Indonesian law has no provision for crimes against humanity, the most serious charges that anyone involved in the atrocities committed in East Timor could face in Indonesian courts would be 'ordinary crimes' such as murder, arson or rape. The Amendment will effectively provide an amnesty to the main organisers of the violations of human rights in East Timor. This amendment was a concession offered to the Indonesian military and police in order to facilitate the election of Abdurrahman Wahid to the presidency.[49]

In September, Indonesian prosecutors named 19 persons, including three lower-level generals and a former provincial governor, as suspects in the wave of killing and property destruction carried out in September 1999 in East Timor. But the list did not include senior generals, most notably General Wiranto and leaders of the pro-Indonesia militia groups. The chairperson of the Indonesian Human Rights Commission, Albert Hasibuan, said that this was a 'very big disappointment'. Early in 2000, this Commission had accused 33 persons, including six top generals, of orchestrating a campaign of mass killings, torture, forced deportation and rape in East Timor.[50]

In UN-administered East Timor, the Justice Department has created the Serious Crimes Panel at the Dili District Court as a joint national/international body. The Panel consists of one Timorese and two international judges. It has the exclusive mandate to try those suspected of having perpetrated serious crimes. As of July 2001, its Office of the Prosecutor General had 30 investigators examining major incidents of mass killings, deportation, as well as individual offences of murder, rape committed in East Timor between 1 January and 25 October 1999. On 9 July, the Panel started its first Crimes Against Humanity trial in Dili. Ten suspects were on trial, an eleventh suspect, the former second-in-command of the Indonesian Kopassus special forces in Lautem district, was still at large. The suspects were accused of perpetrating 13 murders, torture and the forcible transfer of civilian population in Lautem disctrict between April and September 1999. Eleven accused have been convicted in other cases brought to trial. The first sentence was delivered on 25 January 2001, with a former militia man sentenced to 12 years' imprisonment for a murder committed in Lolotoe, Bobonaro district, in September 1999.[51]

Through a lack of political will, the Security Council has deferred to the Indonesian government rejection of an international criminal tribunal on the model of the ICTY and ICTR. In spite of the valiant efforts of the UNTAET, the Dili

---

[49] *IHT*, 19–20 August 2000; *Le Monde*, 20–21 August 2000.

[50] *IHT*, 2–3 September 2000.

[51] See UN 'East Timor Government', www.gov.east-timor.org/showpage.php?dept_id=030000&lang_id =1, 5 November 2001.

Serious Crimes Panel will probably only prosecute and judge a few lower-level actors in the violence and atrocities committed in East Timor: the main, senior Indonesian political and military 'deciders' will not be brought to national or international justice. UN investigators have encountered difficulties in gathering evidence from Indonesian citizens, in spite of an agreement signed by the UN and the Indonesian government to cooperate on investigative matters. UN prosecutors have also been hindered by a lack of resources from the UN, particular a shortage of cars, translators and seasoned investigators.

To be fair, one should add that Indonesia faces significant economic, political and institutional obstacles to successful prosecutions and trials. Resources and focus within Indonesia have been addressed more to corruption charges than to human rights abuses. Secondly, the violence in East Timor is but one case of interethnic and separatist violence occurring throughout the Indonesian archipelago. However, unless there is accountability for past human rights abuses, including those committed in East Timor, there will be little incentive to deter the commission of similar abuses by the Indonesian military and police authorities in the future in other parts of the country.

The Lockerbie Trial

On 31 January 2001, the Scottish High Court of Judiciary, sitting at Camp Zeist, a former US military base, in the Netherlands, rendered its verdicts in the Lockerbie trial. While the Court is a national, not an international tribunal, the extraordinary fact that it sat in another country to judge two Libyan nationals, and that the case had involved the British, the US, the Netherlands and the Libyan governments, and such international bodies as the UN Security Council, the UN Secretary-General and the International Court of Justice, may justify its inclusion in this Chapter as a national trial with strong international connections. Besides the UN, the governments of South Africa and Saudi Arabia also played a key role in the negotiations leading to the transfer of the accused to the Netherlands.

On 21 December 1988, Pan Am Flight 103 from London to New York exploded at 31 000 feet over Lockerbie in southern Scotland, killing all 259 on board and 11 town people on the ground.[52]

A major police investigation followed and ran for several years, involving law enforcement officers from around the world, including the FBI. By early 1991, it was clear that the tragedy was not the result of mechanical failure or pilot error, but was instead the direct consequence of an explosive device placed in luggage in one of the plane's holds. On 27 November 1991, the Scottish Lord Advocate obtained a warrant for the arrest of two Libyans, Abdelbasset Ali Ahmed al-Megrahi and Ali Alim Khalifa Fhimah on charges of conspiracy to murder,

---

[52] Information in this section is based on the University of Glasgow School of Law's 'Lockerbie Trial Briefing Site' and in particular www.ltb.org.uk/backgroundsummary.cfm, 6 November 2001.

murder and breaches of the Aircraft Security Act of 1982. An indictment in similar terms was issued by the US District Court of the District of Columbia on the same day. Thereupon, the British and American governments demanded that the two Libyans be surrendered so that they could stand trial in either Scotland or the US. Libya refused to surrender the suspects, claiming that it had no extradition treaties with either the UK or the US and that, in any case, Libyan law prohibited the extradition of its own nationals.

At the initiative of the UK and US, the UN Security Council adopted resolution 731 of 21 January 1992 which expressed its deep concern over results of investigations which implicated officials of the Libyan government. The resolution condemned the destruction of Pan Am flight 103 (and of UTA flight 772) and the resultant loss of hundreds of lives and, inter alia, urged the Libyan government immediately to provide a full and effective response to the requests addressed by the UK and the US (and France). On 3 March, Libya filed an application against the UK and the USA in the International Court of Justice for a declaration that it was entitled to rely on the Montreal Convention of 1971 on sabotage against aircraft and to try the Libyan suspects in Libya; and that the UK and the US were in breach of the Convention in demanding the surrender of the suspects. The UK and the US countered by arguing that the Security Council resolutions over-rode the Convention. On 23 March, Libya offered to surrender the suspects to the Arab League.

Libya's refusal to surrender the two accused for trial in Scotland or in the USA prompted the US and the UK to go back to the Security Council to seek a binding resolution. By resolution 748 of 31 March 1992, acting under Chapter VII of the UN Charter, the Council decided that Libya 'must now comply without any further delay' with its previous requests and, inter alia, imposed air and arms sanctions. On 11 November 1993, the Council adopted another binding resolution (res. 883) extending sanctions against Libya to a freeze on Libyan assets and an embargo on oil-related equipment.

Early 1994, Professor Robert Black of Edinburgh University and Dr Ibrahim Legwell, the head of the Libyan defence team agreed on a trial in a neutral venue before a panel of international judges. However, the UK and the US refused to accept this compromise, demanding a trial in either Scotland or the US.

Four years later, a compromise was found: in a letter of 24 August 1998, the UK and US representatives informed the Security Council of their initiative for the trial of the two accused before a panel of three Scottish judges and with no jury,[53] sitting in the Netherlands, with the willingness of the Netherlands government to cooperate in the implementation of the initiative. The Security Council welcomed this initiative by resolution 1192 of 27 August 1998. This offer

[53] The case was heard by three judges at the request of the defence, which argued that a Scottish jury could not render a fair verdict. As the trial was to take place in The Netherlands, jurors could not have been sequestered for more than a year. The prosecution agreed: *IHT*, 5 May 2000.

was broadly accepted by Libya, which reiterated its stance that it was for the two suspects and their legal advisers to decide whether they would appear in the Netherlands for trial.

On 5 April 1999, the two suspects surrendered for trial in the Netherlands and were extradited to Scottish jurisdiction at Camp Zeist. A high-security jail cell and courtroom had been built. The Base had been declared Scottish territory for the duration of the trial, by agreement between the UK and the Netherlands governments.

On 31 January 2001, the Scottish Court rendered its judgement. As prosecutors had previously dropped charges of conspiracy and violation of air safety, al-Megrahi, a senior official in the Jamahiriya Security Organisation (the Libyan secret services), was convicted of murder and sentenced to life imprisonment with the possibility of parole in 20 years. He filed notice of appeal to the Scottish court on 7 February 2001. He maintained his plea of innocence, stating that the Court's findings did not constitute proof of his guilt beyond reasonable doubt, and claimed that the bombing was actually carried out by Palestinian terrorists. His appeal will be heard by a panel of five Scottish judges. If his appeal is unsuccessful, al-Megrahi will serve his sentence in Barlinnie prison in Glasgow under UN supervision. The judges held that it had been 'amply proved' that the cause of the Pan Am crash was the explosion of a device from within the aircraft. As there was no proof of either suspect's involvement in the bombing, the prosecution built its case around circumstantial evidence, witness accounts and scientific facts. The judges said that they were convinced that al-Megrahi did not act alone and that he was part of a wider plot by the Libyan government to avenge the 1986 bombing raid, in which Colonel Gadhafi's adopted daughter was killed along with 36 other persons. But the judges said that more evidence would be needed for any further prosecution. The other accused, Fhima, was acquitted on the basis that the evidence was inconclusive that he was aware that any assistance he provided to al-Megrahi related to a plan to blow up an aircraft. He returned to Libya to a hero's welcome shortly after the verdict was announced. In February 2001, Colonel Ghadafi ridiculed the 'triviality' of the evidence in the case, a 'very funny [case] and a farce'. For him, the prosecution had been made up by the US and British information services to overpower Libya because of its support for revolutionary movements in the world. The Libyan foreign affairs minister affirmed that Libya, as a State, had no responsibility in the Lockerbie crash.

Researchers have raised doubts as to the identity of the 'real' culprits: other options include Iran, Syria or the Palestinian Front for the Liberation of Palestine.[54] Leaving aside these doubts and judiciary controversies before and during the trial, the Lockerbie Trial and verdict have been heralded as symbolizing the increasing power of international law over national sovereignty. The Trial also gave a measure

---

[54] *Le Monde*, 2 and 7 February 2001; *IHT*, 2 and 6 February 2001.

of relief to the families of those who died in the crash of the aircraft. It was important that the accused be brought to court, before a fair tribunal and that sentences be rendered.

Conclusion

Mixed national/international criminal tribunals have been created as an alternative, as the 'second best' to genuine international criminal tribunals, or, more positively, as an expected improvement over unwilling or incapable national tribunals. In the examples given above, the substantial cause of their creation was the evidence of grave breaches of international humanitarian law in a specific country or territory and the lack of any real national effort to try the alleged perpetrators of the crimes. The creation of these tribunals has required a strong pressure by the 'international community', or more precisely by the UN Security Council, with the support of the UN secretariat, and the outspoken denunciations and proposals of the major international human rights organisations, relayed by local NGOs, based on the strong feelings of the victimized populations.

The best alternative to the unwillingness or genuine inability of a state to carry out an investigation or prosecution of human rights crimes is international criminal justice, as exemplified by the ICTY and the ICTR and the future International Criminal Court (ICC). However, members of the Security Council, following the creation of the ICTY and ICTR, were suffering from 'tribunal fatigue' and were reluctant to set up yet other international criminal tribunals for political (expected lack of a consensus) and financial reasons, and the advent of the future ICC. Furthermore, the resistance offered by the Cambodian and Indonesian governments to setting up an international criminal tribunal on the unlikely grounds, disproved by foreign experts and observers, that their national justice system was both willing and able to judge the perpetrators of genocide in Cambodia, or the acts of extreme violence and atrocities in East Timor, shows the difficulties of convincing sovereign governments that their justice system is faulty and that they have to accept the interference of international justice. Similar difficulties are expected to be faced by the ICC when it will have to determine unwillingness and/or inability of a state in investigating or prosecuting cases, in accordance with Article 17 of the Rome Statute.

In the case of Cambodia, in spite of the particular heinous character of the organised massacres, the strong head of a poor country, largely dependent on UN and other external resources, has still been able to reduce international efforts to create an independent international tribunal to a national tribunal with minority international presence, which will only judge a few elderly leaders among the Khmer Rouge clique. In his long battle with the UN legal experts, Hun Sen's open priority for peace and reconciliation has successfully overcome the other overriding priority that the main organisers and perpetrators of the genocide should be made accountable for their crimes: he has assured them impunity. The weakness of the main powers in this case are no doubt linked with their own participation or past support for the Khmer Rouge and their fear that the actions of their own leaders may be internationally exposed.

Sierra Leone is an admirable counter-example. The government of a fragile country also poor and heavily dependent on UN support and external resources has asked the Security Council for assistance in creating a nationally and internationally credible, independent, tribunal. The Special Court, a mixed national/international court, will be composed of a majority of international judges, a minority of Sierra Leone judges and its prosecutor will be appointed by the UN Secretary-General. Its jurisdiction is based on both international humanitarian law and Sierra Leonean law. Its Statute contains two important innovations: the specific provisions applying to the Court's jurisdiction over persons of 15 years of age, including the constitution of a Juvenile Chamber (Art. 7) – the reference, in revised Article 1, to the accountability of peacekeepers alleged to have committed transgressions. The required relationship and cooperation to be established between the Special Court's Prosecutor and the National Truth and Reconciliation Commission, including the use of the Commission as an alternative to prosecution, and the prosecution of juveniles, is also particularly noteworthy, as creating, as in South Africa, a broader system including both criminal justice and non-judiciary truth and reconciliation. The limitation of its jurisdiction to the prosecution of 'persons who bear the greatest responsibility for serious violations of international humanitarian law ... ' is reasonable, considering the Court's limited staffing and funding. A similar formulation could have helped both the ICTY and ICTR to initially focus more quickly on the senior level suspects, rather than on 'small fish'.

Close links are maintained with the UN. The Statute of the Special Court has been the object of negotiations between the UN secretariat, the UN Security Council and the government. The Registrar will be a staff member of the UN. UNAMSIL will provide the Court with material and administrative support, technical assistance and security. A link is also established with two other international organisations, the Economic Community of West African States and the Commonwealth, members of which may forward nominations of judges, at the invitation of the UN Secretary-General (Art. 2.2.(a) of the Agreement). Several references are made in the Special Court's Statute to the Statutes, procedures and practices of the ICTY and ICTR. The Rules of Procedure and Evidence of the ICTR should serve as a model for the Statute of the Special Court (Art. 14.1). In determining the terms of imprisonment, the Special Court's Trial Chamber may have recourse to the practice regarding prison sentences in the ICTR and the national courts of Sierrra Leone (Art. 19.1). While imprisonment will normally be served in Sierra Leone, if circumstances so require, imprisonment may also be served in any of the States which have concluded with the ICTR or the ICTY an agreement for the enforcement of sentences (Art. 22).

The Special Court will have primacy over the national courts of Sierra Leone and may formally request a national court to defer to its competence. This primacy, however, does not extend to the courts of other states. The Court also lacks the power to request the surrender of an accused from a third state and to induce the compliance of its authorities. In contrast with Article 29 of the Statute of the ICTY and Article 28 of the Statute of the ICTR, the Statute of the Special Court does not include an article on required cooperation of other states with the Court in the investigation and prosecution of suspects. There is no obligation of other states to comply with any request of the Court in the identification and location of persons, the taking of testimony and the production of evidence, the service of documents, the arrest or detention of persons, the surrender or the transfer of the accused to the Court. In view of the involvement of neighbouring countries such as Liberia in the civil war, the responsibility of foreign heads of states in supporting the RUF and its exactions, and the flight of Sierra Leone suspects to those countries, the Court may be severely restricted in its prosecutions, unless the Security Council decides to extend the Court's jurisdiction in specific cases, at the request of the Sierra Leone government.

The Special Court's other weak point is its financing by voluntary contributions. The UN Secretary-General has insisted on this point, considering that the only realistic solution is financing through assessed contributions. Even though the Security Council's members have rejected this solution, a compromise might still be proposed: the General Assembly might be requested to include a basic regular budget provision for the Special Court as 'expenses of the Organisation' (as for the more expensive ICTY and ICTR), to be supplemented by voluntary contributions from governments, international organisations, individuals, corporations and other entities.

East Timor, currently under a temporary UN administration, is setting up its own judicial system, which was totally disrupted by the Indonesian violence. The Dili Serious Crimes Panel, a small mixed national/international body, will only be able to try a few low-level Indonesian suspects. Indonesia has denied all wrongs, passed an amnesty law and rejected all proposals to set up an international human rights tribunal, on the implausible ground, as in Cambodia, that its judiciary was independent, willing and able to try those responsible for the violence and atrocities. Indonesian senior military responsible for the campaign of terror in East Timor will continue to enjoy total impunity.

Finally, the Lockerbie Trial was not carried out by an international tribunal, but by a national Scottish court sitting in the Netherlands, to judge two alleged Libyan terrorists. Terrorism as such is not included in the Statutes of the ICTY, nor in the Statute of the ICC. 'Acts of terrorism' are part of the Statute of the ICTR (Art. 4(d)) and of the Statute of the Special Court for Sierra Leone (Art. 3(d)). In the event, the Lockerbie suspects were judged for murder, not for terrorism, thus leaving aside the direct implication of Libya.

While some may consider the Lockerbie Trial as a unique sui generis case, the ingenuity of international negotiators and jurists which produced this innovative judicial arrangement may well serve as an example of a successful effort to introduce a peaceful judiciary process in the midst of an apparently inextricable and potentially dangerous political dispute.

CHAPTER 7

CONCLUSION

Today, we live in a world where a man has more chances to be judged if he kills only one person than if he kills 100 000

(Kofi Annan, Secretary-General of the United Nations, December 1998[1])

Looking back on past massacres, and now faced with an unending series of wars and renewed terrorism, the main sources of exactions, suffering and poverty, observers may feel discouraged by the apparently chronic inhumanity of man to man. The optimistic prediction of Harry Truman, at the end of World War II, that 'if we don't make too many mistakes, the world cannot fail to become a paradise' has proved as wrong as the 'workers' paradise' promised by the Bolshevik leaders to the peoples of the Soviet Union.

The 21st century seems primed to renew the horrors of the 20th. Among others, the Russian war in Chechnya, the long civil wars in Angola and Sudan, the yet unsettled 'diamonds' war' in Sierra Leone, the ferocity of the Liberation Tigers of Tamil Eelam in Sri Lanka, the Kashmir dispute, the Israel/Palestinian conflict, the Basque killings, the 11 September terrorist attacks, are some of the more glaring samples of innocent blood shed by civilian victims.

Most of the leaders mainly responsible for initiating and carrying out genocide, massacres and atrocities still enjoy impunity, except for former head of state of Yugoslavia, Milosevic, being tried by the ICTY in The Hague, former Prime Minister of Rwanda, Kambanda, sentenced to life imprisonment by the ICTR in Arusha, Foday Sankoh, leader of the Sierra Leone Revolutionary United Front (RUF), jailed in Freetown, to be judged by the Sierra Leone Special Court. However, most of the senior surviving Khmer Rouge leaders are unlikely to be tried; there is no international attempt to prosecute and judge President Charles Taylor of Liberia, about whom Richard Holbrooke said 'Taylor is Milosevic in Africa with diamonds'. Taylor, a former warlord, is alleged to have terrorized Liberian voters into electing him in 1997, to have ruined his country and to have backed the RUF, whose rebels have given him diamonds in exchange for guns. According to diplomats and international workers, he has become the single most destabilizing force in West

---

1 Kofi Annan in 'Droits de l'homme au-delà du rêve ... ', *Le Nouvel Observateur*, 3–9 December 1998, p. 27.

Africa and has been the direct instigator of the Sierra Leone civil war.[2] Other possible targets may include Jonas Savimbi, who has led the UNITA rebels in Angola in a devastating civil war of more than 30 years, North Korea's absolute leader Kim Jong Il who, together with his defunct father Kim Il Sung, has destroyed his country and probably caused the death by famine of 2 million of their citizens. France's Cour de Cassation ruled on 13 March 2001 that the Libyan leader, Moammar Gadhafi was immune from trial in France during his tenure as head of state: he could not be prosecuted in connection with the destruction on 19 September 1989 of a French UTA DC-10 airliner over Niger that killed 170 persons.[3] International custom would also prevent the prosecution of other heads of state or of governments during their tenure, such as Cuba's Fidel Castro and Israel's Ariel Sharon.

The obstacles to establishing individual criminal accountability of past and current leaders are many. The genuine respect generally accorded to state leaders – the respect for autocrats and despots enforced through oppression or terror, often backed by foreign powers on ideological or trade grounds; a long-term impunity assured for leaders on the excuse of patriotism or nationalism; the refusal of authorities to shatter national myths either to justify their grip on power or to hide past abuses in the name of God and country; defence of the army's honor and the country's glory not to be defamed by 'treators'; the confusion of roles, the head of state assuming all powers;[4] the dependence of national justice on the executive; the weakness or incompetence of prosecutors or judges; the belief that amnesty will erase hidden massacres and absolve its perpetrators; the rejection of a disturbing justice in favour of peace and reconciliation, a preference for a 'clean slate' in the words of Hun Sen; hiding unpleasant facts through censorship, cover up; chasing investigating journalists, closing access to television teams, refusing access to independent fact-finding missions, human rights NGOs and other observers,

In spite of these depressing accounts, a few positive signs show a slow popular awakening to the fact that leaders should be accountable for their deeds, their violations of the law and their crimes, like ordinary citizens. As noted previously, this trend has been buttressed by the reinforcement of international humanitarian law created in the 19th century, by the invention and growth of a human rights regime after World War II, by the development of an international criminal law, by the expanded scope of universal jurisdiction, by the creation of ad hoc international criminal tribunals and by the expected establishment of the International Criminal Court.

Together with these legislative, legal and judiciary developments, two parallel phenomena have appeared. One, the discovery or re-discovery of long hidden facts,

---

2 *Newsweek*, 28 August 2000; *IHT*, 8 December 2000.

3 *Le Monde*, 15 March 2001.

4 French King Louis the XIVth said that 'L'Etat, c'est moi' (I am the State). Even De Gaulle seemed to have a similar view: for him, justice was to be subordinate to state's interests.

which time allowed to come to the public conscience of their people, thanks to the research of historians, the opening of archives and the testimony of witnesses and actors. Examples: the atrocities and torture carried out by the French army in Algeria from 1954 to 1962 (in the face of similar atrocities committed by the Algerian rebels), under the authority and protection of the French political authorities, finally came to light in the French press in the 1990s (see Chapter 1). In a book published in France in May 2001, General Paul Aussaresses described torture sessions and summary executions of Algerian rebels that he ordered and committed during the 'dirty war'. He said that he had no regrets about his actions, which were well known to top public officials and supported by the public. At the same time, a number of French young men drafted for the Algerian war started confessing in the media, sometimes with horror and regret, what they were ordered to do. In the USA, former Senator Bob Kerrey admitted, also in May 2001, his involvement in the killing of women and children in February 1969 in Vietnam.[5] Commentators observed that, rather than those who obeyed orders, American political leaders in the government who set policy and those in Congress who approved and financed the war were those primarily responsible for the deaths and suffering of more than 58 000 American soldiers and of between 2 and 3 million Vietnamese.[6] Similar revelations emerge in Asian countries. In October 2001, it was belatedly reported that a series of massacres on Mount Halla, over Jeju Island, between October 1948 and February 1949, are estimated to have killed 30 000 people. The slaughter, executed by South Korean authorities, with the possible involvement of the US, was alleged to be a brutal effort to eliminate those suspected of being Communists on the eve of the country's civil war. On the Japanese island of Okinawa, demands have grown for official recognition of the killing of large numbers of local residents by Japanese troops to prevent them from surrendering to US forces in 1945. In Taiwan, civic groups have mounted increasing pressure for an official accounting of the deaths of between 15 000 and 30 000 people by Chinese Nationalist forces in 1947.[7]

The other phenomenon is repentance by senior officials for war crimes or crimes against humanity committed by their state or institution years or centuries before, as an acknowledgement of collective responsibility, in an effort to erase lies, clean up history and face a people's own past, even if the repentants are only late successors to those who ordered or committed the crimes, and repentance is generally cost-free. West Germany's Chancellor Willy Brandt led the way at the Old Jewish Ghetto in Warsaw in December 1970, when he fell to his knees in front of the granite slab that memorializes the 500 000 Jews from the city's ghetto who were massacred by the Germans during World War II. He said: 'No people can escape from their history'. French President Jacques Chirac recognised in July 1995 the responsibility of the French state in the persecution of foreign, then French, Jews during the German

5 *Newsweek*, 7 May 2001.

6 *IHT*, 4, 5–6, 7 May 2001.

7 *IHT*, 25 October 2001.

occupation of France during World War II, a responsibility ignored or rejected by General de Gaulle and his successors. In May 1997, Prime Minister John Howard of Australia made a personal apology to tens of thousands of Aborigines who were taken from their parents under a former policy of forced assimilation. His government has published a human rights report stating that the forced assimilation amounted to genocide. Digging further and more broadly into the past, Pope John Paul II delivered an act of repentance for the errors of the Roman Catholic Church on 12 March 2000 in St. Peter's Basilica. In calling for a 'purification of memory', the Pope acknowledged the mistakes and cruelty imbedded in church history, including the Inquisition, the forced conversions of native peoples in Africa and Latin America, and support for the Crusades, whose victims included Jews, Muslims and members of the Eastern Orthodox Church. However, the apology was offered on behalf of the church's 'sons and daughters' but not the church itself. A widely noted omission was the lack of a specific reference to the Holocaust.[8]

Who should indict, prosecute and judge criminal leaders?

The primary jurisdiction is, or should be, the traditional and natural one, national justice. Built within the history and culture of a particular country, it benefits from national state authority, police and investigative powers, rights to effect custody, to ensure that sentences are carried out. It applies national law, a law which evolves in accordance with the evolution of mentalities, themselves submitted to internal and external influences, at the initiative of political leaders and legislators. Sited in their own country, national courts are close to the people, justice agents speak its language, its procedures should be easily understood and should, if properly administered, be well accepted. Its sentences are those contained in national law, which may include the death penalty, a penalty excluded from the Statutes of the international criminal courts. Its costs are in line with national standards, they are part of the public administration budget.

The Preamble of the Statute of the International Criminal Court affirms that it is the duty of every state to exercise its criminal jurisdiction over those responsible for international crimes. Article 1 of its Statute establishes that the Court 'shall' be complementary to national criminal jurisdictions. An exception is however made: the unwillingness or inability of a national court in a particular case (Art. 17), a sensitive issue for the Court to assess and decide. In many countries, national justice is exposed to non-judiciary concerns of power, revenge, fear, prestige, established impunity of the powerful. In non-democratic countries, prosecutors and judges are generally dependent on the government's good or bad will, making the national court unable to exercise its jurisdiction fairly, or even preventing all prosecution. In such circumstances, national judges may be unwilling to risk their career or their life in trying to trigger a judicial process. The winners in a national political combat will

[8] See 'Willy Brandt: On the Road to a New Reality', www.time.com/time/special/moy/1970.html, 17 November 2001; Beigbeder (1999), pp. 201–202; *IHT*, 15 March 2001.

be tempted to exercise victors' justice towards their defeated opponents. Judiciary procedures may not adequately protect the rights of the accused.

A few national judges, in Spain, Italy, France and Latin America have been playing a key role in promoting the independence of national courts and in trying to expand the principle of universal jurisdiction, building on the Pinochet precedent.

International criminal justice finds its place when national justice fails to play its legitimate role.

The Nuremberg and Tokyo Tribunals were created as an attempt to substitute a fair judicial process to raw vengeance, even if they applied 'Victors' justice'. No German or Japanese Court of Justice would, at the time, have prosecuted and judged their own senior leaders for aggression, war crimes and crimes against humanity.

The establishment of the ICTY, the first genuine international criminal tribunal, was caused first by considerations of political expediency, but also by the assessment that the Yugoslav and Croat courts would certainly be unwilling to judge alleged Yugoslav and Croat criminals. The creation of the ICTR was first requested by the government of Rwanda, in order to give international credibility to the trials of the genociders. The main assets of international criminal courts is their international status, independent from any one government authority, thus offering more guarantees of impartiality than a national tribunal judging its own nationals. Prosecutors and judges have an independent status, only limited by the Statute of their tribunal. They apply international law, their procedures conform to international standards, the rights of the accused are fully protected. Through their Statute and the international composition of their court, they should enjoy a high level of international legitimacy.

The main handicap of the international criminal tribunals is that they have no enforcing powers, a substantial weakness. They entirely depend on the voluntary cooperation of states in such matters as the arrest and surrender of accused, extradition, the taking of evidence, the questioning of any person being investigated or prosecuted, the service of documents, the examination of places and sites, the production of documents, the identification, tracing and freezing of proceeds, property and assets, the enforcement of sentences of imprisonment. The international tribunals are also financially dependent on governments' contributions and other voluntary resources. Their costs are relatively high, as shown by the increased budgets of the ICTY and ICTR. Their work has been slow – in part, because of the time needed to set up entirely new institutions – in part, because of financial constraints – in part, because of the time taken to adhere strictly to exacting rules of procedures – in part, because they have not focused, or have not been able to focus on those persons mainly responsible for the most serious crimes of international concern. Their slowness, their international procedures, the languages of their debates, their geographical location may distance their prosecutions and judgements from the people whose nationals they judge.

On the positive side, the creation and achievements of the ICTY and the ICTR have made an essential contribution to the negotiations which led to adoption of the

Statute of the International Criminal Court. Furthermore, an important lesson has been learned from the experience gained in the work of the two international criminal tribunals. These tribunals, and the future ICC, should concentrate on a few senior persons accused of the most serious violations of international human rights and international humanitarian law, leaving other cases to national courts. Besides establishing a judiciary hierarchy in the levels of cases, this should reduce the current overloading of the ICTY and ICTR, and enable a quicker disposition of future cases.

The creation of international criminal tribunals has been and still is, controversial. International criminal justice has been the object of sharp criticisms. Critics submit that the ICTY and ICTR are, as the Nuremberg and Tokyo Trials, a new form of 'Victors' justice'. For Chandler,[9] 'in practice, the prosecution of international justice turns out to be the prerogative of the West' ... 'The truth is that the 'impartiality of the Tribunal [ICTY] is a farce'. James Shea, NATO spokesman during the Kosovo conflict, replying to a question at a press conference on 17 May 1999 as to the possibility of NATO leaders being investigated for war crimes by the Tribunal: 'Impossible. It was the NATO countries who established the Tribunal, who fund it and support it on a daily basis'. More generally, other critics have argued that the international courts are doubly selective: not only are very few people tried, but very few wars are considered for judicial investigation. Kramer[10] believes that courts are the wrong instruments for dealing with large-scale war, devastation, destruction and crimes against humanity. Judicial procedures are designed to judge the guilt or innocence of individuals, but developing stable democratic societies and limiting the loss of human life require 'prudent political calculations, not judicial findings'. Another argument is that attempts to bring even the leader of an abhorrent regime to trial could make it more difficult to promote democracy by making such leaders and their accomplices more desperate to maintain their hold on state power. Finally, war crimes trials are alleged to prolong wars and thwart postwar efforts to build peace, a charge also levelled against humanitarian assistance.

Bass[11] replies that trying war criminals is a better option than its alternative: vengeance. His adversaries in the debate are the realists in the field of international relations: political leaders, diplomats, scholars and philosophers who oppose using moral standards to restrict the behaviour of states outside their borders, not to mention applying the principle of due process to war crimes. Bass recognises that there is insufficient evidence that war crimes tribunals deter war criminals, place the blame for atrocities on individuals rather than on whole ethnic groups, and establish the truth about wartime atrocities. 'At a minimum', Bass concludes, 'long-term deterrence of war crimes would require a relatively credible threat of prosecution: that is, a series of successful war crimes tribunals that became so much an expected

---

9 D. Chandler, 'International Justice', *New Left Review 6*, November–December 2000, pp. 61, 64.

10 Stephen D. Kramer, *IHT*, 16 January 2001.

11 G.J. Bass, *The Politics of War Crimes Tribunals* (Princeton University Press, Princeton, 2000), and Chuck Sudetic, 'Justice is Better than Revenge', *New York Times Book Review*, 29 October 2000, p. 29.

part of international affairs that no potential mass murderer could confidently say that he would avoid punishment'.

At the national and international levels, politics and law are indissolubly intertwined. International criminal justice was born of international politics and cannot escape from political constraints and influences. Its growth and maturation needs to gain worldwide political acceptance, at the cost of a few compromises, on the expectation that its main institution, the International Criminal Court, will progressively assume all its powers and develop a respected jurisprudence. It is true that powerful states are reluctant to engage in any regime that may significantly impede their political and military freedom of action. It is true that national power and interests still prevail. However, the trend towards the expansion of universal jurisdiction and more international criminal justice, encouraged by a few statesmen and military officials, but mostly by public opinion, outspoken national and international prosecutors and judges, human rights activists and promoters of democracy and the rule of law in their own country, may compel realists to accept this unwanted evolution.

However, existing and future international criminal courts alone will never be able to try all cases of serious violations of international humanitarian law. National courts retain their basic role as the main agents for rendering justice. Laucci[12] believes that the rule according to which the ICC's jurisdiction is a complementary one to national courts is wise and also a guarantee for the court's success. The international courts should actively seek to establish cooperation agreements with national jurisdictions and facilitate the transfer of cases, in particular those of minor importance. In Laucci's view, the future of criminal justice lies in an invigorated domestic justice system.

Also noteworthy is the recent creation or proposed creation of mixed national/international tribunals, as a compromise between the two. In part due to expediency, the reluctance of the Security Council to set up new, costly, international criminal tribunals, the creation of the Special Court for Sierra Leone appears to be a useful model, combining a majority of international judges together with Sierra Leone judges, a mixed jurisdiction of international and Sierra Leone law, a location in Sierra Leone. Its Statute usefully specifies that the Special Court will have personal jurisdiction over persons who bear the greatest responsibility for the commission of crimes, including crimes against humanity, war crimes and other serious violations of international humanitarian law, as well as crimes under relevant Sierra Leonean law committed within Sierra Leone. In spite of its less international character, the Cambodia court, when created, may still play a useful role.

In the words of Ferencz, 'There can be no peace without justice, no justice without law, and no meaningful law without a court to decide what is just and lawful under

[12] Cyril Laucci, 'Juger et faire juger les auteurs de violations graves du droit international humanitaire, Réflexions sur la mission des Tribunaux pénaux et les moyens de l'accomplir', International Review of the Red Cross, June 2001, Vol. 83, No. 842, pp. 407–438.

any given circumstances'.[13] National, international and mixed national/international courts are taking their place in the long struggle aimed at strengthening the rule of law, bringing justice to the victims, and eroding the impunity of criminal leaders.

[13] Benjamin B. Ferencz, *An International Criminal Court, A Step Toward World Peace: A Documentary History and Analysis*, Vol. 1 (Dobbs Ferry, N.J., Oceana Publications, 1980), p. 1.

SELECT BIBLIOGRAPHY

Akhavan, P., 'Beyond Impunity: Can International Criminal Justice Prevent Future Atrocities?' (January 2001) 95 *American Journal of International Law*.

Amnesty International, *Amnesty International Report 2000* (Amnesty International Publications, London, 2000).

Bass, G.J., *The Politics of War Crimes Tribunals* (Princeton University Press, Princeton, 2000).

Bassiouni, M.C., *Crimes Against Humanity in International Criminal Law* (Kluwer Law International, The Hague/London/Boston/New York, 1999).

Beigbeder, Y., *Judging War Criminals, The Politics of International Justice*, Foreword by Theo van Boven (Macmillan Press Ltd and St. Martin's Press, Inc., now Palgrave, Basingstoke/New York, 1999).

Brocheux, P., 'Pol Pot et la destruction du Cambodge' (October 2000) *L'Histoire* 247.

Bronkhorst, D., *Truth and Reconciliation, Obstacles and Opportunities for Human Rights* (Amnesty International Dutch Section, Amsterdam, 1995).

Chandler, D., 'International Justice' (November–December 2000) *New Left Review* 6.

Coombs, M., 'Fifth Circuit decision on the constitutionality of and probable cause for extradition to the International Criminal Tribunal for Rwanda' (2000) 94 *American Journal of International Law*.

Courtois, S., Werth, N. *et al.* (eds), *Le livre noir du communisme* (Laffont, Paris, 1997).

Dedering, T., 'The Annihilation of the Herero in German South West Africa, 1904', in Levene, M. and Roberts, P. (eds), *The Massacre in History* (Berghahn Books, New York/Oxford, 1999).

Des Forges, A. (for Human Rights Watch and Fédération internationale des droits de l'homme), *Aucun témoin ne doit survivre, Le génocide au Rwanda* (Ed. Karthala, Paris, 1999).

Destexhe, A., *Rwanda and Genocide in the Twentieth Century* (Pluto Press, London/East Haven, CT, 1995).

Domenach, J.L., 'Le modèle chinois' (October 2000) *L'Histoire* 247.

Fanon, F., *The Wretched of the Earth* (Penguin Books, London, 1990).

Ferencz, B.B., *An International Criminal Court, A Step Towards World Peace: A Documentary History and Analysis* (Dobbs Ferry, N.J., Oceana Publications, 1980).

Ginsburgs, G. and Kudriavtsev, V.N., *The Nuremberg Trial and International Law* (Martinus Nijhoff Publishers, Dordrecht/Boston/London, 1990).

Gourevitch, P., *We wish to inform you that tomorrow we will be killed with our families, Stories from Rwanda* (Picador USA, Farrar, Straus and Giroux, New York, 1998).

Hazan, P., *La justice face à la guerre, De Nuremberg à La Haye* (Stock, Paris, 2000).

Hitchens, C., 'The Case Against Henry Kissinger' (February, March 2001) *Harper's Magazine*.

Hochschild, A., *King Leopold's Ghost, A Story of Greed, Terror, and Heroism in Colonial Africa* (Houghton Mifflin Company, Boston/New York, 1998).

Holbrooke, R., *To End a War* (Random House, New York, 1998).

Lee, R.S. (ed), *The International Criminal Court, The Making of the Rome Statute* (Kluwer Law International, The Hague/London/Boston/ New York, 1999).

Kissinger, H.A., 'The Pitfalls of Universal Jurisdiction' (July/August 2001) 80 *Foreign Affairs* 4.

Laucci, C., 'Juger and faire juger les auteurs de violations graves du droit international humanitaire, Réflexions sur la mission des Tribunaux pénaux et les moyens de l'accomplir' (June 2001) 83 *International Review of the Red Cross* 842.

Mercier, M., *Crimes Without Punishment, Humanitarian Action in Former Yugoslavia* (Pluto Press, London/East Haven, CT, 1995).

McColm, R.B. (Survey Coordinator), *Freedom in the World, Political Rights and Civil Liberties, 1991–1992* (Freedom House, Lanham/London, 1992).

Miquel, P., *Histoire de la France, de Vercingétorix à Charles de Gaulle* (Marabout, Librairie Arthème Fayard, Paris, 1976).

Mundis, D.A., 'Improving the Operation and Functioning of the International Criminal Tribunals' (2000) 94 *The American Journal of International Law*.

Murphy, S.D. (ed), 'US Assistance Regarding Information on Former Chilean President Pinochet' (April 2000) 94 *American Journal of International Law*.

Murphy, S.D., 'International Criminal Law' (July 2000) 94 *American Journal of International Law*.

Popovski, V., 'The International Criminal Court: A Synthesis of Retributive and Restorative Justice' (December 2000) 15 *International Relations* 3.

Röling, B.V.A. and Cassese, A., *The Tokyo Trial and Beyond* (Polity Press, Cambridge (UK), 1993).

Ronzitti, N., 'Is the *non liquet* of the Final Report by the Committee Established to Review the NATO Bombing Campaign Against the Federal Republic of Yugoslavia Acceptable?' (December 2000) 82 *International Review of the Red Cross* 840.

Sassoli, M. and Olson, L.M., 'The judgment of the ICTY Appeals Chamber on the merits in the Tadic case' (September 2000) 82 *International Review of the Red Cross* 839.

Schalk, D.L. 'Reflections d'outremer on French colonialism' (March–June 1998) 28 *Journal of European Studies* 1–2.

Scharf, M.P., *Balkan Justice, The Story Behind the First International War Crimes Trial Since Nuremberg* (Carolina Academic Press, Durham, 1997).

Soutou, G.-H., 'La Première Guerre mondiale, une rupture dans l'évolution de l'ordre européen' (Autumn–Winter 2000) *Politique étrangère* 3–4.

Taylor, T., *The Anatomy of the Nuremberg Trials* (BackBay Books, Little, Brown and Company, Boston/New York/Toronto/London, 1992).

Ternon, Y., *L'Etat criminel, les génocides au XXe siècle* (Seuil, Paris, 1995).

Tessitore, J. and Woolfson, S. (eds.), *Issues Before the 45th General Assembly of the United Nations, An annual publication of the UN Association of the USA* (Lexington Books, D.C. Heath and Company, Lexington, Mass./ Toronto, 1991).

Tessitore, J. and Woolfson, S. (eds.), *A Global Agenda, Issues Before the 47th General Assembly of the United Nations, An annual publication of the UN Association of the USA* (University Press of America, Lanham/New York/London, 1992).

Tessitore, J. and Woolfson, S. (eds.), *A Global Agenda, Issues Before the 51st General Assembly of the United Nations, An annual publication of the UN Association of the USA* (Rowman & Littlefield Publishers, Inc., Lanham/New York/Boulder/London, 1996).

Tessitore, J. and Woolfson, S. (eds.), *A Global Agenda, Issues Before the 52nd General Assembly of the United Nations, An annual publication of the UN Association of the USA* (Rowman & Littlefield Publishers, Inc., Lanham/New York/Boulder/Oxford, 1997).

Tessitore, J. and Woolfson, S. (eds.), *A Global Agenda, Issues Before the 53rd General Assembly of the United Nations, An annual publication of the UN Association of the USA* (Rowman & Littlefield Publishers, Inc., Lanham/New York/Boulder/Oxford, 1998).

Tessitore, J. and Woolfson, S. (eds.), *A Global Agenda, Issues before the 54th General Assembly of the United Nations, An annual publication of the UN Association of the USA* (Rowman & Littlefield Publishers, Inc., Lanham/New York/Boulder/Oxford, 1999).

Tessitore, J. and Woolfson, S. (eds.), *A Global Agenda, Issues before the 55th General Assembly of the United Nations, An annual publication of the UN Association of the USA* (Rowman & Littlefield Publishers, Inc., Lanham/New York/Boulder/Oxford, 2000).

Wieviorka, A. (ed.), *Les Procès de Nuremberg et de Tokyo* (Editions Complexe, Paris, 1996).

Tronchon, J. *L'insurrection malgache de 1947* (Karthala, Paris, 1986).

Vidal-Naquet, P., *La torture dans la République (1954–1962)* (Les Editions de Minuit, Paris, 1998).

Weinhard, W., *Petite histoire du colonialisme* (Bélin, Paris, 1997).

Williams, P. and Cigar, N., *A Prima Facie Case for the Indictment of Slobovan Milosevic* (Alliance to Defend Bosnia-Herzegovina, London, 1996).

INDEX

www.ingramcontent.com/pod-product-compliance
Lightning Source LLC
LaVergne TN
LVHW102227300926
849160LV00005B/52
* 9 7 8 9 0 4 1 1 1 8 1 5 8 *